TREASURES OF IRISH CHRISTIANITY

Treasures of
Irish Christianity

People and Places,
Images and Texts

Edited by
SALVADOR RYAN
and
BRENDAN LEAHY

VERITAS

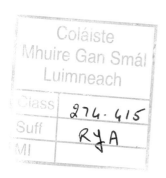
Published 2012 by
Veritas Publications
7–8 Lower Abbey Street
Dublin 1, Ireland
publications@veritas.ie
www.veritas.ie

ISBN 978-1-84730-364-6

Designed by Lir Mac Cárthaigh, Veritas
Printed in Northern Ireland by W. & G. Baird, Antrim

Veritas books are printed on paper made from the wood pulp of managed forests. For every tree felled, at least one tree is planted, thereby renewing natural resources.

Contents

IV – New Realities

Introduction

I N RECALLING the achievements of the Irish Christian past in his letter to the Catholics of Ireland on 19 March 2010, Pope Benedict XVI highlighted how its 'ideals of holiness charity and wisdom' have helped to consolidate the spiritual identity of Europe. He expressed the hope that a contemporary reflection on the contribution of past generations of Irish men and women might 'provide the impetus for honest self-examination and a committed programme of ecclesial and individual renewal'.

Inspired by the theme chosen for the 2012 International Eucharistic Congress – 'Communion with Christ and with one another' – we invited a number of scholars to offer a short reflection on a particular aspect of the Irish Christian experience – something that they might consider a gem or, indeed, a 'treasure' and one which might resonate with this eucharistic theme. The response to this invitation was overwhelmingly enthusiastic and generous and we soon found the collection growing larger than we had initially anticipated.

The title we have chosen for this collection is *Treasures of Irish Christianity*. At first, this might suggest a work consisting of entries on such well-known 'treasures' as the Ardagh Chalice, the Book of Kells or, indeed, any number of other precious items that have their origin in the so-called 'Golden Age' of Irish Christianity. However, we have decided to interpret the word 'treasure' much more broadly than this. Here 'treasures' are understood as some of the texts, images, people and events that have shaped – in varying degrees – the landscape of Irish Christianity over its long history. Indeed, these might be considered some of the 'living stones' of 1 Peter 2:5 which built Irish Christianity into a 'spiritual house'.

With this in mind, this collection does not pretend to be in any way exhaustive. In fact, with very few exceptions, the topics featured were chosen by the contributors themselves. It follows that while some subjects will already be well known, many others will not. Furthermore, given the nature of the compilation and the manner in which it has been assembled, many of the most famous features of Irish Christianity do not appear. It is our hope that many of the less-well-known subjects included here will more than compensate for the well-trodden tracks that we have decided not to retrace. These eighty entries should be considered as interesting tiles in their own right, each of which has their place in the much larger mosaic of Irish Christianity. However, it would take thousands of additional entries and hundreds of additional volumes for the most modest of images to emerge from the mosaic as a whole.

The entries are arranged largely chronologically, beginning with St Patrick's fifth-century letter to a British warlord named Coroticus, who had preyed on Patrick's early community of converts, to the work of reconciliation in Northern Ireland in the late twentieth century. They trace aspects of the foundations of Christianity in Ireland through its subsequent flowerings in the Middle Ages and fragmentations in the age of Reformations and beyond. The repeal of the penal code, culminating in the granting of Catholic emancipation, gave way to a period of new realities in the mid-nineteenth through twentieth centuries. As will be seen, however, even in the most recent of times, the Irish Christian story has remained rooted in its past, as the discovery of an early Christian psalter in an Irish bog at Faddan More in 2006, discussed in one of the later entries in the volume, reminds us. In other ways, thankfully, it has gained the courage and strength to move beyond a sectarian past, as exemplified in an especially moving piece by Ken Newell.

The Irish Christian story continues. As always, though, it will be those 'living stones' of 1 Peter 2:5, oftentimes unnoticed and unacknowledged, that will carry that story into what we trust will be a brighter future.

Brendan Leahy & Salvador Ryan

—I
Foundations

The Church as Christ's Body in St Patrick's Letter to Coroticus

PATRICK MULLINS

MANY ASPECTS of the life and ministry of St Patrick are disputed but one of the few points on which there seems to be universal scholarly agreement is the authenticity of his *Confession* and his *Letter to Coroticus*, which are the oldest surviving texts of Irish literature.[1]

Patrick's *Confession* includes a profession of faith in 'One God in Trinity of sacred name' (n. 2)[2] and the section on the Holy Spirit reads:

> And [the Father] has plentifully poured upon us the Holy Spirit, the gift and pledge of immortality (cf. 2 Cor 1:22), who makes those who believe and are obedient into children of God (cf. Rm 9:26) and fellow heirs with Christ (cf. Rm 8:17).

The new life that the baptised receive is something that supersedes their ethnic and family identities (n. 18): 'They have become the people of the Lord (cf. Hos 1:10), and they are now called the children of God' (cf. Rm 9:26). We are already God's children and heirs but our share in Christ's reign awaits the coming of the kingdom (n. 24):

> We shall arise in the brightness of the sun, that is in the glory of Christ Jesus our redeemer, we shall be children of the living God and fellow heirs with Christ (cf. Rm 8:16-17) and conformed to his image (cf. Rm 8:29); for from him and through him and in him (cf. Rm 11:36) we shall reign.

---

1. For a scholarly introduction to the figure of Patrick, the Patrician texts and their various manuscripts, see the Saint Patrick's Confessio Hypertext Stack Project at www.confessio.ie
2. The numbering system is here taken from *Saint Patrick: Confession et Lettre à Coroticus*, ed Richard P. C. Hanson, *Sources Chrétiennes* 249 (Paris: Cerf, 1978).

The practical implications of having become children of God and fellow heirs with Christ thanks to baptism are very clearly spelled out in Patrick's *Letter to Coroticus*. Although himself baptised as a Christian, Coroticus and his soldiers had killed a number of recently baptised Christians and had sold others into slavery. Patrick addresses them (n. 1) as 'those who by their evil deeds are servants of the demons' and as among those who 'live in death' like the wicked tenants (cf. Mt 21:33-46; Lk 20:9-16). He refers (n. 3) to

> the tyranny of Coroticus who fears neither God nor his chosen priests, whom God has chosen and to whom God has granted the highest, the divine and the sublime power: those whom they shall bind on earth shall be bound in heaven (Mt 16:19).

The holy and humble of heart must neither eat nor drink with them until they 'free the baptised "servants of God" and the handmaids of Christ' whom they have sold into slavery (n. 4). Patrick recognises that failing to show brotherly love to anyone is something that estranges an individual from the Christian community (cf. 1 Jn 3:14-15) but he points out that Coroticus and his men went much further:

> So how much more guilty is the one who stains his or her hands with the blood of the children of God whom [God] has acquired recently in the very ends of the earth through the preaching of us who are so insignificant?

Because (n. 5) Christ's disciples are one fold (cf. Jn 10:16) and have one God and Father (cf. Eph 4:6), those who have been baptised constitute a vast corporate body in such a way that (n. 8) 'if one member suffers, all the members suffer with it' (cf. 1 Cor 12:26).

Coroticus and his men had distributed 'baptised young women as prizes and all for the sake of a wretched temporal kingdom that will vanish' (n. 10) and Patrick hopes that they will 'release the baptised captives they have taken'. By their murder and enslavement of their fellow Christians, Coroticus and his soldiers had implicitly rejected the communal and ecclesiological implications of Christian initiation. This apostasy from what they had publicly professed to believe on the day of their baptism necessarily meant the loss of salvation unless they repented: 'He that believes ... will be saved, he who does not believe will be condemned' (Mk 15:15-16). God has spoken.

Patrick clearly recognised that, because of what they had done, Coroticus and his band should be excluded from the community life of the Church. In sometimes graphic language, he underlines the contradiction between what they have done and what they had professed to believe when they had been baptised. He is not without hope, however, and his strong words of condemnation are revealed at the end of the letter as an invitation to repentance and reconciliation with the Church and with God:

> For though it be very late, it may be they will repent of their impious actions – being the murderers of the Lord's brothers and sisters – and release the baptised captives they have taken. Thus they would merit to live in God and be healed for this life and eternity. (n. 25)

Penance, Atonement and the Eucharistic Community

HUGH CONNOLLY

The people complained to St Meog that they had no water: 'Dig at the foot of yonder tree and you shall find a spring', he replied. They did so and found water and a stream began to flow.

TODAY, AS we seek to recover the communal nature of the Eucharist and a corresponding sense of repentance and atonement and to move away from more individualistic, clericalist and authoritarian models of Church, we could perhaps do worse than dig into the living tree of our own spiritual tradition. In this regard, it may be that the Irish Penitentials, which were used so successfully as a pastoral instrument in the restoration of the life of the Church during the Middle Ages, have something to teach us. Although the Penitentials have traditionally suffered from something of a bad press, it might be said in their favour that they were part of a more complete pastoral system in which personal prayer, the psalms, the Eucharist and various elements of Christian life were made available both within the monasteries and to lay people dwelling around them.

Considering that the monastery was a focal point of life in Ireland, where there were no great cities, it tended to serve both a secular and religious purpose. This community, centred upon the monastery, aimed at being a forgiving, reconciling and atoning centre of life. St Finnian, for instance, prescribes that all who have repented, atoned and carried out the requisite penance should be 'received back into communion' (Vi 34-35).[1]

---

1. For the texts of the Penitentials, see Ludwig Bieler, ed., *The Irish Penitentials* (Dublin: Dublin Institute for Advanced Studies, 1963).

It is interesting to note that responsibility is placed squarely here upon the community. There is an emphasis upon corporate accountability. There is a real sense that the founding fathers of Irish monasticism had a vision of a Church that could not content itself with being a mere dispensary of penance and of absolution to individuals; instead, it had to be committed to the praxis of conversion and atonement. All were called to do penance and to convert others. The example par excellence of this way of life was provided by the monks themselves, who, unlike their desert forefathers, did not completely abandon the world but merely remained a little apart, that they might provide a witness of ascetic life. In this type of community, the differences and divisions of ecclesiastical rank were muted; even the bishop was, in a sense, merely one of the monks, consecrated for the sacramental moments which required episcopal office but otherwise remaining firmly under the jurisdiction of the abbot.

This close association of the monks with the society to which they gave spiritual counsel and guidance was a hallmark of their pastoral approach. In this ascetic and intensely spiritual context, ecclesiastical rank and clerical status came very much in second place to the individual's personal faith response to the Gospel and their call to conversion. Throughout the penitential literature there is an identification of priest and people, cleric and lay, single and married, all united in doing penance. It is not as though one is the 'possessor' of spiritual power and the other is being asked to somehow 'measure up'. The principal divisions of the penitential literature are therefore not those of status, rank, age or gender; they are, rather, the divisions of the various kinds of sinful human behaviour and the corresponding virtues. The Irish monastery was thus a locus for a remarkable union. Newly evangelised people joined in the activity of ascetic penance alongside monks of long standing. Monks rubbed shoulders with the married, bishops with laymen, and saints with sinners. People repenting of distractions at prayer did penance beside those guilty of sexual offences. What was happening here was truly a living sign of repentance and atonement. The monastery and the Church were opened up to the people. The Irish monastic community thus bridged the gap between the official Church and the masses in a way that older Churches of Europe had been unable to do among 'civilised' people. Not only was penance reinterpreted, but so too was the inter-relation of Church (monastery) and society. Irish monasticism was therefore in closer contact with the world and actively entered it with ascetic and moral demands. Indeed, perhaps part of the outstanding missionary successes of the Celtic monks is explained by the observation that the Irish Church was already 'missionary' at home.

There is a case to be made, therefore, that in the early Irish Church, unifying and reconciliatory activity was not simply confined to the explicit practice of penance, but was in fact more typically representative of its whole spiritual, eucharistic and penitential ethos. It may be that there is a timely resonance here for the contemporary Irish and indeed the universal Church as it gathers to reflect once more on Eucharist, atonement and new beginnings.

St Columbanus (c. 543–616): Missionary of Unity

FINBARR G. CLANCY

AINT COLUMBANUS (also known as Columban) is one of Ireland's most important missionary saints. Tomás Cardinal Ó Fiaich once referred to him as 'Ireland's first European', while Robert Schuman, architect of the European Union, described him as 'the patron saint of those who seek a united Europe'.[1] The preservation of unity among his monks, between the Churches and among the peoples of Europe was always a passionate concern for Columbanus. It is also one of the fruits of the Eucharist.

Columbanus's early monastic training took place under the monk Sinell, a man renowned for piety and his love of scripture, in Cleenish on the shores of Lough Erne. He later joined the monastery of Bangor, on the shores of Belfast Lough, under its famous abbot Comgall. This monastery was renowned for its austerity, learning and liturgy. Columbanus immersed himself in the study of the classics, scripture and the Fathers of the Church.

Columbanus's missionary journey to Europe is thought to have begun in AD 590, or even as early as AD 575. He was responsible for several new monastic foundations, the most famous being at Bobbio, in northern Italy. It was there that he died and was buried in AD 616. His missionary journeys were important for the spread of Celtic monasticism in Europe and helped popularise the use of a new private form of penance. Columbanus also helped to spread the love of learning and the study of scripture and the early Fathers.

---

1. T. Ó Fiaich, *Columbanus in His Own Words* (Dublin: Veritas, 1974; revised edition, 2012), p. 8, p. 170.

Columbanus was a prolific writer and Ireland's second great author after St Patrick. His surviving works include *Monastic Rules*, a penitential, letters, a number of sermons or *instructiones*, and some poems.[2] The varied genres in which he wrote attest to his knowledge of a variety of sources, his skill in composition and his notable adaptability to different contexts.

Columbanus was fond of the image of life as a pathway and of seeing the Christian as a pilgrim on that pathway, an association no doubt conditioned by his own missionary experience. The path of discipleship was one of conformity to Christ, his example and teaching. Christ's true disciple must be 'moulded to the example of his Redeemer and the pattern of the true Shepherd' (letter 2.3). Such a disciple seeks to follow Christ's footsteps. Columbanus evocatively captures this aspect of discipleship in *Instructio* XI.2, where he says: 'Let Christ paint his image in us.' If the fourth gospel speaks of the Eucharist effecting a mutual indwelling between Christ and the believer (cf. Jn 6:56), we find an echo of this in Columbanus's phrase 'Live in Christ, that Christ may live in you' (*Instructio* X.2).

Columbanus advises a Synod of Bishops meeting in Gaul that they should imitate Christ's exemplary humility, root out all hatred and love one another with their whole hearts (letter 2.5). It should never happen that a quarrel among Christians should rejoice their enemies (letter 2.7). Faithfulness to the Gospel message is the sure recipe for preserving harmony between the members of the body of Christ, under Christ as head.

Having a concern for charity, peace, humility and concord in the community were essential elements for Columbanus's vision of harmony in the midst of the 'stormy discords of this age' (letter 2.2). In letter 2.8 he cites Jesus' teaching about mutual love (cf. Jn 15:1-17), warning his readers that 'the fiction of peace and charity between the imperfect will be such as is the measure of disagreement in their practical pursuits'. In other words, our practice of love and our quest for unity and peace must be sincere and genuine. Columbanus concluded his letter to the Synod of Bishops (letter 2.9) with a famous quotation:

> Pray for us as we also do for you ... Refuse to consider us estranged from you; for we are all joint members of one body, whether Franks or

---

2. For these texts see *Sancti Columbani Opera*, G. S. M. Walker, ed. (Dublin: Dublin Institute for Advanced Studies, 1970).

Britons or Irish or whatever our race be. Thus let all our races rejoice in the unity of faith and our knowledge of the Son of God, and let us all hasten to approach to perfect manhood, to the measure of the completed growth of the fullness of Christ, in whom let us love one another, praise one another, correct one another, encourage one another, pray for one another, that with him in one another we may reign and triumph.

Columbanus encourages his readers to ponder carefully the Lord's commands and to hasten to fulfil them. His message is ever timely and the Eucharist, the great sacrament of unity, enables us to become the canvas where Christ can paint his image. It also helps foster our sense of mutual solidarity with others.

St Columbanus overseeing the foundation of the monastery of Bobbio, Italy. College Chapel, Maynooth, Co. Kildare

St Columbanus's *Instructio* XIII on the Eucharist

FINBARR G. CLANCY

COLUMBANUS' *INSTRUCTIO* XIII is a precious gem in the Irish treasury concerning Eucharistic belief. It is the final sermon in the series which he probably composed at Bobbio. This treatise is deeply scriptural and is noteworthy for its mystical character. There are resonances with certain lines from some of the hymns and communion antiphons in the late seventh-century Antiphonary of Bangor. We can also detect echoes of some Patristic sources, with which he was familiar.

The dominant image throughout *Instructio* XIII is the fountain. This is the spiritual magnet around which Columbanus assembles his key scriptural texts (Jer 2:13; Is 55:1; Sir 1:5; Ps 35:10; Jn 4:14, 7:37). Notable in the sermon is Columbanus's use of the language of 'thirsting', 'drinking', 'tasting' and 'longing'. He also displays a predilection for terms like 'desiring' and 'loving' as he articulates the power of the Bread of Life to attract us and to fulfil our deepest desires. Columbanus stresses the centrality of union with Christ in his understanding of the Eucharist. He links the fountain image with the Bread of Life discourse from John's gospel:

> Thus the Lord himself, our God Jesus Christ, is the Fountain of Life, and so he calls us to himself the Fountain, that we may drink of him. He who loves drinks of him, he drinks who is satisfied by the Word of God, who sufficiently adores, who longs sufficiently, he drinks who burns with the love of wisdom ... Thus let us eat the same our Lord Jesus Christ as Bread, let us drink him as the Fountain, who calls himself 'the living Bread, who gives life to the world' (Jn 6:33), as it were to be taken by us, and who likewise shows himself as the Fountain when he says:

'Let him that is thirsty come unto me and drink' (Jn 7:37), of which Fountain the prophet also says: 'since with you is the Fountain of life' (Ps 35:10). (*Instructio* XIII.1)

Columbanus emphasises that we must always hunger and thirst for Christ in the Eucharist, even though we never exhaust the Living Bread or the gushing Fountain by our hunger and our thirst:

Observe whence that Fountain flows; for it flows from that place whence also the Bread came down: since he is the same who is Bread and Fountain, the only Son, our God, Christ the Lord, for whom we should ever hunger. For though we eat him in loving, though we feast on him in desiring, let us still as hungering desire him. Likewise as the Fountain let us ever drink of him with overflow of love, let us ever drink of him with fullness of longing, and let us be gladdened by some pleasure of his loveliness. For the Lord is lovely and pleasant; though we eat and drink of him, yet let us ever hunger and thirst, since our food and drink can never be consumed and drained entire; for though he is eaten he is not consumed, though he is drunk he is not lessened, since our Bread is eternal, and our Fountain is perennial, our Fountain is sweet. (*Instructio* XIII.2)

Columbanus next quotes Psalm 33:9, 'Taste and see how lovely, how pleasant is the Lord', one of the communion antiphons in the Antiphonary of Bangor.

Towards the conclusion of his sermon, Columbanus lapses into a prayer-like address to God:

Would that you would deign to admit me there to that Fountain, merciful God, righteous Lord, so that there I, too, with your thirsty ones might drink the living stream of the living Fount of living water, gladdened by whose overflowing loveliness I might ever cleave to him on high and say: 'How lovely is the fountain of living water, whose water fails not, springing up to life eternal' (cf. Jn 4:14). O Lord, you are yourself that Fountain ever and again to be desired, though ever and again to be imbibed. Ever give us, Lord Christ, this water (cf.

Jn 4:15), that it may be in us too a Fountain of water that lives and springs up to eternal life. (*Instructio* XIII.3)

Almost in crescendo-like fashion, Columbanus continues his prayerful petition:

> I ask great gifts indeed, who knows it not? But you, the King of glory, know how to give greatly, and you have promised great things, nothing is greater than yourself and you have given yourself to us, you gave yourself for us. Wherefore we beseech you that we may know the thing we love, since we pray for nothing other than yourself to be given to us; for you are our all, our life, our light, our salvation, our food, our drink, our God. (*Instructio* XIII.3)

Skellig Michael

DIARMUID SCULLY

SKELLIG MICHAEL lies in the Atlantic some nine miles off Bolus Head, the westernmost point of Kerry's Iveragh peninsula. The rock is a numinous presence in the ocean: dark, twin-peaked and towering more than seven hundred feet above sea level. Even in summer, storms sever it from the outside world. But the fortunate visitor lands on a rock teeming with and surrounded by life: birds, seals, dolphins and basking sharks, glinting shoals of fish.

From perhaps the sixth to the twelfth or thirteenth centuries, Skellig was a monastic settlement. The monks lived on its sheltered, broad north-eastern summit, where six dry-stone, corbelled beehive cells and two oratories huddle together, along with a church dedicated to St Michael. Like St Cuthbert's settlement on Northumbria's Farne Island, this is a monastic city, a spiritual fortress. Lacking a spring, the monks cut channels into the rock above the monastery to collect rainwater. Below, there is a garden with rich soil, and there are carefully maintained pockets of earth suitable for growing vegetables throughout the island. The rock appears barren from afar, but this desert has been made to bloom; it recalls Bede's account of Cuthbert transforming the bleak Farne into a fertile place of prayer. Cuthbert on Farne imitated the first monks, the Desert Fathers, who entered the North African wilderness to become closer to God. Their inspiration also lies behind Irish monasticism, 'a veritable vine transmitted from Egypt'. Like Cormac of Iona, who sailed deep into the North Atlantic, the men who went to Skellig sought 'a desert in the ocean'.

Cuthbert went to Farne as a hermit, and Skellig too has space reserved for anchoritic practice. There is a lone cell on its slender western peak, with access via a rock chimney, 'the Needle's Eye', to the island's highest point, for centuries a place of pilgrimage. To the modern eye, the accompanying

Skellig Michael

panorama of boundless sea and sky is exhilarating; we cannot be sure how it was interpreted in the Middle Ages. On Farne, Cuthbert built a high wall so that he could not be distracted from divine contemplation by nature around him. In seeming contrast, many lives of the Irish saints emphasise contemplation through communion with nature. But Bede (c. 672–735) also presents Cuthbert on Farne as a new Adam in a restored creation, living harmoniously with the creatures of the sea and sky, who accept his dominion. Bede's account of Farne recalls his own Genesis commentary's description of Eden, which invokes Isaiah's prophecy of a new heaven and a new earth, where no creature will do harm or hurt on God's holy mountain (Is 65:25). These are powerful, resonant images, and help to explain why holy men soaked in scripture chose Skellig Michael as their dwelling place, with heaven their destination.

The rock's location and its dedication to Michael further clarify its attraction. Following Graeco-Roman tradition, the medieval Irish located themselves at the ends of the earth. Europe, Asia and Africa encircled by ocean comprised the known world, with Ireland as the last inhabited place in the oceanic west or northwest. Classical mythology locates sacred islands like the Isles of the Blest – perfect, fertile, temperate – in the farthest western ocean. Like Eden, they inspired the Irish imagination: thus Tír na nÓg and the Promised Land of the Saints in the Voyage of St Brendan. To live on Skellig Michael, then, is to inhabit an island that evokes paradise and the realms of pagan myth, and lies between the world of men and the unknown.

Scriptural commands and prophecies shaped the symbolic meaning of this ocean and its western islands. Missionaries viewed the conversion of Ireland and Britain as the climax of the extension of salvation from Jerusalem at the centre of the earth to its uttermost places: 'Go therefore and make disciples of all nations' (Mt 28:19). Patrick in Ireland declares that the Gospel has been preached 'at the limit beyond which no one dwells'. Leaving the Irish mainland for Skellig and other remote islands, from Lindisfarne to Iona and the far North Atlantic, Irish holy men were completing the Christianisation of 'the islands of the gentiles' granted to Noah's son Japheth (Gn 10:2), whom they recognised as their ancestor. The eleventh-century *Lebor Gabála* (Book of Invasions), recounting the origins of the Irish, gives Skellig a role in its narrative of their arrival from Spain: Ír, son of their leader Míl, was buried there. The text refers simply to 'Sceilig', but by the eleventh century the rock was dedicated to the archangel Michael, leader of heaven's army. If, like Farne and Egypt, Skellig was demon-haunted before the monks' arrival (as many remote, high places were believed to be), then Michael was its ideal patron – his patronage further signals Ireland's place in the universal Church and the communion of saints. At world's end, it is an integral part of the Church on earth and in heaven.

Seeing the Face of God: An Example of Conversion in the Seventh-Century Patrician Lives

ELIZABETH DAWSON

THE EARLIEST extant Hiberno-Latin saints' lives, which date from the seventh century, are particularly illuminating because of the attention they give to Christian conversion; importantly, they are the first extant Irish written narratives that deal with this transformation. Here we discuss two specific portrayals of conversion in the lives of St Patrick written by the clerics Tírechán and Muirchú – Tírechán's description of the conversion of the daughters of Loíguire, the legendary king of Ireland, and Muirchú's story of Monesan, daughter of an illustrious British king.[1] While very different writers, both in motivation and production, their separate accounts share a considerable number of elements, which point to a common appreciation of conversion and early Christian practice and so may help us to better understand this enigmatic period.

Hagiographical texts are not truly historical in conception – for example, they include miraculous stories – but they are historicist in practice, as it was the aim of the authors to preserve the stories and traditions of their Christian communities. However, in doing so, these writers unconsciously reveal a huge amount about the state of Irish Christianity in their own time, as well as consciously presenting various perspectives on earlier conversion. As a result, the lives ultimately enlighten our understanding of the seventh-century communities in which they were produced and, potentially, those that came before them. It is in this light that the stories

---

1. *The Patrician Texts in the Book of Armagh*, Ludwig Bieler, ed. (Dublin: Dublin Institute for Advanced Studies, 1979). For the episode concerning Monesan in Muirchú's text, see pp. 98–101; for Tírechán's episode concerning the daughters of Loíguire, see pp. 142–5.

concerning Loíguire's daughters, Ethne and Fedelm, and the British
Monesan are so important. The two episodes separately relate how the
women, fascinated with gaining knowledge of the true God, are preached
to and ultimately baptised by Patrick. Tírechán's depiction of the daughters
of Loíguire is the most lengthy in this regard, and in response to Ethne
and Fedelm's questions, Patrick preaches a version of the creed to them.
Muirchú's portrayal of Monesan's thirst for knowledge is slightly different,
however, as her questions regarding the 'maker of the sun' are answered
by her mother and nurse. Nonetheless, both episodes demonstrate
the importance of true faith and belief in God as a pre-requisite for
conversion – something which is not always a seminal feature in other
conversion stories found in the works. The reasons for this enlightenment
soon become clear however, as following baptism, the women request to
see the face of God. This crucial aspect of the stories is directly inspired
by the biblical topos which calls on people to seek out the face of God
through prayer and submission to the Lord.[2] The women can therefore
only aspire to such heights if their Christian transformation is absolute.
And it is possibly for this reason that, following their baptism, Tírechán
has Loíguire's daughters receive the Eucharist – in this way cementing their
Christian conversion. More specifically, the texts are inspired by Moses's
encounter with the Lord described in Exodus where, after requesting to
see God's glory, the Lord tells Moses that no one shall look upon his face
and live, and so Moses must be content with a glimpse of his back.[3] In
contrast, the wishes of Ethne, Fedelm and Monesan are met, but in line
with the biblical story they die in order to achieve their objective.

The elements shared by both works – the women's quest for the true
God, their baptism, demand to see the face of the Lord, and eventual death
– are heavily influenced by biblical conventions, and their reoccurrence
indicates that these features of the Bible were important to an early
Irish Christian audience, especially in relation to conversion. But the
comparisons do not end here and both authors include strikingly similar
descriptions of the women's burials, as well as the veneration of their relics.
Muirchú tells us that Monesan was buried on the spot where she died
and that her body was transferred to a nearby church twenty years later,

2.   See, for example, 1 Chr 16:11; 2 Chr 7:14; Ps 11:7, 24:6, 7:8 and 105:4; and Dn 9:3.
3.   In particular, see Ex 33:20.

while Tírechán says that Loíguire's daughters were buried in a *ferta* (burial mound) as 'the heathen Irish used to do', and that an earthen church was eventually built over their bones. As such they must be representative of an Irish custom associated with the reclamation of relics, and more generally are illustrative of the transfer from pagan to Christian social practices. Moreover, the fact that the memories of these women were subsequently valued as part of the greater Patrician cult suggests an attempt by the authors, or the Christians who came before them, to bring them into a general understanding of Irish conversion. Indeed, their association with a common conversion and martyrdom story that took inspiration from well-known biblical stories is a further extension of this resolve.

Adomnán's Life of St Columba

KATJA RITARI

S AINT COLUMBA (c. 521–97), also known as Colm Cille, is one of the foremost saints of Ireland along with the national saint of the island, Patrick, and the female saint, Brigid. Columba is known as the founder of the monastery of Iona in the Inner Hebrides on the coast of Scotland. He belonged to the Uí Néill, the ruling family of the northern part of Ireland, and died on 9 June AD 597. His life was written by his eighth successor as the abbot of Iona, Adomnán, at the end of the seventh century, approximately a hundred years after the saint's death.[1]

The *Life* is considered to be the most historically reliable of texts on Irish saints' lives since it is based on oral and written memories of their founding saint preserved by the monastic community. It is divided into three parts, dealing with prophecies, miracles and heavenly apparitions, which all give evidence of Columba's God-given miraculous powers and of his sanctity.

The *Life* includes lively vignettes of monastic life at Iona, and some of these depict eucharistic scenes involving the saint and his monks.[2] Columba's first thaumaturgical act, which began his career as a miracle worker, follows the model of Jesus changing water into wine in John 2:1-11.[3] This happened when Columba was studying as a young man with bishop Finbarr and there was a lack of wine for the Eucharist. The saint, who was serving as a deacon, solved the problem by drawing water from a well and changing its nature

---

1. Adomnán of Iona, *Life of St Columba*, trans. Richard Sharpe (Harmondsworth: Penguin, 1995). The Latin text has been edited with translation by Alan Orr Anderson and Marjorie Ogilvie Anderson, *Adomnán's Life of Columba* (Oxford: Clarendon Press, 1961; revised edition, 1991).
2. Eucharist is mentioned in chapters i.1, i.40, i.44, ii.1, ii.39, ii.45, iii.11, iii.12, iii.17 and iii.23.
3. *Life of Columba*, ii.1. This miracle is also briefly mentioned at the beginning of the work in chapter i.1.

into wine. According to medieval thinking, this miracle was a sign from God manifested through the saint and a corroboration of his holiness.

The Eucharist had a central role in the life of the monastic community as an occasion of communal celebration. Adomnán tells how the saint suddenly called his brethren together to celebrate the feast days of St Brendan and the bishop Colmán, both of whom he had seen ascending to heaven accompanied by choirs of angels.[4] The death of a saint was commemorated as his or her day of birth (*dies natalis*) to true life in heaven and this solemn feast involved 'the sacred mystery of the Eucharist' and a special meal as an addition to the austere diet of the monks. By this liturgical celebration the monks commemorated those who had already gone to heaven and in whose footsteps they themselves hoped to follow one day.

As the Eucharist was a holy sacrament, there was concern for its purity. Once, when Columba was staying in Ireland, he witnessed the Mass being celebrated by a priest deemed to be deeply religious by the local monastic community.[5] The saint, however, perceived by his divine powers that this celebrant of 'the sacred mystery of the Eucharist' was unworthy because of a hidden sin and pronounced these words: 'Clean and unclean are now seen mixed up together – the clean ministry of the sacred offering here administered by the unclean man who at the same time hides in his heart the guilt of a great sin.' In this episode, there is not yet any sign of *opus operatum*, the doctrine that the spiritual effect of the sacrament is inherent in it and not dependent on the virtue of the person administering it, a teaching that was based on the thought of Augustine and further developed by theologians later in the Middle Ages.

Another miracle recounted in a eucharistic setting involved a humble bishop who came to visit the monastery and tried to conceal his identity.[6] The saint, however, was able to perceive the true identity of the visitor and gave him honour by asking him to break the bread 'according to the rite of a bishop'. Once, when Columba himself was acting as the celebrant, a column of light was seen rising from his head as a sign of his holiness just

---

4. Ibid., iii.11–12.
5. Ibid., i.40.
6. Ibid., i.44.

at the moment when he was standing at the altar and consecrating the sacred oblation.[7]

Penance held a central place in the Irish monastic practice and Irish monks had a crucial role to play in the development of private penance.[8] In the *Life of Columba*, a man guilty of killing came to Iona and was sent to do seven years of penance in a community attached to the monastery.[9] Only after this was he allowed to approach the altar and receive the sacrament as a sign of having completed the penance.

All of these episodes demonstrate the importance of the Eucharist for the monastic community of Iona. It was a holy sacrament that brought the community together to enjoy a foretaste of the heavenly liturgy and communion with God. It involved not only the community here on earth, but also the saints who had already gone to heaven and led the way for others to follow. For Adomnán, the Eucharist was a sacrificial offering and a sacred mystery that brought heaven and earth together in a communion with Christ.

7. Ibid., iii.17.
8. For more on penance, see Thomas O'Loughlin, *Celtic Theology* (London: Continuum, 2000), pp. 48–67.
9. *Life of Columba*, ii.39.

St Kilian of Würzburg: An Irish Monk in the Golden Age

GABRIEL FLYNN

IN THE period following the deposition of Romulus Augustus (AD 476), the last Western Roman Emperor, the Empire slowly disintegrated and Europe descended into incessant warfare as the Germanic tribes who took over fought first the Romans and then each other. Such was the extent of the tragedy in this disintegrating world that Pope Gregory the Great (AD 590–604) experienced deep distress and pessimism as he watched Europe plunge into barbarism and chaos. Gregory's fears were dissipated by a light from the world's western periphery as Irish missionaries crossed the European continent in what was perhaps the greatest evangelisation of all time. The honour roll of 'Irish monks in the golden age' includes Columba (or Colm Cille of Iona), Aidan of England, Gall of Switzerland, Columbanus of Bobbio, Feargal (or Virgilius) of Salzburg, and Kilian of Würzburg.[1] There are various sources for the life of Kilian from the eighth century onwards, but little can be said with certainty concerning his early life. In this regard, the comments of Ó Fiaich are germane:

> If I were to speak to you today simply about what we know for certain of St Kilian's life before he and his companions left Ireland, I could sum it all up in a single sentence. But we can derive a certain amount of extra information from his name, from his probable birthplace, from the names of his companions and from what we know otherwise about Irish monasticism during the 7th century.

---

1. For the most authoritative work of reference on the early Irish saints and their cults, see Pádraig Ó Riain, *A Dictionary of Irish Saints* (Dublin: Four Courts Press, 2011).

There are several different versions of Kilian's name in Irish sources. The name which is closest to the modern Kilian or Killian is the old Irish name Cilline, which is sometimes spelled Cillene, Cilleine or Cilleni. Cilline may have been derived from *ceall* or *cill*, meaning 'a church'. St Kilian, in common with Columbanus and other famous Irish missionary saints, does not appear in any of the early Irish annals or genealogies but he does feature in some of the early Irish martyrologies. According to John O'Hanlon's *Lives of the Irish Saints*, Kilian hailed from an illustrious family and may even have been of royal descent. While the claims concerning his lineage cannot be verified, it may safely be said that Kilian had a disposition towards study and the acquisition of knowledge from an early age and became an erudite scholar and persuasive preacher.

The parish of Mullagh in County Cavan, close to the border with County Meath, has for centuries been regarded as the birthplace of Kilian. He is traditionally believed to have been born there about AD 640. The Church in Ireland at the time of Kilian's birth was predominantly monastic rather than diocesan. The Irish monastery of his era was much closer to the monastic settlements of the Nile Valley than to the great medieval monasteries such as Clairvaux. Some of the early Irish monasteries had very large communities. Furthermore, Irish monks carried copies of the Bible with them to Britain and the continent, many of which may be seen in libraries and museums throughout Europe. As Ó Fiaich remarks, 'There are more Irish manuscripts from before 1000 in St Gallen today than in all the libraries of Ireland.' In the library of the University of Würzburg are to be found the earliest examples of the Irish language, in the shape of glosses on the Latin text of the Pauline letters (M.p.th.f. 12). These glosses are mostly of the eighth century but some are in a hand that goes back close to the year 700. The university library also has an eighth-century Gospel of Matthew written in Irish majuscules by an Irish scribe (M.p.th.f. 61).

Kilian, the priest Kolonat and the deacon Totnan are said to have arrived in Würzburg in the autumn of 686, from where they launched a mission of evangelisation in Franconia and Thuringia. Kilian's ministry was to be brief; he and his companions would suffer martyrdom, probably in 689. Their deaths are recorded in Bede's martyrology. The remains of Kilian and his companions were located by St Burkhard, the first bishop of Würzburg, and were transferred in 752 to the newly finished cathedral.

≈

They were solemnly placed in their final resting place in the church on 8 July 788. A Gospel book said to have been found in Kilian's grave is in Würzburg's university library (M.p.th.q. 1a). The cult of the Irish martyr quickly spread, and his feast day on 8 July was celebrated with increasing devotion. The new cathedral in Würzburg, built in 1042–45, was dedicated to Kilian. Churches and chapels were dedicated to him in Bavaria and far beyond its borders, and he was celebrated in art and literature. Irish links with Würzburg were maintained after Kilian's death and continued almost unbroken down to the present day.

FURTHER READING

Ó Fiaich, Tomás, 'St Kilian: His Irish Background and Posthumous Influence', *Seanchas Ardmhacha*, 13 (1989), pp. 61–80.

Ryan, John SJ, ed., *Irish Monks in the Golden Age* (Dublin: Clonmore and Reynolds, 1963), esp. pp. 1–15.

Wittstadt, Klaus, *Sankt Kilian: Leben - Martyrium – Wirkung* (Würzburg: Echter, 1984).

The Eucharist in Medieval Irish Narrative: A Brief Survey of Themes

ROBYN NEVILLE

HAGIOGRAPHY, OR the study of saints' lives as both a literary genre and cultural-historical production, reveals a number of ways in which the Eucharist figured in the imaginations of medieval Irish writers. Several early narratives feature the Eucharist as the very setting for miracles that justify or legitimate the power of the saint. In Adomnán's early eighth-century *Life of Columba* of Iona, for example, an esteemed visitor to the monastic foundation of Iona, Brendan moccu Altae, envisions a column of holy fire rising 'like a column of light' from Columba's head during the celebration of the Eucharist, specifically at the moment of consecration. The fact that the fire extrudes from the saint at this particular liturgical moment hints at a kind of early medieval practical piety, a reverence for the consecrated host that only alludes to the very whisper of a sacramental theology: the moment of consecration is so sacred, so transformative, that the celebrant is himself transformed, enveloped in light yet unconsumed.

Moreover, and perhaps in imitation of the first public miracle of Christ, Columba turns water into wine (as does the female Irish saint, Darerca of Killeavy), but here the miracle occurs not as an activity within the liturgy per se, but rather as a kind of narratological statement about the saint's provisional abilities. Here the saint is asked by others to fetch the elements for a future celebration of the sacrament; upon searching and finding the storehouses empty, the saint then blesses simple water and it becomes wine through the power of God.

An example of a miracle that further underscores the importance of the Eucharist involves the miraculous bi-location of the saint in order to either consecrate or receive the Eucharistic elements. For example, the

Eucharist functions as the site of a miracle in the vernacular life of Ciaran of Saighir, who gives 'communion' (*cumaine*) to his monks at his monastic community at Saighir (in present-day County Offaly) on Christmas Day, but then miraculously transverses a great distance to give his foster mother the sacrament on the same day at her residence in Ross Banagher. This example highlights the pastoral function of the Eucharist within medieval Irish narrative.

Vernacular narratives echo the importance placed on receiving the Eucharist immediately before the moment of death. Ciaran of Saighir himself receives 'communion and sacrifice' (*cumaoin agus sacarbaidh*) immediately prior to his death, as do the eponymous saints in the vernacular lives of Máedóc of Ferns, Mochuda of Lismore and Berach of Termonbarry. Bairre of Cork takes the Eucharist, here called the body of Christ (*cuirp Crist*), from the hand of Fiama mac Eogan, a cleric of Disert Mor. Indeed, the reception of the body and blood of Christ from the hand of a high-status religious figure immediately before the time of death constitutes a narrative trope in these early Irish lives. Saints alone do not take Eucharist directly before their deaths; lay persons also benefit from this practice. For example, in the Latin life of Áed Mac Bricc from the medieval collection of Irish saints' lives known as *Codex Salmanticensis*, Áed confronts a wealthy pagan and, after converting him through the demonstration of a miracle, offers him the choice of either departing immediately for heaven, or remaining in this life. The man chooses to enter heaven, so Áed gives him the Eucharist, and the man immediately dies – happily, we are told. This Eucharist only occurs after the saint has demanded that the man first 'believe in God and do penance'.

The Patrician literature features an earlier example of this theme. Tírechán's seventh-century *Collectanea* depicts a narrative episode in which the two daughters of King Loíguire engage with Patrick in a catechetical conversation on issues of Christian belief and practice. After a lengthy catechetical discussion, and apparently in accord with the two girls' wishes, Patrick baptises and then veils them. This is not enough; the girls demand to see the face of Christ directly, but the saint responds that 'unless you taste death, you cannot see the face of Christ and [also] unless you receive the sacrifice'. Demanding the Eucharist, the girls insist on seeing 'the Son, our spouse', but after taking the sacrament, the girls immediately

47

and peacefully 'fall asleep' in death. In this way, the girls' earnest desire for immediate subjective experience of the divine has resulted in the practice of Eucharist, and yet the girls do not meet Christ directly in the eucharistic elements. Rather, the girls must die and enter heaven in order to encounter Christ; they cannot meet him in the consecrated host. Such adumbrations of Eucharistic piety point to the diverse application of liturgical theologies in early medieval Irish narrative, for although the Eucharist figured as an important symbol in medieval hagiography, the specifics of its sacramental character were not set in stone.

The Book of Kells, Folio 114

JENNIFER O'REILLY

THE BOOK of Kells, folio 114, is a rare example among early medieval Latin Gospel books of a figural image positioned within the Gospel text. Its depiction of Christ, standing between two figures who hold his raised arms, has often been seen as an illustration of his arrest, but a number of features question or qualify this understanding.[1] First, the picture appears some five pages *before* Matthew's words: 'Then they came up and laid hands on Jesus and held him' (Mt 26:50). Moreover, the text on the verso of the picture, the beginning of Jesus' prophecy of his passion and resurrection before going with his disciples to Gethsemane to pray (Mt 26:31), is enlarged, ornamented and framed.

Second, the picture is a not a narrative illustration of one event but a monumental hieratic image. The orant pose of Christ, set between two crosses which form the capitals of a magnificent arch, evokes the crucifixion; the letter *chi*, the Greek initial of his sacred title *Christ* (Messiah), is revealed in the diagonal cross formed by his arms and legs.[2] The composition radically renews early Christian iconographic conventions, deriving from the art of late antiquity, in which the exalted Christ, often represented by the triumphal cross or the christogram, is manifested beneath an honorific arch or symmetrically flanked and sometimes touched by attendant figures or creatures.

Third, the inscription overhead provides a further aid to interpretation: 'And a hymn being said, they went out to Mount Olivet' (Mt 26:30). The words conclude Matthew's account of the Last Supper. The preceding page

1. George Henderson, *From Durrow to Kells: The Insular Gospel-books 650–800* (London: Thames and Hudson, 1987), pp. 162–63; Carol Farr, *The Book of Kells: Its Function and Audience* (London: The British Library, 1977), pp. 104–34.
2. Suzanne Lewis, 'Sacred Calligraphy: The Chi-Rho Page in the Book of Kells', *Traditio* 36 (1980), pp. 139–59.

The Book of Kells, folio 114. Image courtesy of the Board of Trinity College Dublin

of text, which faces the picture, consists entirely of Christ's institution of the Eucharist and allusion to the risen life of which it is a foretaste (Mt 26:26-29). The Book of Kells has the 'mixed Irish text' of the Gospel, incorporating Old Latin or pre-Vulgate readings, but there is an insertion in Matthew 26:26 on this page which is not paralleled in other Insular Gospel books and probably represents a liturgical reminiscence. It occurs in the words of Christ, when he took bread, blessed and broke it and gave it to his disciples: 'Take and eat this all of you. This is my body which is broken for the life of the world (*quod confringitur pro saeculi vita*)'. The verb *confringere* is not found in the Roman canon of the Mass but appears in other early liturgical contexts in the western rite. St Ambrose's treatise on the sacraments, for example, quotes the commemoration of the institution of the sacrament in the Mass prayers as *hoc est enim corpus meum, quod pro multis confringetur*.[3] The Irish Stowe Missal has the Roman canon, but one of the prayers or confessions of faith at the breaking of the bread speaks of the breaking of Christ's body (*in hac confractione corporis*).[4]

The Stowe Missal has a fixed lection beginning: 'As often as you eat this bread and drink this cup, you show forth the Lord's death till he come' (1 Cor 11:26). The belief, developed by the fathers and expressed in the liturgy, that the passion and resurrection are made present at the eucharistic altar, and that through the breaking of bread the faithful partake of the Body of Christ and become one body with him (1 Cor 10:16-17), came to be expressed through detailed parallelism in which bringing the offering of the paten and chalice to the altar calls to mind Christ being brought to his passion. In the Irish commentary on the Mass appended to the Stowe Missal, the breaking of the host is a figure of the seizure of Christ, the host on the paten his flesh on the cross, the fraction on the paten the body of Christ broken with nails and spear.[5]

The enigmatic gesture of the attendant robed figures in Kells, who lay their hands on Christ's outstretched arms, may be reminiscent of the liturgical ceremony of *sustentatio*, derived from imperial ceremonial and described in the earliest Roman ordines. Two flanking deacons support

---

3. *De sacramentis* IV, 5.21.
4. See Martin McNamara, 'The Eucharist in the Stowe Missal: Words and Actions in the Mass Figures, Symbols of Higher Truths', an essay in this book, pp. 57–9.
5. *The Stowe Missal*, George F. Warner, ed. Vol. II.3 (London: Henry Bradshaw Society, 1915), p. 41.

the outstretched arms of the vested celebrant, who bears the priestly role of Christ, as he enters the sanctuary, at the offertory and at the communion.[6] In the Book of Kells the attendant figures are flanked by two columns ornamented with vines rising from chalices, an early Christian motif representing the eucharistic and eschatological incorporation of the faithful into Christ (Jn 15:5). Christ is robed in red; his high priestly gesture of oblation offers a visual exposition of the means by which the fruits of his life-giving offering continue to be received. His gaze invites the faithful to draw near. At a critical juncture in the Gospel text the image dwells on the mystery of the body of Christ, at once crucified, exalted and sacramental.

6. Jennifer O'Reilly, 'The Book of Kells, Folio 114r: A Mystery Revealed Yet Concealed', *The Age of Migrating Ideas: Early Medieval Art in Northern Britain and Ireland*, ed. R. M. Spearmann and John Higgitt (Edinburgh, 1993), pp. 106–14; Éamonn Ó Carragáin, '"Traditio evangeliorum" and "sustentatio": The Relevance of Liturgical Ceremonies to the Book of Kells', *The Book of Kells*, ed. Felicity O'Mahony (Aldershot, 1994), pp. 399–436 (417–22).

The Holy Island of Loch Cré: Monaincha, the Thirty-First Wonder of the World

GEORGE CUNNINGHAM

Perhaps no other church ruin in Ireland is so attractive in site, completeness, interesting detail and appearance as that at Monaincha.[1]

S o WROTE the late Harold Leask, Inspector of National Monuments, about this place. And yes, this little, now-dry bog island in the great Red Bog of Éile, three kilometres east of Roscrea town, Co. Tipperary, was once the thirty-first Wonder of the World and Munster's most famous place of pilgrimage in the Middle Ages. These holy bog islands are the 'Skelligs' of the Midlands. Roscrea's Holy Island – for such it is still called, although it has been drained for over two hundred years – was once the hermitage of local saints: Molua of Kyle, Cronán of Ros Cré (Roscrea) and Canice from Aghaboe in nearby Ossory. Indeed, Canice's journey to the island was one of wonder, 'who without ship, without boat came dryshod to the island', and his *vita* or *beatha* continues: 'neither rain nor storm nor darkness nor hunger nor thirst nor any man disturbed him'. Here he wrote a copy of the four Gospels, *Glas Cainnigh*, the green book of Canice, now unfortunately lost to us. And here, according to the Irish Annals, Maelpatraic Ua Drugáin, 'paragon of the wisdom of the Irish, chief lector of Ard Mhaca [Armagh], head of the council of the west of Europe in piety and devotion, died on his pilgrimage at the island of Loch Cré on 2 January, 1138'. But the strangest 'pilgrim' of all must have been Flaithbheartach, abbot of Scattery Island, off the coast of County Clare,

---

1. Harold Leask, *Irish Churches and Monastic Buildings* (Dundalk, 1955), Vol. 1, p. 29.

View of Romanesque west doorway, Monaincha Abbey, Roscrea, Co. Tipperary. Photo courtesy of George Cunningham

and ex-king of Munster, who, fleeing from the Norsemen, took refuge here in 923.

Much later, on a Sunday in June in the early seventeenth century, the Lord Deputy complained that over 15,000 people – 'and some say many more' – had gathered there as pilgrims, led by the Franciscan Bishop of Down and Connor, Conor O'Devany, who was martyred in 1612, for in 1607 Pope Paul V had granted an indulgence to penitents here. In our time too, pilgrims in great numbers have gathered at this holy place, notably in 1974 and more recently during Jubilee Year 2000, led by the then Bishop of Killaloe, Dr Willie Walsh, himself a proud native of Roscrea parish. And those of us privileged to have been present on a Saturday in early November 2000 will never forget the office of vespers sung by the Cistercian monks of Mount St Joseph Abbey as the evening sunlight streamed through the portals of the west doorway – yes, indeed, the 'very stones did speak and sing'.

Monaincha has a recorded history of over 1,400 years. Following the deaths of the early saints as detailed above, it next appears, around 800, as the site of the Culdees or *Céle Dé* – translated as 'servants or clients of God', a reform group of the early ninth century. Led by the anchorite and scribe, Hilary, from nearby St Cronan's in Roscrea town, they set up a hermitage on Monaincha, bringing, we are told, nothing with them from Roscrea but its bread!

The reputation of the holy place grew over time – a second island, now known as Lady's Island, came into use and pilgrims flocked to the area. Monaincha was taken over in the twelfth century by the Augustinian Canons, who erected the beautiful nave and chancel Romanesque church with its exquisite carvings and the now much-weathered high cross.

The Norman chronicler, Gerald Barry of Wales, heard of Inis Locha Cré, on which, the story was related to him, no one could die. He lectured and wrote of this marvel in his book on the topography of Ireland, calling it *Insula Viventium*, the 'Island of the Living', later known in Irish as *Inis na mBeo*. Through his writings and commentaries, the tale travelled around the then-known world, eventually returning to Ireland to be recorded in the late fourteenth-century *Book of Ballymote* as the thirty-first Wonder of the World. Indeed, one German 'tourist/pilgrim' recorded his visit here –

the primary purpose of his long journey to Ireland in 1590 – in diary form, which has recently been published.[2]

Following the dissolution of the monastery in the sixteenth century, the island remained a place of prayer. It became the property of the Birch family in the eighteenth century, who drained large portions of the bog, thus rendering the island dry. The grassy mound on the main island, raised by centuries of burial, was encircled by a wall, and burials inside were denied to all but members of the landlord's family and friends. Family homes were built on the second smaller island and a road was built through it from Roscrea to service turf cutting at Monaincha and Timoney bogs.

Today, Monaincha remains a place apart, one of the truly sacred places of Ireland. The exquisite twelfth-century Irish Romanesque church, the tranquillity of the surrounding bog and the traditions and atmosphere of spirituality that still permeate this venerable and ancient place make any modern journey to and sojourn at this little bog island memorable. It continues to speak silently through every season, through every year, century and millennium. Its ruins are conserved and left alone, just as they should be. Say a prayer there sometime.

2. Dagmar Ó Riain-Raedel, 'A German Visitor to Monaincha in 1591', *Tipperary Historical Journal* (1998), pp. 223–33.

The Eucharist in the Stowe Missal:
Words and Actions in the Mass
Figures, Symbols of Higher Truths

MARTIN MCNAMARA

T HE MASS was central to Irish Christian life from earliest times. We can presume that the churches and oratories had all the liturgical books required for its worthy celebration – missals, lectionaries, hymnals and such like – although most of them are now lost. We are fortunate to have one of these early missals, what is known as the Stowe Missal. It was written about 830 for a church or religious community in Tallaght, near Dublin, or more probably for one in Lorrha, Co. Tipperary. The missal and related texts are in Latin, and the canon of the Mass is closely related to our present Roman Canon, or First Eucharistic Prayer.

At the end of the manuscript there is a text in Old Irish (before 900), generally referred to as a 'Treatise on the Mass'. The purpose of this 'treatise' seems to be to give a deeper appreciation of the Mass by raising the minds of its readers or users from the sacred furniture, vessels, actions or readings to a spiritual truth regarded as 'figured' by these. It is not easy to say for whom the treatise was first intended. It may have been compiled as a text from which sermons could be composed, thus with a larger congregation in view. Or it might have been for the private devotion of the compiler only. The treatise, however, seems to have enjoyed a certain circulation. We have a later, and somewhat expanded form of it preserved in the early fifteenth-century Irish manuscript, known as the *Leabhar Breac*.

Behind the approach of the 'Treatise to the Eucharist' there seems to stand texts of 1 Corinthians 10:6, 11 – in which Paul tells the Corinthian community that certain events of Israel's desert wanderings were a 'figure' (Latin *figura*, Greek *typos*), a foreshadowing, of the Christian community, the new Israel. Earlier Western liturgies had actions (bowing, stepping backwards and forward, covering or half-covering the chalice, the bread and wine) which could be given an allegorical interpretation. This allegorical interpretation of the Eucharist is in keeping with a similar approach which became common in contemporary (ninth-century) continental Europe. On first reading, the Old Irish treatise might seem trivial and forced to us, but on deeper consideration we see in it the riches of Christian doctrine that the author wished to convey. Towards the end of the treatise, after his lengthy explanation, the author reminds his first readers and now us: 'This is what God deems worthy, the mind to be in the figures of the Mass, and that this be your mind.' Let us follow some of his examples.

The Stowe Missal text begins abruptly on the altar. The *Leabhar Breac* text has an introduction, with a Latin heading, as follows: 'On the figures [*De figures*] and the spiritual senses of the order of the sacrificial oblation.' The figure of the incarnation of Christ from (his) conception to his passion and his ascension explains the Order of the Mass. The church that shelters the people and the altar are a figure of the shelter of the Godhead divine, of which was said: 'You guard me under the shelter of your wings' (Ps 16:8, cited in Latin). The Stowe Missal treatise begins with consideration of the altar and the chalice, central to any celebration of the Eucharist: 'The Altar is the figure of the persecution which is inflicted. The Chalice is the figure of the Church which has been set and founded on the persecution and martyrdom of the prophets *et aliorum* [and others].' The Mass altar of sacrifice (and the chalice) recalled for believers that the blood of martyrs is the seed of Christians. The significance of the altar is still worthy of consideration, as we are reminded in the *Catechism of the Catholic Church* (n. 1383).

The text of the treatise goes on to take us through the actions of the Mass as celebrated: first the host on the altar, the water and wine in the chalice, the scripture readings (then apparently chanted), the uncovering, the elevation of the chalice leading to the consecration – the central point of the entire celebration. The treatise lays stress on this: when the words 'Jesus took bread' are sung, the priest bows himself down three times to repent of his sins. He offers the chalice to God and chants, 'Have mercy on me, O God.' The congregation prostrates. No sound must be heard, lest it distract the priest, so that his whole attention may be directed towards God as he chants the words of consecration, in the treatise's words, rightly given the name *periculosa oratio* (the prayer full of danger/perilous prayer). This is all evidence of the early Irish Church's close attention to the significance of the various parts of the Mass.

Abhlann

CAITRÍONA Ó DOCHARTAIGH

THE MODERN Irish word for the eucharistic host, *Abhlann*, derives from the Old Irish word *obla(e)*, which in turn is a borrowing from the Latin word *oblata*, meaning 'that which is offered'. There is a little uncertainty as to the early inflexion of this noun, and therefore we may be looking at a double borrowing process, with some forms of the word derived from the Latin *oblation*. As in Modern Irish, *obla(e)* could mean both altar bread and the consecrated host, but unlike the term *Abhlann Choiscricthe* in contemporary Irish there is rarely a qualifying adjective in the medieval sources. One of the earliest attestations of the word is found in an Old Irish tract on the Mass at the end of the Stowe Missal, which dates to around the year 830 and contains a number of different Masses as well as the order of baptism and the visitation of the sick. As discussed by Martin McNamara in the previous essay, at the end of these texts, which are all in Latin, we find a tract principally in the Irish language which explains each action of the eucharistic rite symbolically and provides an allegorical interpretation of the liturgy. As Pádraig Ó Néill has remarked, the hand which wrote the tract is different to the rest of the missal but does not seem to be much later in date. Therefore, the tract is extraneous to the basic missal texts but roughly contemporary. It is interesting to note that the tract, along with many of the rubrics throughout the manuscript, is in Irish, which provides a fascinating insight into the interaction between the vernacular language and Latin in the ninth-century Irish Church.

Towards the beginning of this tract we find the following statement: *Oblae iarum super altare .i. in turtur.* Some early editors read the last word here as Latin *intrat* ('he/she/it enters'); however, this may be due to confusion regarding the *–ur* abbreviation used in the manuscript.[1] We can

---

1. B. McCarthy, 'On the Stowe Missal', *Transactions of the Royal Irish Academy* 27 C (1885), pp. 135–267 (246); W. Stokes and J. Strachan, eds., *Thesaurus Palaeohibernicus* (Cambridge: Cambridge University Press, 1901–3), Vol. II, 252.8.

translate this phrase as 'The Host, then, above/on top of the altar, i.e. the turtledove.' What can this association between the host, the altar and a turtledove mean in this context?

It has recently been suggested by Neil Xavier O'Donoghue that this is a unique reference to the use of a eucharistic dove, a type of chrismal, in an Irish context.[2] The practice of suspending a dove-shaped vessel containing the reserved eucharist above the altar is recorded in continental European sources as early as the fifth century. In Latin sources this object is usually referred to as *columba*, the Latin word for dove, and doves are also connected to the eucharistic chalice in early Christian iconography. As well as referring to a physical object, this reference to a turtledove in the Stowe Missal may also have an allegorical, symbolic interpretation, in line with the themes explored in the rest of the tract. The turtledove has a special connotation as the offering of the poor in the books of the Old Testament. When Abraham makes one of his first sacrifices to the Lord (Gn 15:9), he includes a turtledove among the animals offered. In Leviticus 12:6 we are told that a turtledove is appropriate as a sin offering after the birth of a child, which is why the Virgin mother offers a pair of turtledoves in Luke 2:24. Therefore, there is a strong association between offerings and the turtledove in a biblical context. One of the most significant biblical allusions for our purposes is the explicit connection made between the turtledove and altars in Psalm 84:3: 'For the sparrow hath found herself a house, and the turtle a nest for herself where she may lay her young ones: Thy altars, O Lord of hosts, my king and my God.'[3]

The turtledove does not figure in most modern translations of this Psalm since they are based on St Jerome's later translation directly from the Hebrew. However, his earlier translations from the Greek Septuagint, which include the reference to the turtledove, were the most widely disseminated in medieval Western Europe, in particular the so-called *Gallicanum* text of the psalms that predominated in Ireland at the period.[4]

---

2. See Neil Xavier O'Donoghue 'The Eucharistic Chrismal in Early Christian Ireland', an essay in this book, pp. 67–70.

3. Ps Iuxta LXX 83, 4: *etenim passer invenit sibi domum et turtur nidum sibi ubi ponat pullos suos altaria tua Domine virtutum rex meus et Deus meus.*

4. An etymology for the word *turtur* is supplied in a gloss to this Psalm in a Vatican manuscript which contains glosses in both Old English and Old Irish; see M. McNamara, ed., *Glossa in Psalmos: The Hiberno-Latin Gloss on the Psalms of Codex Palatinus Latinus 68*, Studi e Testi 310 (Vatican City, 1986).

I
Foundations

In addition, the psalms, because of their role in the Office, were particularly important in the medieval Irish Church with its monastic emphasis. In monastic schools children were taught to read using the psalms, and the importance of knowing the entire psalter by heart is stressed in many texts. From the evidence of the surviving commentaries, it is evident that the psalms were not only the best known but also the most studied text of the Bible in medieval Ireland. Therefore, this intimate knowledge of the psalms results in many references to the psalter when allegorical interpretations are sought, including perhaps here. The association of the altar with the turtledove in the Stowe Missal may also have been reinforced by the commentaries of the sixth-century writer Cassiodorus, whose work was known in Ireland during this period. In his commentary on the psalms he equates the turtledove in this psalm with human flesh, then continues by interpreting the turtledove on the altar in the following manner:

> Since he had earlier spoken of the house of the sparrow and the nest of the turtle, he now shows what meaning we should have taken from them. On these altars the faithful soul chirrups as though giving thanks for a most pleasing house; on these altars such works of the flesh as are holy are placed.[5]

FURTHER READING

McNamara, Martin, *The Psalms in the Early Irish Church* (Sheffield: Sheffield Academic Press, 2000).

O'Donoghue, Neil Xavier, *The Eucharist in Pre-Norman Ireland* (Notre Dame, IN: University of Notre Dame Press, 2011) esp. 72–3.

Ó Néill, Pádraig, 'The Old-Irish Tract on the Mass in the Stowe Missal: Some Observations on its Origins and Textual History', *Seanchas: Studies in Early and Medieval Irish Archaeology, History and Literature in Honour of Francis J. Byrne*, Alfred P. Smyth, ed. (Dublin: Four Courts, 2000).

---

5. P. G. Walsh, ed., 'Cassiodorus: Explanation of the Psalms', Vol. II, *Ancient Christian Writers: The Works of the Fathers in Translation* 52 (Mahwah, NJ: Paulist Press, 1991), pp. 315–6. *Patrologia Latina* 70, 602.

The Derrynaflan Paten: Discovering an Ancient Theology

THOMAS O'LOUGHLIN

WHEN, ON a cold spring morning in 1980, the news came of a spectacular find of early Christian metalwork on the monastery site of Derrynaflan (not far from Cashel, Co. Tipperary), most interest focussed on the chalice – 'another Ardagh chalice' ran one headline – but my own curiosity was sparked by the reference to the paten. Now, at long last, we had the basic set of eucharistic vessels: both chalice *and* paten together. This was so important because patens survive far less often than chalices. We have only a handful of patens from the Latin churches, so each example tells us much about the evolution of the celebration of the Eucharist, and how it was understood, in specific places and at specific times. Now we had an Irish example as well. I can still remember my excitement as I went to the National Museum when they were first put, uncleaned, on display – and my curiosity was justified.

But why get excited about a paten? For us, a paten is an almost flat, saucer-sized disk which can sit atop a chalice, designed to hold, during the liturgy, a single unleavened wafer, about five centimetres in diameter, shown at the elevation and then consumed by the priest – this has been the Latin practice for a millennium. If others are 'going to communion' – until the 1960s this was presumed to be a minority (if anyone at all) – then their particles are separate smaller, unleavened wafers, cut into roundels, and held throughout in another vessel: the ciborium.[1] For us, a paten looks paltry beside a chalice, a ciborium or a monstrance, but in the first millennium the paten was as significant as the cup.

---

1. For how vessels reveal how the Eucharist is understood see T. O'Loughlin, 'The Liturgical Vessels of the Latin Eucharistic Liturgy: A Case of an Embedded Theology', *Worship* 82 (2008), pp. 482–504.

The Derrynaflan paten, view from above. © National Museum of Ireland

The word 'paten' originally meant a big bowl (Greek: *patené*) because the bread of the Eucharist was a single large, leavened loaf. The loaf had to be large enough for each member of the congregation to have a piece – we have no evidence of celebrations with more than a hundred present – and the loaf (according to the law of the time) had to be whole, white, round, fresh and 'living' (i.e. leavened – unleavened bread begins to appear only around the later tenth century). This loaf rested on the dish until the singing of 'the Lamb of God' when the deacons broke it into the number of pieces needed – and then arranged these carefully, often in a special pattern, on the paten so that the now-broken loaf could be shown to the assembly with the words 'This is the Lamb of God' – we still do this, but to appreciate its significance then, we should remember that there was then no elevation of the host. This is why the Derrynaflan paten is approximately thirty-six centimetres in diameter, and the decorations were probably to guide the deacons in arranging the pieces.

This attention to having a single loaf and to breaking it so that each had her/his share of the one loaf was seen as the basic symbolism of the Eucharist. It is the ritual action already being commented upon and interpreted by Paul when he wrote:

> The cup of blessing that we bless, is it not a sharing in the blood of Christ? The loaf that we break, is it not a sharing in the body of Christ? Because there is one loaf, we who are many are one body, for we all partake of the one loaf. (1 Cor 10:16-7)

This action of each having a part – a particle – of a single loaf, and each drinking from a single common cup, expresses not only our solidarity with the Lord, but with one another. What Paul reflected on we find expressed in the prayers of the *Didache* (a first-century Christian treatise only rediscovered in 1873) and then expressed in large chalices and patens such as those from Derrynaflan.[2]

We already suspected that Irish Christians understood the Eucharist this way because we have hymns which were sung during the action of breaking and arranging the loaf's pieces on a paten and a detailed description in Old

---

2. For details, see T. O'Loughlin, 'The Praxis and Explanations of Eucharistic Fraction in the Ninth Century: The Insular Evidence', *Archiv für Liturgiewissenschaft* 45 (2003), pp. 1–20.

Irish about arranging them.[3] But there were always doubts: were these just archaic survivals? The Derrynaflan paten confirmed the whole picture.

Now you can appreciate my excitement: the paten is a theology in metal. Visiting the museum today, I am still struck by it – and wonder when we shall return to that practice of showing ourselves that we are in Christ 'one body, for we all partake of the one loaf' (1 Cor 10:16-17).

---

3. See T. O'Loughlin, *Celtic Theology: Humanity, World and God in Early Irish Writings* (London: Continuum, 2000), pp. 141–5.

The Eucharistic Chrismal in Early Christian Ireland

NEIL XAVIER O'DONOGHUE

O N VISITING the newly restored Treasury of the National Museum on Kildare Street in Dublin, the most obvious artefacts that relate to the Mass are the magnificent Ardagh and Derrynaflan chalices. But before you reach these you have to pass a display case with a number of other metal objects resembling small houses. Although often identified as 'house-shaped reliquaries', these may well be examples of another eucharistic vessel in use in the early Irish Church, the eucharistic chrismal.

The celebration of the Eucharist has been at the centre of Catholic devotion since its institution at the Last Supper. But many of the forms of devotion that are common today date from the second Christian millennium. The first generations of Irish Christians would not have known Corpus Christi processions, Holy Hours or the Exposition of the Blessed Sacrament. But this is not to say that devotion to the Blessed Sacrament was foreign to them. Indeed, other forms of devotion to the Eucharist would have been commonplace. Some of these, such as a desire to have someone prayed for at Mass or a devotion to the altar as the place of the Eucharistic sacrifice, were common throughout Western Christendom. However the use of a eucharistic chrismal was a more local devotion that Christians in early Christian Ireland would have been familiar with.

The eucharistic chrismal was a type of reliquary that held a portion of the Blessed Sacrament and was carried around the neck of a priest or a monk. From the literary descriptions and the few remaining chrismals in different museums, it seems that they were made of metal (or metal overlaying a wooden core) and had a chain for hanging around the neck. In early Christian Ireland, the administration of Holy Communion as *viaticum* for the dying was very important and mention is sometimes made

Eucharistic chrismal in the Cathedral Treasury of Chur, Switzerland. © Cathedral Treasury, Chur

of a saint using the Blessed Sacrament stored in his chrismal to give a dying person the *viaticum*. But the main purpose of the chrismal seems to have been devotional. It was understood to be a type of portable tabernacle where Christ could be adored. The early Irish penitentials often speak of the importance of the chrismal and the solemn duty the monk or priest had to safeguard its contents. In addition, some of the earliest texts written in Ireland mention the use of chrismals. The first life of St Brigid, which dates from the eighth century, mentions a miracle pertaining to a chrismal that St Brigid gave to Bishop Brón:

> The holy Bishop Brón returned to his part of the country and took with him a chrismal from saint Brigit. Now he lived by the sea.
>
> One day the bishop was working on the shore and a boy with him. And this chrismal was left on a rock on the shore and the tide came in up to high water mark.
>
> Then the boy remembered the chrismal and began to cry. But the bishop said, 'Don't cry. I'm confident that saint Brigit's chrismal won't get lost.'
>
> And so it turned out. For the chrismal was on the rock dry and had not been shifted by the waves of the sea and when the tide went out they found it just as it had been left.[1]

Another later text mentions an incident where St Comgall is working in a field and he takes off his chrismal and lays it on his cloak. Some pagan bandits come and are unable to lay hands on him because they are filled with fear as they see the chrismal, which they understand to be the God of St Comgall.[2] In the slightly later life of St Laurence O'Toole, we are informed that he carried a host on his person 'as *viaticum* and as a safe guide on the journey, as was then the custom'.[3]

Travelling Irish monks were to bring their chrismals to different places on the Continent and the cathedral church in Chur, Switzerland, still

---

1. Sean Connolly, '*Vita Prima Sanctae Brigitae*', *Journal of the Royal Society of Antiquaries of Ireland* 119 (1989), p. 39.
2. See *Vita S. Comgalli* 22, in Charles Plummer, ed., *Vitae Sanctorum Hiberniae* (Oxford: Oxford University Press, 1910), 2:11.
3. G. J. C. Snoek, *Medieval Piety from Relics to the Eucharist: A Process of Mutual Interaction*, (Leiden: Brill, 1995), p. 95.

≈

preserves a beautiful eighth-century chrismal that may well have come from Ireland. We know that St Columbanus passed through Chur on a number of occasions and perhaps this chrismal was brought there by one of his disciples. In addition, the whole collection of Irish house-shaped shrines in different museums need to be examined again to determine whether they were in fact shrines to hold the Eucharist and not simply saints' relics.

While this devotion was not to last and it is not proper today for a priest to carry the Eucharist on his person for devotional purposes, it was an important stepping stone in the development of the use of the Tabernacle and a more developed liturgical worship of the holy Eucharist. It shows how the Early Irish Church was an integral part of the Universal Catholic Church even in the first millennium and was ahead of its time in many things. Today we can appreciate the love and the devotion of those who have gone before us in the faith and renew our own eucharistic devotion knowing that, as St Columbanus taught, in the eucharistic presence of Christ we find a fountain of sweetness for our whole lives.[4]

FURTHER READING

Blindheim, Martin, 'A House-Shaped Irish-Scots Reliquary in Bologna and Its Place among the Other Reliquaries', *Acta Archaeologica* 55 (1984), pp. 1–53.

O'Donoghue, Neil Xavier, *The Eucharist in Pre-Norman Ireland* (Notre Dame, IN: University of Notre Dame Press, 2011).

_____ 'Chrismals and House-Shaped Shrines in Early Medieval Ireland', *Insular and Anglo-Saxon: Art and Thought in the Early Medieval Period*, Colum P. Hourihane, ed. (University Park, PA: Penn State University Press, 2011).

Ó Floinn, Raghnall, 'A Fragmentary House-Shaped Shrine from Clonard, Co. Meath', *Journal of Irish Archaeology* 5 (1989/1990), pp. 49–55.

4. St Columbanus, *Sermon* 13.2, *Sancti Columbani Opera*, G. S. M. Walker, ed. (Dublin: Dublin Institute for Advanced Studies, 1957), pp. 116–19.

Aonghas of Tallaght

PÁDRAIG Ó RIAIN

ONGHAS, SON of Aonghabha, who died about AD 830, was the author of Ireland's earliest known martyrology, a term commonly used for a universal calendar of saints' feasts. Aonghas was attached to the church of Tallaght (Tamhlachta), positioned in what is now a modern suburb on the south side of the city of Dublin. Although sometimes styled a bishop, the churchman was in fact more usually remembered as a noted *céile Dé* (God's client) and, as such, he was an outstanding representative of a group of anchoritic clergy active in Ireland in the period 750 to 850. Many new churches were founded during this period, including Tallaght and Finglas – the so-called 'two eyes of Ireland' – and several liturgical texts were compiled.

Aonghas also has the rare distinction of being an early Irish saint whose personality can be glimpsed, however dimly, in the prologue and epilogue of his metrical martyrology, the so-called *Féilire Aonghasa*. Martyrologists usually required skill in the science of *computus*, but Aonghas, while no doubt knowledgeable in this area of study, piously attributed his own text to the inspiration of the host of saints whose feasts determined its arrangement by the days (or dates) of 'their perfect deaths'. Warming to his theme, the martyrologist contrasted the abiding glory of these saints with the forgotten state of their tormentors, and compared the decline of such pre-Christian centres of authority as Tara with the flourishing state of churches such as Armagh.

In the epilogue to his very influential work, which survives in more copies than any other Irish martyrology, Aonghas describes himself both as a *páipearán* ('mendicant'– a term often used for a cleric) and as a *deidhbhléan de thuaith Íosa* ('a poor man of Jesus' family'). He also makes an appeal to the 'thousands and thousands that had gone to heaven every day from the earth' – headed by his teacher and abbot, Maol Ruain, the founder of Tallaght – not only for assistance in attaining his own salvation, but also for the privilege of dying at the sacred feast of Easter or, at least, during Lent. A poem composed some centuries after his death states that Aonghas died on a Friday, but offers no information on the time of year. His name was added, however, to his other great work, the prose *Martyrology of Tallaght*, at 11 March, which would have placed his death during Lent.

As bishop, a title accorded him in the notice of his feastday, Aonghas would have had primary responsibility for the liturgy at Tallaght, and he may have compiled his two martyrologies in response to a decree promulgated at a council held in Aachen in 817. The decree required that a reading be made from a martyrology each day at the beginning of the monastic chapter, immediately after the office of Prime. Despite his boast of having drawn on many authorities, the sole source of his metrical text seems to have been his other work, the prose *Martyrology of Tallaght*. This was an abbreviated copy of the so-called *Martyrology of Jerome*, which is also known as the *Hieronymian Martyrology*. The version used by Aonghas was probably originally drawn up on Lindisfarne in Northumbria and brought to Tallaght via Iona in Scotland and Bangor in County Down.

A preface was added to Aonghas' popular metrical martyrology in the late twelfth century. This purports to record episodes in the life of the saint, bringing him from a church named after him at Dysert (Díseart Aonghasa), near Croom in County Limerick, to Coolbanagher (Cúil Bheannchair), a short distance north of Dysartenos (Díseart Aonghasa) in County Laois. He allegedly began work on his metrical martyrology at Coolbanagher, before leaving for Tallaght, where he completed it. The saint's genealogy attached him through his father Aonghabha to the Uí Eachach Cobha, who gave name to the baronies of Iveagh Upper and Lower in County Down.

Since the time of the Irish Franciscan John Colgan, who was at work on the acts of the Irish saints during the second quarter of the seventeenth century, a litany of Irish saints, beginning with an invocation of 150 Roman pilgrims who reached Ireland in coracles, has also been attributed to Aonghas, but there is no manuscript evidence to support this. Finally, a late (perhaps twelfth-century) poem states that Aonghas was reared at Clonenagh in County Laois, and was later buried there.

Saint Brendan and the Crystal Pillar
JOHN CAREY

STORIES ABOUT other worlds, whether in ancient myths or in modern science fiction, are in fact usually stories about our own world, essential aspects of which are revealed through analogies or symbols. Accordingly, it is not surprising that the monks who, in medieval Irish tales, venture to strange regions beyond the ocean, encounter there the mysteries of their faith. We find this illustrated in one of the most enigmatic scenes in the ninth-century *Voyage of Saint Brendan*:

> On a certain day, then, when they had celebrated Mass, a pillar appeared to them in the sea. And it did not seem to be far away from them; but it took them three days to approach it. When the man of God had approached, then, he gazed toward its summit, but could not see it at all on account of its height; for it was higher than the air. It was covered, moreover, by a veil with broad meshes – so broad that the boat was able to pass through its openings. This had the colour of silver, but was harder; it seemed to them like marble. The pillar was of clearest crystal. Saint Brendan said to his brethren: 'Put the oars in the boat, and the mast, and the sail; and let some of you in the meantime hold the fastenings of the veil.' For the aforementioned covering occupied a great expanse: outward from the pillar in every direction, as it were a mile; and it extended on into the depths.
>
> When they had done this, the man of God said to them: 'Bring the boat inside through one of the openings, so that we may carefully behold the wonders of our Creator.' When they had entered within, and gazed this way and that, the sea seemed to them as clear as glass, so that they could see everything beneath it. For they were able to see the base of the pillar and also the extremities of the net lying upon the ground. The light of the sun was no less within the sea than outside

it. Then Saint Brendan was measuring a single opening between four [strands of?] the veil, four cubits on each side.

And so they were sailing for a whole day along a single side of that pillar; and through its shade they were able to feel the heat of the sun on the far side. So it was until noon. And the man of God himself was measuring one of its sides: the length of each of the four sides of that pillar was 1,400 cubits. Thus for four days the venerable father was busy between the four corners of that tower.

Then on the fourth day they found a chalice of the same sort as the veil, and a paten of the colour of the column, lying in a certain window in the side of the pillar facing the east. Saint Brendan immediately took these vessels, saying: 'Our Lord Jesus Christ has revealed this wonder to us. And in order that it may be revealed to many, and believed, he has given me these two gifts.' At once the man of God instructed the brethren to celebrate the divine office and afterwards to refresh their bodies; for they had not been worried about taking food or drink since they saw that pillar.[1]

What are we to make of this vivid, mysterious vision? Those who have sought to use the *Voyage* as evidence for actual Irish expeditions across the Atlantic have seen it as a fantastically exaggerated reminiscence of an iceberg. But even if some such traveller's tale lies somewhere in the background of the scene – and I am far from persuaded that it does – to regard this as adequately *explaining* what is described would be to ignore all of the details which the author has so carefully enumerated. Here, as elsewhere in the *Voyage*, our only hope of understanding the story lies in attempting to enter into its spirit. I am not sure that my own attempt has been successful, but I will offer it for what it is worth.

The precious materials, the radiant light and the precise measurements all recall John's description of the 'New Jerusalem'; but this resemblance does not seem to go any further. Rather, I suggest that the pillar can be taken as an image of Christ. In Irish, words for 'pillar' can be used of heroes,

---

1. Carl Selmer, ed., *Navigatio Sancti Brendani Abbatis from Early Latin Manuscripts* (Notre Dame, IN: University of Notre Dame Press, 1959), p. xx. For useful background information, see Jonathan Wooding, ed., *The Otherworld Voyage in Early Irish Literature: An Anthology of Criticism* (Dublin: Four Courts, 2000).

of kings, and of God himself; and this is a pillar which links earth – and, indeed, the lower deeps – with the height of heaven, even as one text describes Christ as a tree growing downward from heaven to reach the earth. The clarity of its crystal renders it a peerless vehicle of light, warmth and vision; but its summit, in the changeless spaces above the atmosphere, is beyond mortal sight. And just as Christ is God clothed in human flesh, so the pillar is covered with a veil: also of radiant beauty, but differing from the crystal in its opacity.

Blood and water burst from Christ's side as he hung upon the cross, and it is in the pillar's side that Brendan finds the precious vessels: a chalice and paten, of the same substances as the veil and the pillar. These 'gifts' are to be carried back as a testimony of the wonders witnessed upon the ocean: 'Blessed are they that have not seen, and yet have believed.'

～II
Flowerings

St Brendan and the Eucharist: Liturgical Imagination in High Medieval Irish Narrative

ʼROBYN ʼNEVILLE

ELIGIOUS NARRATIVES from the high medieval period feature the Eucharist as a dramatic site for miraculous encounter; chief among these is the *Betha Brenainn*, the vernacular life of Brendan of Clonfert. Although the text technically inheres to the literary category of hagiography, the vernacular life of Brendan comprises its own discrete set of narrative topoi, and it is here that we begin to see the narrative treatment of liturgical space emerging as a unique concern. Here the imaginary of liturgical action is expanded to include a universe filled with wonder and mystery, such that the sacramental setting for the Eucharist extends beyond the bounds of natural law into the unbounded and unknowable frontier of eternity. A full year into his great sea journey, for example, Brendan looks for dry land, presumably for the purpose of either kindling the paschal fire or for finding stable ground upon which to stage the Easter liturgy. Instead of finding an island, Brendan and his companions famously celebrate the Easter Eucharist on the back of an obliging whale (called Iascanius in the earlier *Navigatio Sancti Brendani Abbatis*), who, in the vernacular life, provides them with *talam tirim* ('land of dry/stable earth'). This phrase offers a narrative clue to high medieval Irish attitudes towards the Eucharist (a place of firmness, of stability in the world of chaos): the very image of monstrosity and threat – the sea monster – becomes a place of stability and calm, a liturgical haven in the wild and reckless emptiness of the sea.

Brendan also extends his eucharistic ministry to otherworldly beings, and here again the imagined world of the liturgy is expanded to encompass non-human recipients. For example, in the vernacular life of Brendan, the saint revives a dead giantess, baptises her and then gives her communion, whereupon she dies and goes directly to heaven, but not before first identifying herself as one whose people dwell beneath the sea. She has golden hair, her skin is as white as sea foam and she is a hundred feet tall (her nose alone is four feet long). Although Brendan offers her the possibility of miraculously restoring her to her people, she chooses to receive the Eucharist and depart immediately for heaven. In this way, the narrative expands the Eucharist beyond the limits of the human: all of the mysterious and wondrous universe may participate in the sacrament, for even non-human beings are invited to partake in the consecrated elements.

Finally, the vernacular life of Brendan depicts the first Irish example of a true eucharistic miracle in the consecrated host itself. Brendan makes a visit to the isle of Britain, and when Brendan's British host, Gildas, comes to receive the elements from Brendan at the moment of distribution, he sees a 'human form on the paten, and human blood in the chalice' (*is annsin atconnairc Gillas duine forin teiscc, agus a fhuil isin coilech*). Gildas is immediately seized with great fear. Indeed, the eucharistic vision is portrayed in the narrative as a kind of punishment or judgement against Gildas, for earlier in the narrative, Gildas tests the purity of his congregation by locking the church doors with great iron bolts (presumably only the pure in heart can open the doors; Brendan, of course, is so holy and pure that he commands the doors to open, calling the church 'the Mother of Christ', and the bolts spontaneously explode into tiny pieces, thus admitting the saint's egress). Gildas begs for Brendan's protection against the eucharistic vision, the harbinger of his coming judgement; Brendan promises the zealous Briton that he will intercede on his behalf, thus sparing him from punishment in the afterlife. The appearance of the 'human form' in the host implies a new direction in the narrative representation of true presence.

These narrative episodes in the vernacular life of Brendan point to the development of the discursive significance of the Eucharist as both a spiritualised destination for its participants and as a site for miracles within the consecrated elements themselves. More than merely a practical description of the liturgy, the fanciful depictions of the Eucharist on the back of the whale and the distribution of consecrated eucharistic elements to the giantess demonstrate an expansion of the sacramental imagination in popular legend. Similarly, the vision of the human form within the consecrated host suggests an evolution in the miracle stories associated with the actual host on the paten. In this way, the Brendan narratives represent a later developmental phase in the treatment of eucharistic tropes in medieval Irish hagiography.

Some Aspects of Early Irish Eucharistic Devotion

MARTIN MCNAMARA

THERE IS a multitude of manners in which Irish eucharistic devotion over the centuries could be considered. In keeping with the theme of the 2012 International Eucharistic Congress – 'The Eucharist: Communion with Christ and with one another' – in this essay I shall first consider texts that have a bearing on this theme and then move on to other aspects of early Irish eucharistic devotion.

The Eucharist and concern for the poor and destitute
Concern for the poor and needy seems to have been intimately connected with the celebration of the Eucharist in medieval Ireland and earlier still. It appears to have been emphasised in Irish catechesis. We find it in eleventh-century Irish homilies, where the three elements for the celebration of any solemnity are indicated as the word of God, scripture and its explanation, the sacrifice of the Body and Blood of Christ, and concern for the poor and destitute. Thus in a homily for the feast of St Michael:

> It is proper to make three commemorations in solemnities of the saints and of the faithful. The first commemoration is celebration and preaching of the word of God. This is the second commemoration: the sacrifice of the Body of Christ, Son of the Living God, and of his blood on behalf of the Christian people. This is the third commemoration: to give food and clothing to the poor and destitute of the great Lord of the elements.

We have an almost identical text in a homily on the celebration of Easter, where, however, the second commemoration is 'the giving of alms in honour of the Lord, through love and pity for the poor'. The principle of concern for the poor holds for every eucharistic celebration, not merely those for major celebrations. In another eleventh-century homily from the *Leabhar Breac* on the Last Supper and the words of consecration we read:

> If we go in this fashion to receive the Body of Christ and his Blood, that is with faith and perfect works, with alms and mercy for the Lord's poor and destitute, that sacrifice will make us holy and separate us from every stain of soul and body as long as we are here in this world and will finally bring us to inhabit the heavenly kingdom in God's presence for ever.

The Body of Christ: that born of Mary, the Holy Church, the Word of God
In an eleventh-century bilingual homily (Latin and Irish) on the Last Supper and the words of Institution, preserved in the fifteenth-century Irish manuscript, the *Leabhar Breac*, the following explanation of 'this is my body' is given in Latin:

> The Body of Christ is understood in three ways: in the proper sense the body that was born of the Virgin Mary; secondly the Holy Church, whose head is Christ; thirdly holy scripture.

The Irish text spells out each of these. 'The second Body, that is the Holy Church, that is the perfect assembly of all the believers, whose head is the Saviour Jesus Christ Son of the living God.' How holy scripture can be called the body of Christ presents a problem. The Irish text paraphrases: 'The third Body, sacred scripture in which is narrated the pure mystery of the body of Christ and of his Blood.'

It may be that behind the Latin text there stands an influence from St Augustine. Augustine delivered four sermons to catechumens (Sermons 56–59) on the Our Father, part of which concerned the meaning of 'Give us this day our daily bread'. Apart from that of natural sustenance, Augustine interprets the bread as the Eucharist, but also as the Word of God; 'the daily lessons which you hear in church are daily bread'; 'the Word of God which is laid open to us, and in a manner broken day by day, is *daily bread*'. Christ's identification of the bread as his body could easily lead to the identification of Christ's body as holy scripture.

The Eucharist, the Mass uniting the people of heaven and earth

Christ is the ladder linking heaven and earth (cf. Jn 1:51), a very important truth in an age becoming ever more secular, with a belief in one-dimensional humans, without regard for the spiritual. The opposite was true in Irish tradition. In a sermon in the *Leabhar Breac* for the celebration of Easter we read:

> And although it is proper to commemorate every solemnity in their own ways, all the more so is it proper to commemorate this solemnity, since this is the solemnity of the meeting of the people [*muinnter*] of heaven and earth.

In the *Leabhar Breac* we have another text in which the uniting of heaven and earth at the consecration of the Mass is made clear:

> What believer would doubt that when the priest raises his voice at the sacrifice, that heaven opens and the choirs of angels descend, and the heavenly and the earthly church are united and joined together?

The Irish Book of Hymns

PÁDRAIG Ó MACHÁIN

T HE *LIBER Hymnorum*, the Book of Hymns, survives in two manuscript copies from the eleventh century. It is an anthology of prayers and hymns that formed part of the liturgy of the medieval Irish Church. Most of the hymns are associated with native saints or church personages. A small handful is attributed to more universal figures such as the Virgin Mary, St Zachariah and St Hilary.

Most of the thirty-four hymns are in Latin. They include the earliest surviving poem (fifth century) composed in that language in either Ireland or Britain. This is St Sechnall's hymn praising St Patrick's missionary work. Nine of the hymns are in Irish, and six of these are early compositions dating from the seventh to the ninth century. In language and theme these Irish hymns illustrate the strong native element in community worship in early Irish Christianity.

A number of the texts in the Book of Hymns are of a general devotional nature in praise of God, Jesus or, as in the eighth-century poem by Cú Chuimhne, of 'Mary the marvellous mother, who gave birth to her [own] father'. Cú Chuimhne's Hymn – '*Cantemus in omni die*' – is of interest also, in that it refers explicitly to the choral element in the performance of these hymns.

Other hymns were probably intended to be sung on the feast days of particular saints: non-native saints such as St Michael, St Martin, and St Philip; or, more often, one of Ireland's great trinity – Patrick, Brigid and Colm Cille. Fiacc's Hymn, for example, is a metrical life of St Patrick, while Broccán's Hymn is devoted to an account of the miracles performed by St Brigid during her lifetime. The latter hymn also refers to something mentioned more than once in these texts: the time-honoured identification of Brigid with the Virgin Mary: 'It was clear from her deeds that she was the unique mother of the Son of the Great King.' Another

text, Colmán's Hymn, ends with an invocation to all three of these saints,
and also emphasises the community element of this part of the liturgy:
'A blessing on the patron Patrick, with the saints of Ireland about him, a
blessing on this monastery and on all within it.'

A prominent theme of the hymns, particularly those in Irish, is the
appeal for protection, both physical and spiritual. Recitation of some of
the poems, we are told, acted as a defence against dangers such as plague,
poison and sudden death.

The more powerful of the hymns are distinguished by personal
requests to God or Christ to act as a bodyguard. In the words of Sanctán's
Hymn: 'God behind me, God on my left, God before me, God on my
right; may God help me against every danger that I risk; let there be a
bridge of life beneath me, and the blessing of God the Father above me.'
This reaches its apogee in St Patrick's Hymn, a renowned eighth-century
incantation which, in invoking protection against the 'spells of women,
smiths and druids', reflects in part the concerns of the early Irish Church
with countering paganism. It belongs to a wider genre known as *lorica*
or *lúireach* ('protective breastplate'), and its recital was said to give to
St Patrick's followers the power to pass undetected by their enemies. It
summons the powers of heaven and nature against every evil, and asks
Christ to be present in all places:

> Christ with me, Christ before me, Christ behind me, Christ in me,
> Christ beneath me, Christ above me, Christ on my right, Christ on my
> left, Christ where I lie, Christ where I sit, Christ where I stand, Christ
> in the heart of every man who thinks of me, Christ in the mouth of
> everyone who speaks of me, Christ in every eye that sees me, Christ in
> every ear that hears me.

Later than any of the other compositions in the Hymn Book is a short poem
by Máel Ísu Úa Brolchán, a famous poet of the community of Armagh who
died in the monastery of Lismore in 1086. This is one of the finest lyrics of
the period, in which Máel Ísu addresses the Holy Spirit and reprises the
theme of seeking protection against spiritual and physical harm. Like many
other hymns in the Hymn Book, although composed centuries ago, it has

travelled well over time, retaining its relevance and beauty of expression to the present day.[1]

In Spirut nóeb immun,
innunn, ocus ocunn;
in Spirut nóeb chucunn
táet, a Chríst, co hopunn.

In Spirut nóeb d'aittreb
ar cuirp is ar n-anma,
díar snádud co solma
ar gábud, ar galra.

Ar demnaib, ar pheccdaib,
ar iffern co n-ilulcc,
a Ísu, ron-nóeba,
ron-sóera do Spirut.

May the Holy Spirit be about us, in us, and with us; let the Holy Spirit, o Christ, come to us speedily.

May the Holy Spirit dwell in our body and our soul; may he protect us readily against peril, against diseases.

Against devils, against sins, against hell with many evils, o Jesus, may thy Spirit hallow us and deliver us.

---

1. Sources: J. H. Bernard and R. Atkinson, *The Irish Liber Hymnorum* (2 vols, London 1898); Whitley Stokes and John Strachan, *Thesaurus Palaeohibernicus,* Vol. 2 (Cambridge, 1903), pp. 298–359.

Echtgus Úa Cúanáin's Poem on Eucharistic Doctrine

ELIZABETH BOYLE

'THE PERSON who believes that they consume only bread and wine at the eucharistic feast will receive "rough judgement with fury"' (*breith ngairbh co ngail*). So begins Echtgus Úa Cúanáin's Middle Irish poem on eucharistic doctrine. But the fearsome threat of his text's opening lines only serves to emphasise the importance for the salvation of the soul of believing 'correctly' (*íar cóir*) in the transformation of the bread and wine into the body and blood of Christ on the altar. Echtgus tells his audience to place their trust in God's miraculous power, rather than letting their perception be limited to 'that which your hard sense sees' (*a n-aicenn do chédfaidh crúaidh*); and he proceeds to call on the testimony of numerous miracles, such as the parting of the Red Sea, the Virgin birth, and indeed Creation itself, as evidence of God's ability to act outside and beyond the everyday rules of nature: 'If he makes without material, the elements of heaven and earth, he will make from bread and from wine, body and blood without falsehood' (*Ma dorighne cen adbar/ dúile nimhe acus talman/ doghéna d'abhlainn is d'fín/ corp acus fuil cen anfír*).

Echtgus probably composed his text in Roscrea (in County Tipperary) in the first half of the twelfth century, or perhaps in the last decades of the eleventh. He was writing at a time when there was great concern about the perceived lack of uniformity of belief across the Christian world. This concern was part of a wider European movement for ecclesiastical reform which found vocal supporters in eleventh- and twelfth-century Ireland, and therefore it is not surprising to find Echtgus highlighting certain reform-minded themes in his poem. Thus we see him emphasising the role of the priest, not only in conducting the eucharistic feast, but also in ensuring correct belief among his congregation. He characterises Jesus as 'the best priest under heaven' (*in sacart is ferr fo nimh*), and expresses the ideal of Jesus being 'as one with his Church' (*mar aen risan eclais*). Indeed, even the fact that the text is written in the Irish language, rather than Latin, suggests Echtgus's desire to communicate his ideas to a wide audience, perhaps both lay and ecclesiastical, in order to ensure uniformity of belief at all levels of society.

What might potentially be a dry work of doctrinal discourse is enlivened and humanised by its use of miracle stories, and Echtgus devotes particular space to a miracle which he found in the ninth-century Latin work *De corpore et sanguine Domini* by the Carolingian author, Paschasius Radbertus. In this miracle, which Paschasius himself took from an eighth-century text composed at Whithorn, the eucharistic host is transformed into the infant Jesus after a priest prays that the host reveal its true form. The priest touches and kisses the Christ-child before the infant resumes the form of a wafer. This moment of intimacy between the priest and the Christ-child becomes, in Echtgus's poem, a clever metaphor which represents the intimacy with Christ that is enjoyed by each recipient of the eucharistic feast.

This medieval text survives today because it is preserved in two seventeenth-century manuscripts, which were compiled within the context of the doctrinal debates of the Catholic Reformation. In addition to these manuscripts, scribes in nineteenth-century Munster copied an abbreviated and modernised version of Echtgus's text in the mistaken belief that it had been composed during the Protestant Reformation, in order to counter Protestant objections to belief in the Real Presence of Christ in the bread and wine. The fact that this text is known to us only through its survival in modern manuscripts shows how resonant its concerns have been throughout the ages, and reminds us of the ways in which texts can be reshaped and reconceived by new audiences.

Echtgus's poetic treatise is an accomplished work, which combines theological orthodoxy with poetic imagination and a touching humanity. In the last few verses of his poem, Echtgus asks for forgiveness of his sins and tell us:

For the Lord's sake pray (all of you) with me, that I may attain union with the king of the stars; I have practised my calling without aversion,

Echtgus my name, I am a descendant of Cúanáin' (*Ar in Choimdhidh guided lem/ co rís aentaidh Rígh na renn/ rochlechtas mo gairm gan gráin/ Echtgus m'ainm, im úa Cúanáin*).

These words provide us with a rare moment of connection with an individual from Ireland's rich – but largely anonymous – medieval literary past. Thus, this important Irish contribution to the centuries-old European debates about eucharistic doctrine also gives us a glimpse of a medieval Irish author who saw his own salvation as being intimately tied to that of his fellow believers.

Fig. 88.

NORTH DOORWAY, CORMAC'S CHAPEL, CASHEL.

The north portal of Cormac's Chapel, Cashel. From Margaret Stokes, *Early Christian Architecture of Ireland* (1878)

Terribilis est locus iste: hic domus Dei est et porta coeli: The North Portal of Cormac's Chapel, Cashel, Co. Tipperary

DAGMAR Ó RIAIN-RAEDEL

'HOW AWE-INSPIRING this place is! This … is a house of God; this is the gate of heaven' (Gn 28:17). This inscription often appears above the entrances of churches on the Continent as an expression both of forewarning and of reassurance. Originally uttered by Jacob on awaking from his dream, it can be interpreted in terms of a *rite de passage* comprising three stages: separation, a transitory liminal period, and eventual re-assimilation. The approach to the church is expressed in terms of initial awe, while the actual crossing of the threshold (*limen*) implies a period of transition, followed by acceptance into membership of God's house, with the hope of eventually reaching heaven. Although no Irish church is known to have borne this inscription, the concept would have been a familiar one, as the biblical passage is also cited in an antiphon used for the dedication of churches. Moreover, examination of the north portal of Cormac's Chapel on the Rock of Cashel, Co. Tipperary, suggests that the symbolism of the biblical passage was also fully understood in Ireland.

The portal, which is one of the most sumptuously sculpted of Irish Romanesque doorways, is flanked on its eastern side by a tomb recess or *arceosolium*, generally believed to have been intended for the church's patron, Cormac Mac Carthaigh (d. 1138), king of Munster. Before the thirteenth-century construction of the nearby cathedral obscured both the north portal and the tomb recess, the latter would have faced a High

Cross placed in a central position in the open space in front of it. In this way, placed between the image of the Saviour on the cross and the entrance to the 'house of God and gateway to heaven', Cormac's tomb would have formed an integral part of the sacred topography of the rock on which he had founded his royal chapel, and from where he no doubt hoped to make his way towards eternal life.

The probable influence of the passage from Genesis on the location of Cormac's tomb can be inferred from a number of twelfth-century documents which refer to architectural details redolent of the concept of approach to the *domus Dei*. The *Visio Tnugdali*, for example, written by an Irish monk in the Irish Benedictine monastery (*Schottenklöster*) at Regensburg in Bavaria a decade or so after Cormac's death, describes how the king had already advanced on the road to ultimate redemption. Although he was still obliged to perform daily penance, Cormac had nevertheless by now reached the *campus laetitiae* (plain of joy) beyond the gate of the Lord (*porta domini*), through which 'the virtuous may enter' (Ps 118:20). The just were the blessed who 'wash their robes … and may enter in by the gates into the city' (Rv 22:14) and thus make their way to heaven.

A second contemporary document, the life of the Irish saint Malachy, provides comparable particulars. The author, St Bernard of Clairvaux, tells of a vision in which he saw his recently deceased sister standing, dressed in a black robe, in front of a church into which she had not been allowed entry. This, we are told, was due to the fact that St Bernard had not said sufficient prayers on her behalf. However, after having offered additional Masses for her soul, he now saw her dressed in a white robe, moving towards the altar. Then, after more effort on Bernard's part, his sister was shown to him in splendid garments in the company of the choir of angels. The progression towards redemption illustrated in this passage re-enacts the kind of conditions experienced by the biblical just who sang: 'Let us go to the house of Yahweh (the Lord) … our feet are standing in your gateways (*in portis tuis*), Jerusalem!'(Ps 122:1, 2).

The position of Cormac's tomb near what would have been the *porta regia*, the triumphal entrance gate for solemn processions connected with his royal chapel in Cashel, would have allowed the king, aided by the prayers of the *paureres* and *peregrini* who, according to the *Visio Tnugdali*, he had supported during his lifetime, to enter through the heavenly gate. Bearing in mind the saying: 'If the pagan tomb was designed to keep alive a man's memory on earth, the purpose of the Christian one was to secure him a place in the queue for heaven on the day of judgement,' Cormac Mac Carthaigh, king of Munster, appears to have taken all necessary steps to ensure that, when the last trumpet sounded, his place in the queue was secure!

FURTHER READING

Colvin, Howard, *Architecture and the After-Life* (New Haven and London: Yale University Press, 1991).

Ó Riain-Raedel, Dagmar, 'Cashel and Germany: The Documentary Evidence', D. Bracken and D. Ó Riain-Raedel, eds., *Ireland and Europe in the Twelfth Century: Reform and Renewal* (Dublin: Four Courts Press, 2006), pp. 176–217.

_____ 'Wie der deutsche Kaiser' Sakraltopographie und Krönungskirche in Cashel/Irland', *Places of Power – Orte der Herrschaft – Lieux du Pouvoir. Deutsche Königspfalzen*, ed. *Caspar Ehlers. Beiträge zu ihrer historischen und archäologischen Erforschung 8* (Göttingen: Vandenhoeck & Ruprecht, 2007), pp. 313–71.

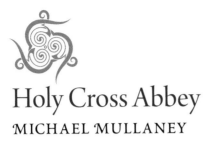

Holy Cross Abbey

MICHAEL MULLANEY

HOLY CROSS Abbey, as the name suggests, has since its foundation been associated with the relic of the True Cross. A manuscript dating from around 1640, *Triumphalia Chronologica Monasterii Sanctae Crucis* (The Triumphant History of the Monastery of Holy Cross), recalls the legend that gave Holy Cross its ancient and now obsolete name as *Ochtar Lamhann* ('eight hands'). King Donal Mór O'Brien's Foundation Charter dates the founding of the Cistercian monastery to 1182, at a place then known as *ceall Uachtar Lamundi* (the church of upper Lamhann). The use of *ceall* indicates an earlier religious or monastic settlement. The monastery was founded for the purpose of enshrining a fragment of the True Cross, the gift of Pope Pascal II to King Donal's grand-uncle Muircheartach O'Brien (d. 1119), who had laid claim to the High Kingship of Ireland. The founding charter is now in the National Library.

The Cistercian monastic life was a reform of earlier monasticism centred on prayer, work and a community life lived in silence and frugality. The austerity and simplicity of the abbey is in keeping with the Cistercian spirit. The architectural features are Gothic, a style imported to Ireland by the Cistercian monks and which gradually replaced Irish Romanesque architecture (exemplified by Cormac's Chapel on the Rock of Cashel).

The monastery at Holy Cross remained Gaelic in the wake of the Anglo-Norman invasion despite the fact that all of Tipperary was under the influence of the Butlers, Anglo-Normans. At one time the monastery owned 8,000 acres worked on by monks, tenants and serfs. The monks were not known, however, for their financial acumen and they often ran into financial difficulties. Throughout this whole time, Holy Cross continued to receive many pilgrims who came to venerate the relic of the True Cross.

Under the protection of the Butlers, the monastery thrived and many of the surviving and beautiful features of the monastery were commissioned under their patronage: the tower, the cloister and the ornate *sedilia*, described as one of the finest examples of the skill of Irish artists of the time. The Ormond reliquary, a silver fifteenth-century cross with an aperture with a ring on the front for viewing the relic of the True Cross, also dates from this period.

The general suppression of monasteries by Henry VIII was decreed in 1539, but although those in the Irish sphere of influence survived for some time longer, Holy Cross Abbey was in decline as a monastic community. Elizabeth I granted the buildings and estates to her cousin Thomas, Earl of Ormond, in 1563. Still pilgrims came to venerate the relic. In 1567, Sir Henry Sidney, Lord Deputy of Ireland, complained to the Queen of 'the detestable idolatry used to an idol called Holy Cross, whereunto there is no small confluence of people daily resorting'. Pilgrims of that time included the Archbishop of Cashel, Dermot Hurley, during the short period he spent in his diocese before he was executed in 1584. Both Hugh O'Neill and 'Red' Hugh O'Donnell would visit the abbey for a blessing on their way to take part in the famous Battle of Kinsale.

The final break with the Cistercians came with their replacement by diocesan priests by the mid-eighteenth century. The roofless abbey became a burial ground and travellers came to view the ruins. The history of the relic after the seventeenth century is not altogether clear. However, it is thought that the Ormond reliquary may have passed into the hands of Thomas Butler. In the early 1800s it had come into the possession of the newly-founded Ursuline convent in Blackrock, Cork, one of the first religious congregations to be established after the 'penal laws'.

The abbey was restored after legislation to mark the fiftieth anniversary of Dáil Eireann (21 January 1969) exempted it from the Irish Church Act (1869), which prevented worship in national monuments. By the autumn of 1975, the relic, which had been safeguarded by the Ursulines in Cork, had been divided into two sections and the larger part, along with the fifteenth-century Ormond reliquary, was returned to the newly restored abbey church. Two years later, an authenticated relic of the True Cross was gifted to the abbey by the Sacristan of St Peter's Basilica, Rome, to mark the abbey's opening day.

Holy Cross Abbey and its monastic ruins continue to be a powerful monument to the enduring power of faith and a sanctuary of the relic of the True Cross, reminding the pilgrim people of God, through the vicissitudes of our history, of the saving mystery of the wood of the cross.

FURTHER READING

Hayes, William J., *Holycross: The Awakening of the Abbey* (Roscrea: Lisheen Publications, 2011).

The Lismore Gradual

FRANK LAWRENCE

T HE LISMORE Gradual, a book of Gregorian chant for the entire year, was written at Lismore, Co. Waterford, in the mid-twelfth century. Destined for use by the cantor of a cathedral church, it is the oldest complete musical source from Ireland. This beautiful manuscript draws us into the rich liturgical and theological world of Lismore, a spiritual powerhouse of twelfth-century Ireland.

Before the Council of Trent (1545–63) many regional variants of the Roman liturgy existed, akin to the dialects of a language. The Lismore Gradual bears witness to a fusion of diverse influences ranging from Ottonian Germany and Anglo-Saxon Winchester to Anglo-Norman Canterbury and the Benedictine monasteries of Normandy. The spiritual vitality and confidence of the monastic and ecclesial community at Lismore shine through this book.

Much has been written about the twelfth-century Irish Church: it was a period of reforming synods when dioceses that still endure were established. We often neglect, however, the spiritual programme of these twelfth-century 'reforming' bishops. Malachy of Armagh and Laurence O'Toole of Dublin come to mind immediately, but we should remember other equally important figures: Malchus of Waterford, Gilbert of Limerick, Christian of Lismore and Ailbhe of Ferns. These holy bishops created institutional structures to serve as a framework within which the sanctification of the people of God could take place. And the primary locus of sanctification was the celebration of the liturgy centred on the diocesan bishop. Here the Body of Christ – the Christian Church – has always been nourished and grown.

The feast *par excellence* of Christ's body is Corpus Christi. Although a thirteenth-century feast, it is pre-figured in the Palm Sunday procession rite of the Lismore Gradual. The medieval Palm Sunday procession was the most impressive of the year. This commemoration of Christ's entry into Jerusalem, opening the great drama of Holy Week, lends itself to dramatic or mimetic representation. The structure of the procession at Lismore with bishop, clergy and laity moving through the city reflects a fusion of traditions from Canterbury and the Benedictine monastery of Fécamp in Normandy.

In northern Europe, figural representations of Christ were carried in the procession, but in Normandy, and later in England, the consecrated host was carried – a practice probably designed to assert the Real Presence in response to theological controversies of the time.

The Lismore Gradual stipulates that the 'corpus Christi' is to be carried in procession and accompanied by a series of chants based on the Gospel account of Palm Sunday. The processional route consisted of four stations where a section of the Gospel was read, a sermon preached and the reliquary containing the Blessed Sacrament adored. One of the chants is striking in its emphasis on the presence of Christ, here and now, today – the *hodie* of all liturgical celebrations.

Cum audisset populus, based on John 12:12, was sung in many places on Palm Sunday until recently. The unusual feature of the Lismore version is twofold: firstly, the text divides between the participants – children, clergy and bishop; secondly, in no other place is such a direct connection made between this text and the Eucharist. The children sing out three times asking: Who is he? What is he? How great is he? The clergy, behaving 'as if they were Christ's disciples' respond to each question in turn: this is he who has come for the salvation of the people; he is our salvation and the redemption of Israel; and finally to the question 'How great is he?' they add – 'whom the thrones and dominations go out to meet!' Then all present turn to the bishop while he sings 'Fear not, O Daughter of Sion; behold your king comes to you sitting on an ass.' They genuflect to the Blessed Sacrament 'remembering the Passion that is to come', and sing together 'Hail, king, creator of the world who has come to redeem us.'

Lismore was a magnet for European influence in the twelfth century: veneration of the Holy Cross and the Real Presence were prominent there. Bernard of Clairvaux's *Life of Malachy* recounts a story of a Lismore cleric who denied the Real Presence of Christ in the Eucharist. Despite Malachy's attempts, he persisted in his stance, to his own eventual detriment. This manuscript is contemporaneous with the incident recounted by Bernard.

This chant from Lismore provides a glimpse of the splendour of its liturgy. The *hodie* of the psalmist, echoed in the sense of Christ's presence among his people, is grounded in the Paschal Mystery. This awareness of the Paschal Mystery, and of the Eucharist rooted in the paschal dimension, lies at the core of Vatican II's teaching on the liturgy. In twelfth-century Lismore and twenty-first-century Dublin, the challenge is the same – to grow in communion with Christ and one another through the Paschal Mystery.

Richard of Dundalk

MICHAEL DUNNE

RICHARD FitzRalph was born in Dundalk around the year 1300. Aged fifteen, he went to Oxford to study arts and then theology (the full course would take sixteen years of study). At Oxford he acquired a thorough grounding in logic and metaphysics and an impressive familiarity with the Bible, which he would later use to great effect on the pulpit. FitzRalph's writings from his Oxford days became very influential and he was one of the most quoted Oxford theologians throughout the fourteenth century. In 1331, a year after obtaining his doctorate in theology, FitzRalph was elected as chancellor of the University of Oxford.

In 1346, the cathedral chapter of Armagh elected FitzRalph archbishop, and he was consecrated in July 1347 in Exeter Cathedral. He travelled to Ireland early in 1348 and gave his first recorded sermon as archbishop on the Lord's Prayer in the Church of St Nicholas on 24 April 1348. We know this because we have his 'Sermon Diary', a unique document containing ninety-two items, most of them preceded by the title, date and place of delivery, spanning the years 1335–59. We have sermons which were given in London and Avignon but also in places closer to home such as Ardee, Drogheda, Mansfieldstown, Coleraine, Dromiskin, Trim, Kells, Greenore, Screen and Termonfeckin.

FitzRalph defended the primacy of Armagh against the Archbishop of Dublin and brought the matter to Pope Innocent VI (r. 1352–62), who decreed a compromise solution whereby the Archbishop of Armagh would be 'primate of all Ireland' and the Archbishop of Dublin 'primate of Ireland' (titles still in use today).

FitzRalph's attitude to the mendicant friars, whom he had previously respected, altered radically when he became Archbishop of Armagh. He defended the offices of bishop and parish priest, and saw the activities of the friars as disrupting the local parish structures. He began a critical examination of the biblical and legal foundations of the friars' privileges and way of life. The legal proceedings between FitzRalph and the four mendicant orders were formally opened by the archbishop at Avignon on 8 November 1357. However, by the time of FitzRalph's death from plague at Avignon in November 1360, no verdict had been reached and the matter quietly lapsed into oblivion.

The Eucharist was one of the topics that FitzRalph dealt with when giving the lectures required to obtain his doctorate in theology at Oxford in 1329. He would have just been ordained a priest since it was common for the secular clergy to be ordained at the age of thirty, the same age as when Christ began his public ministry. The manner in which he approaches the topic is highly technical, beginning by looking at the views of St Thomas Aquinas and Blessed John Duns Scotus. He concentrates, however, on a particular topic related to the doctrine of transubstantiation, which was then being debated in Oxford owing to some controversial views being put forward by William of Ockham and his supporters, namely on the status of the accidents or appearances of bread and wine after the consecration. FitzRalph's approach is very close to that movement in contemporary thought known as 'analytical philosophy' and his text is full of 'thought experiments' designed to test arguments for logical rigour and consistency.

FitzRalph also dealt with eucharistic doctrine in two of his sermons, both of which were given in England. The first, given in Lichfield Cathedral, where he was Dean, for Holy Thursday 1345, deals again with the problem of substantiation and the eucharistic accidents. We are told that the sermon was first given in Latin and then explained to the people in English. The sermon is a long one and must have taken well over an hour to deliver. The text gives a wealth of quotations from both the Old and New Testaments. The points of doctrine which were treated as philosophical and theological problems in an academic setting at Oxford are now treated as marvels: how one body can be transformed into another; how the accidents can be present without a subject; how the complete body of Christ can be present in the host and completely present in so many different places and times. The second sermon was given in London on the feast of Corpus Christi, 1356, at the Augustinian Priory, Holywell. This sermon is perhaps less technical than earlier treatments but it remains a firm declaration of faith in the Real Presence.

After his death, FitzRalph's bones were brought home and interred in the Church of St Nicholas in Dundalk. Here the local cult to St Richard of Dundalk led to calls for his canonisation and occasioned the famous verses in the margin of a manuscript now conserved at the National Library in Brussels:

> Manny a mile have I gone
> and manny did I walk
> But neuer sawe a hollier man
> Than Richard of Dundalk.

One Bread, One Body, One Borough: Corpus Christi, Drogheda, 1412

COLMÁN Ó CLABAIGH

THE INSTITUTION of the feast of Corpus Christi in Liége around 1230 marked a highpoint in the development of eucharistic devotion in medieval Europe. This solemn commemoration of the Body and Blood of Christ was extended to the whole Church by Pope Urban IV in 1264, and by the fourteenth century its celebration had become universal. In Ireland, as elsewhere in Europe, the feast found expression in a wide variety of liturgical celebrations and popular devotions. These celebrations had both individual and corporate dimensions. Individually, Christians fostered an intense devotion to Christ under the eucharistic species of bread and wine. Reception of the Eucharist by the laity was a relatively rare event, occurring four or five times a year and, ideally, preceded by confession and reconciliation with one's neighbour. Collectively, the feast allowed Christians to celebrate their identity as a redeemed community – the body of Christ – and this corporate emphasis found expression in the eucharistic processions that became regular features of the feast in medieval European cities. References to Corpus Christi processions survive from medieval Dublin and Kilkenny and the ordinances governing the conduct of the Dublin procession issued by Mayor Thomas Collier in 1498 indicate that it was an elaborate and colourful affair, with each of the city's guilds taking responsibility for depicting a biblical tableau. These ranged from the glovers' guild who depicted Adam and Eve being driven from paradise, to the butchers who depicted Christ's tormentors, to the city's young men who, dressed in their finest, represented the nine worthies – heroic figures from scripture, mythology and history who traditionally personified the virtues of chivalry.

The clearest illustration of the corporate, multifaceted nature of the feast comes from the account of its celebration in Drogheda in 1412 that is preserved in Mervyn Archdall's *Monasticon Hibernicum* (1786). Drogheda had developed from two distinct settlements on opposite banks of the River Boyne and the rivalry between the two communities often spilled over into bloodshed, violence and sometimes even death. To counter this, Friar Philip Bennett, a member of St Mary Magdalene's Dominican priory in the town, invited representatives of both communities to attend a sermon on Corpus Christi, 1412, in St Peter's Church, Drogheda. He took as his theme the opening line from Psalm 133: 'Behold, how good and how pleasant it is when brothers live in unity.' He then, in the manner of medieval preachers, proceeded to expand on this phrase with great force and effected a remarkable change in the hearts of his congregation. On finishing his sermon, he invited his listeners to return to the town's Dominican priory where 'they were sumptuously and elegantly entertained'. The preacher's words and the friars' hospitality had a remarkable effect: both factions were reconciled and agreed jointly to petition the king for the charter of incorporation that established Drogheda as a single, united borough. As well as giving an almost unique insight into the impact of a preacher in late medieval Ireland, the incident illustrates how one medieval community understood its call to 'be' the body of Christ and how intimately intertwined liturgy and life could be.

Blessed Bees

EVIE MONAGHAN

D URING THE medieval period, a large corpus of eucharistic miracle stories was established and promoted widely in Europe. These stories were designed to encourage devotion and belief in the Real Presence and were often transposed into specific local contexts for greater effect. One such story, or *exemplum*, is found in the fifteenth-century text known as *Liber Flavus Fergusiorum*, held in the library of the Royal Irish Academy.[1] The story recounts how a priest travelling to visit a sick man, presumably to give him the *viaticum*, encounters a swarm of bees on his way. He captures the swarm and continues his journey but leaves behind the host he was carrying. Realising his mistake, the priest returns but finds the host gone. After spending a year in penitence, an angel appears to him and tells him where to find the host. The swarm of bees had left the priest, returned to where the host lay and brought it to their hive, where they had built 'a fair chapel of wax and an altar, and a Mass-chalice and a pair of priests, fashioning them fairly of wax, to stand over the host'.[2] The priest, instructed by the angel to bring people with him, finds the hive, and many of those who saw the miracle were convinced of the truth of the Real Presence.

This story illustrates a type of eucharistic miracle tale in which the Real Presence is confirmed by the veneration afforded to the host by animals. Indeed, there was a popular *exemplum* of almost exact parallel circulated in the medieval period throughout Europe, in which bees venerated a host that had been placed in a hive by its owner in order to increase the yield of honey.[3] The primary purpose of eucharistic miracle stories was

---

1. For a full discussion of these *exempla*, see Miri Rubin, *Corpus Christi: The Eucharist in Late Medieval Culture* (Cambridge: Cambridge University Press, 1991), pp. 108–29.
2. E. J. Gwynn, 'The priest and the bees', *Ériu*, ii (1905), pp. 82–3.
3. Rubin, *Corpus Christi*, pp. 123–4.

to demonstrate the veracity of the doctrinal claims of the Church, and they operated within a rich symbolic culture. The belief in the corporeal presence of Christ on the altar was a central truth claim of Catholicism, but because of its complex theological basis the Church frequently encountered scepticism on this matter. Nowhere was this more evident than in the sixteenth century when transubstantiation was rejected by the Protestant reformers. Miracles which provided physical proof of the Real Presence were a useful pedagogic tool to convince the laity of the doctrine.

The motif of veneration by animals was a common device and the homage of the bees to the host was drawn from a broader theme that saw the natural world recognise Christ's body in the Eucharist when people did not.[4] The choice of bees has particular resonance for one of the other central themes of eucharistic belief: the fostering of communion within society.

Bees were extremely important to the medieval and early modern world. Their honey was an essential commodity and beeswax was a vital element for religious worship. Aside from their commercial value, the way in which bees organised themselves was seen as a near-perfect model for the way in which a society could function. Writers on beekeeping in the seventeenth century even compared bee colonies to a perfect paradigm of a monarchical state.[5] Indeed, the importance of bees is testified by the fact that many people saw them as an integral part of their property. A court roll from the beginning of the fifteenth century relates a case involving the theft of three swarms of bees in Tipperary. Two centuries later, many of the deponents in the Ulster Depositions testify to the theft of their bees during the 1641 rising.[6] As creatures that were seen as having some sort of supernatural aura, bees were also prominent in stories that involved people in distress. Edmund Nangle, an army officer from Longford, in the midst of a physical and spiritual crisis, recounted how 'blessed bees' descended from heaven and 'entered my belly and all my bowels, driving out as well

---

4. Helena Concannon, *The Blessed Eucharist in Irish History* (Dublin: Browne and Nolan, 1932), p. 8, p. 30, p. 114.
5. Tickner Edwardes, *The Lore of the Honey Bee*, 3rd ed. (London: Methuen & Co., 1909), pp. 32–4.
6. National Library of Ireland, MS D1404; Trinity College Dublin, MS 820, fol. 11r; MS 818, fol. 064v.

the vermin that were in me, as also sucking and carrying away from my body all the scum and filth of them'.[7]

The medieval *exempla* were continued into the early modern period within a more organised doctrinal culture of Tridentine reform. Large compendiums of stories were produced which enabled preachers to supplement their sermons with vivid 'real-life' proofs of doctrine.[8] The stories were perhaps even more useful in a culture in which the Mass was regarded as highly superstitious by Protestant reformers, but also because they alleviated the often theologically heavy sermons of Tridentine preachers. While the age of miracles was widely regarded by Protestants as being over, the miraculous was still a substantial part of Catholic religiosity, even by the promoters of a more austere Tridentine Catholicism.[9] The miracle of the bees in the *Liber Flavus Fergusiorum* thus continued to have resonance for early modern Catholics.

As the Eucharist had become the battleground of reformation controversialists and as Catholics in Ireland faced increasing pressure to conform to the Church of Ireland, the symbolic power of the Real Presence together with the communal harmony of the devoted bees offered a powerful synthesis for their own religious practice and social interaction.

---

7. *Narrative of Edmund Nangle of Cloandarah, 1665* (Dublin, 1665). For an account of bees rescuing the library of a Protestant bishop from destruction, see Raymond Gillespie, *Reading Ireland: Print, Reading and Social Change in Early Modern Ireland* (Manchester: Manchester University Press, 2005), p. 18.
8. Bernadette Cunningham, '"Zeal for God and For Souls": Counter-Reformation Preaching in Early Seventeenth-Century Ireland', Alan J. Fletcher and Raymond Gillespie, eds., *Irish Preaching 700–1700* (Dublin: Four Courts Press, 2001), pp. 120–2.
9. Richard Archdekin, *A Treatise of Miracles Together with New Miracles and Benefits Obtained by the Sacred Relics of St Francis Xavier Exposed in the Church of the Society of Jesus at Mechlin* (Louvain, 1667).

Blood Piety and the Eucharist in Late-Medieval Ireland

SALVADOR RYAN

I T IS a curious fact that during the later Middle Ages, when the chalice had ceased to be offered to congregations gathering for the Eucharist, one finds an explosion of interest in devotions relating to Christ's blood, particularly in northern Europe.[1] This period was characterised by affective devotion – the encouragement of deep meditation on the human suffering of Christ and sympathy with the tribulations of his passion and death, which were ever more graphically portrayed in religious art and forensically elaborated upon in devotional tracts. This was an era in which shrines which claimed to house miracle-working 'relics' of Christ's earthly blood mushroomed across Europe – sites such as Hailes in England, Wilsnack in Germany and Bruges in modern-day Belgium. These pilgrimage sites did not gain universal ecclesiastical approval, for theologians as early as the twelfth-century Guibert of Nogent (1055–1124) pointed out that since Christ's body had been resurrected, he could not have left any part of it behind – and that included any blood!

This was also the heyday of female mystics such as Mechtild of Hackeborn (c. 1240–98), Gertrude of Helfta (1256–1302), Bridget of Sweden (1303–73), Julian of Norwich (c. 1342–1416) and Margery Kempe (c. 1373–1438), all of whom exhibited an extraordinary fascination with images of Christ's saving blood, which poured from his wounds. Some mystics claimed to have been told the exact number of wounds that Christ suffered during his passion (which ran into several thousand) and these numbers often assumed mystical significance in popular prayers

---

1. See especially Caroline Walker Bynum, *Wonderful Blood: Theology and Practice in Late Medieval Germany and Beyond* (Philadelphia: University of Pennsylvania Press, 2007).

and magical charms. Similarly, the exact size of Christ's side wound often appears in devotional tracts in medieval manuscripts, and this wound, or indeed the five wounds as a set, routinely appeared on pendants or religious badges which were worn for protection and blessing.

This broader European devotion to Christ's blood is also evidenced in the devotional literature of medieval Ireland, especially in the religious verse of native Irish bardic poets who composed between the thirteenth and seventeenth centuries. The choice of themes found in these poems also reflects the devotional tastes of the patrons who commissioned them.[2] A dizzying array of images relating to Christ's blood are used to recount the story of mankind's salvation.

The human race is portrayed as encountering difficulty on stormy seas – its boat about to be smashed on the rocks – until a wave of Christ's breast blood rises up beneath the boat and carries it safely into the harbour of Christ's heart wound. In a related image, Christ is portrayed as sitting in the boat with humanity, rowing it to safety with an 'oar empurpled in breast blood' (the lance with which Christ's side was pierced). The so-called 'instruments of Christ's passion' or *arma Christi* were ubiquitously represented during this period and were considered to work for the benefit of those who trusted in them and to the detriment of those who rejected them. The fear of sinners is evoked when Christ is portrayed as an angry hunter chasing his quarry (mankind), which darts away from him and finds refuge in a wood (that of the cross) or, in another image, hides behind a thicket of thorns (the crown of thorns). Even the *titulus* board was said to work for the weal of the Irish – after all, one tradition claimed that the letters INRI spelt *'In Ri'* ('the King' in Old Irish), and thus a fourth language was represented on Calvary when the Irish proclaimed Christ king on the cross.

Agricultural imagery was also used for the shedding of Christ's blood. Christ is portrayed as sowing new seeds of humanity in the ploughed soil (flesh) of his wounded hands and feet (turned over by Longinus' lance) and most deeply in his heart. One poet refers to the blood-rain (of Christ's

---

2. Salvador Ryan, 'Reign of Blood: Aspects of Devotion to the Wounds of Christ in Late Medieval Ireland', Joost Augusteijn and Mary Ann Lyons, eds., *Irish History: A Research Yearbook* (Dublin: Four Courts Press, 2002); and 'Exchanging Blood for Wine: Envisaging Heaven in Irish Bardic Religious Poetry', Carolyn Muessig and Ad Putter eds., *Envisaging Heaven in the Middle Ages* (Abingdon: Routledge, 2006).

crucifixion) as the shower that made this seed grow – the heavier the rain the brighter the sunshine (of Christ's mercy) afterwards. The eucharistic resonances of Christ's blood-letting are captured in the frequent Irish use of the term *fíon-fhuil* or 'wine-blood' from as early as the eighth century to refer to Christ's blood on Calvary. This was considered to presage the drinking of a wine-feast in heaven, a banquet at which no bouncer would be needed, as some poets remarked.

The most striking Irish image of devotion to Christ's blood, however, is a Marian one. The famous *pietà* scene in which the dead Christ lies in Mary's lap was recalled in many popular medieval lives of Christ and Mary which circulated around Europe. When one of these, the *Liber de Passione Christi*, was translated from Latin into Irish in the fifteenth century, however, an additional feature crept into the account. The Virgin Mary was portrayed as bending her head down to kiss and then drink the blood from Christ's wounds, and protesting vehemently when the body was taken away as she had not had her fill. Here the mother of Christ performs an act which resembles part of the Gaelic Irish keening ritual for which there are many references in Irish literature and, indeed, some claims that the action was witnessed historically.[3] Typically, when a male died violently, the principal female mourner (most often a wife or female companion) would drink the blood from the wounds of the dead body, not allowing any of his blood to seep into the ground. This is most famously exemplified in Eibhlín Dubh Ní Chonaill's late-eighteenth-century lament *Caoineadh Airt Uí Laoghaire* ('The Lament for Art O'Leary'). However, in the case of the Virgin Mary, her drinking of Christ's blood almost certainly contains other layers of meaning. This might include a deep respect for Christ's blood and the concomitant fear, seen in a normal eucharistic setting, that it would ever spill to the ground – part of the reason, surely, for the withdrawal of the chalice from the laity in the first instance. Furthermore, Mary's craving to be allowed drink her fill of Christ's blood is reminiscent of medieval mystical literature as exemplified in the fourteenth-century Middle English text, *A Talking of the Love of God*:

3.   Alexandra Bergholm, 'The Drinking of Blood in the Ritual Context of Mourning', A. Ahlqvist and P. O'Neill, eds., *Language and Power in the Celtic World* (Sydney: Celtic Studies Foundation, 2011), pp. 1–12.

I suck the blood from his feet … I embrace and kiss as if I was mad. I roll and suck I do not know how long. And when I am sated, I want yet more …[4]

In this image, then, the figure of Mary is an amalgam of *Mater Dolorosa*, Gaelic Irish keening woman and medieval mystic in her devotion to Christ's blood.

_____

4. Bynum, *Wonderful Blood*, 2.

Annunciation scene with pelican piercing its own breast beneath. Detail. O'Dea crozier. © Diocese of Limeri

The O'Dea Mitre and Crozier

ANTHONY HARPUR

IN 1418, the goldsmith Thomas O'Carryd completed a jewelled and enamelled silver-gilt mitre and crozier for Cornelius O'Dea, Bishop of Limerick. These two treasures were concealed on the orders of a future bishop of Limerick to prevent their destruction during the Reformation, suggesting they were held in very high regard even in the sixteenth century. They are the most important examples of native Irish works of late-medieval religious art to survive today, yet their design conforms completely to the style and standard of goldsmiths' work from England or Continental Europe. The only evidence of Irish manufacture is found in the inscriptions on both the mitre and crozier, which name the patron and craftsman, and give the date of completion.

The mitre is made of leather, covered with gilded silver and decorated with nearly two hundred gems, and at least seven thousand fresh-water seed pearls. Early nineteenth-century sketches show that, originally, many more pearls and gemstones adorned the mitre. The O'Dea mitre displays the largest surviving collection of jewels from ancient or medieval Ireland. Tiny figures depicting the Virgin and child being venerated by Bishop O'Dea are mounted on the front and back of the mitre. This *mitra preciosa* was only used by the bishop on the highest holy days. The silver-gilt crozier is two metres in length and weighs 3.8 kilograms. The elaborate head of the crozier is decorated with two registers of niches displaying moulded silver-gilt and translucent enamelled figures of the Holy Trinity, the Virgin and various saints. The volute, or crook, of the crozier is decorated with twelve pairs of large pearls and a scene of the annunciation. Below this scene is a pelican piercing its breast to feed its blood to its young, a symbol of the crucifixion and the Eucharist.

Because no other Irish examples have survived, Cornelius O'Dea's mitre and crozier must be compared with English and continental examples. Medieval precious mitres are particularly rare items; one of the oldest, preserved in Amalfi (Italy), was made for St Louis of Toulouse before 1295. William of Wykeham's reconstructed mitre, from the late 1300s, is in New College, Oxford, and a later fifteenth-century jewelled mitre is preserved in Salzburg, Austria. The O'Dea crozier has long been compared to William of Wykeham's crozier, made before 1400 and also preserved in Oxford, and has recently been compared to croziers from Haarlem (Netherlands) and Cologne (Germany), both also from the fourteenth century, yet Richard Foxe's crozier in Oxford (early 1500s) is probably a better comparison. What makes the O'Dea mitre and crozier particularly rare is the fact that they were clearly made as a set.

The images on the crozier are an intriguing selection. The six moulded silver-gilt figures in the lower niches depict the Holy Trinity, the Virgin and Child, St Peter as pope, St Paul the Apostle, St Patrick holding the *Bachall Ísu* ('Staff of Jesus', traditionally believed to have been presented to Patrick), and St Munchin, patron of Limerick diocese. The figure of St Peter recalls the election of Pope Martin V on 11 November 1417 by the Council of Constance (1414–18). This election of a single pope ended three decades of scandalous division in the Catholic Church when two, then three, competing popes claimed pontifical authority. The depiction of St Patrick holding the *Bachall Ísu* is unique: there is no other medieval Irish image of St Patrick holding his most famous relic. Above these figures, six translucent enamels depict St John the Evangelist, St Catherine of Alexandria, St Margaret of Antioch, St Barbara, St Brigid of Kildare with a crozier, and St Radegund of Poitiers, who was venerated by pilgrims to Rathkeale before 1435. These saints were likely chosen for their devotion to holy virginity, useful given the difficulties the medieval clergy often had with celibacy. The volute, or crook, encloses the scene of the annunciation to the Virgin Mary. The incident depicted on the crozier is the last act of the annunciation: the Virgin accepts the message of the angel that she would become the mother of Jesus. It is the very moment of the incarnation, in which Jesus was conceived in the Virgin's womb. The pelican positioned below the annunciation transforms that scene from a mere depiction of the account in the Gospel of St Luke. The pelican is a eucharistic emblem, representing Christ's sacrifice on the cross. Here it recalls the miracle of the consecration of bread and wine into the Body and Blood of Christ, which is compared to the miracle of the incarnation of the body and blood of Jesus in the womb of the Virgin. The two images together symbolise the doctrine of transubstantiation in the Eucharist.

O'Dea mitre. © Diocese of Limerick. The O'Dea mitre and crozier are displayed in the Hunt Museum in Limerick on behalf of the Diocese

The Fraternity of St Anne in St Audoen's Parish, Dublin

COLM LENNON

I N THE late middle ages, dozens of religious fraternities of laymen and laywomen were founded in parishes in the area of eastern Ireland, known as the Pale. The primary function was the celebration of Mass by specially appointed chaplains on behalf of the members who wished to have their souls remembered in perpetuity to facilitate their passage through purgatory. Among these foundations was the fraternity of St Anne, located in a specially built chapel in the parish church of St Audoen in central Dublin. Established as a corporation in 1430 by a charter of King Henry VI, the fraternity in honour of St Anne in St Audoen's was entitled to accumulate lands and houses yielding an income of up to 100 marks (£66-13s-4d) per annum, to be used for the equipping and maintaining of the fraternity chapel and the payment of its personnel. Six chaplains were to be appointed by the membership, each to serve at one of the designated altars within the chapel, dedicated respectively to St Anne, the Blessed Virgin, St Catherine, St Nicholas, St Thomas and St Clare. Among the founder members were gentry, merchants, clerics and craftspeople, bearing names such as Cusack, Blakeney, Stafford, White and Barnewall.

By the late fifteenth century, the fraternity of St Anne had become wealthy through the donations and bequests of members and pious benefactors who wished to be commemorated in the prayers and ministrations of the chaplains. The fraternity's portfolio contained dozens of properties, including houses and farms, which yielded an annual income far in excess of the stipulated 100 marks. This allowed for a lively round of devotional activities, as well as the decoration of the fraternity chapel and church, especially on days of the funeral rites of brothers or sisters. At least one elaborate fresco, depicting St Anne and the Virgin, was commissioned for the south wall of the chapel. As well as celebrating the obsequies of dead members, many of whom were interred below the chapel altars, there were perennial obits observed on their anniversaries as requested by testators. Special ceremonies, including a procession and a banquet, marked the celebration of the feast of the patroness, St Anne, on 26 July every year. Each of the chaplains was bestowed with lodgings and the necessaries for the fit performance of his priestly functions. In return, these fraternity priests commemorated the deceased members and assisted in the running of the parish through participation in the liturgy, and also through charitable and educational work.

On the eve of the Reformation, the fraternity of St Anne was an integral part of religious and social life in St Audoen's parish. Besides the well-maintained chapel, a collegiate building for the housing of the chaplains had been acquired in the vicinity of St Audoen's. Many of Dublin's leading families, who worshipped there, provided brothers and sisters and arranged for their own commemoration with tombs in the chapel. Officers of the fraternity served as aldermen of the city council. Ecclesiastical changes under Queen Elizabeth led to the ceding of the church of St Audoen to the small Church of Ireland community in the parish. The majority of the parishioners who remained Catholic, including the members of St Anne's fraternity, moved their worship to private houses, such as the mansion of the chaplains, known as the college of St Audoen's. Despite the Anglican reforms, which anathemised belief in purgatory, however, the religious fraternities were not outlawed in Ireland as happened in England, and St Anne's survived as a corporation into the seventeenth century with its properties and revenues intact. A papal bull of 1569 had enjoined all Catholic fraternity members to husband their resources for bestowal only on their co-religionists.

Down to the 1640s, St Anne's fraternity played a crucial role in channelling support for priests returning to Dublin from continental colleges to establish a renewed Catholic system of worship. This was in spite of the fact that several leading Protestants participated in the affairs of the fraternity, and also notwithstanding the complaints of the rector (prebendary) of St Audoen's to the effect that none of the income from its rentals was going towards the support of the parish church. An attempt

≈

to take over the fraternity by Lord Deputy Wentworth failed due to the outbreak of rebellion in 1641, but when the fraternity resumed its meetings in the 1650s, control had passed to the Anglican membership. Nevertheless, St Anne's continued to dispense charity to distressed parishioners from Catholic as well as Protestant families down to the 1680s. The fraternity was finally suppressed as a religious association by parliament in 1695. As a late-medieval institution which survived the early Reformation and whose membership straddled the confessional divide, the fraternity of St Anne, through its well-documented archive, reveals some of the complexities of change and continuity in Irish religious history.

FURTHER READING

Berry, Henry F., 'History of the Religious Gild of St Anne', *Royal Irish Academy Proceedings*, section C, xxx (1904–5), pp. 21–106.

Clark, Mary and Raymond Refaussé, eds., *Directory of Historic Dublin Guilds* (Dublin: Dublin Public Libraries, 1993).

Empey, Adrian, 'The Layperson in the Parish: The Medieval Inheritance', R. Gillespie and W. G. Neely, eds. *The Laity and the Church of Ireland, 1000–2000: All Sorts and Conditions* (Dublin: Four Courts Press, 2000), pp. 36–41.

Lennon, Colm, 'The Chantries in the Irish Reformation: The Case of St Anne's Guild, Dublin, 1550–1630', R. V. Comerford, Mary Cullen, J. R. Hill and Colm Lennon, eds., *Religion, Conflict and Coexistence in Ireland: Essays in Honour of Monsignor Patrick J. Corish* (Dublin: Gill and Macmillan, 1990), pp. 6–25.

_____ 'The Fraternities and Cultural Duality in Late Medieval Ireland, 1450–1550', Christopher Black and Pamela Gravestock, eds., *Early Modern Confraternities in Europe and the Americas: International and Interdisciplinary Perspectives* (Aldershot: Ashgate, 2006), pp. 35–52.

~III
Fragmentations

Renewal, Reformation and Ruins

HENRY A. JEFFERIES

DOTTED AROUND the Irish countryside are the ruins of many hundreds of medieval parish churches and chapels. Because of their ruinous state today, historians used to see them as evidence that Irish church buildings were 'tumbledown, disused and makeshift places of worship' in the later middle ages. Recent research, however, has revealed that most of those churches had either been newly built, rebuilt or refurbished just before the Protestant Reformation swept across most of northern Europe.

When Martin Luther ignited the Reformation with his protest against indulgences in 1517, most people in Ireland went to Mass in churches that were in sound condition. The churches were generally very small by today's standards: typically between fifteen to sixteen metres long, and six to seven metres wide. Yet they compared very favourably with those other stone buildings in the Irish countryside of the time – the tower houses of the landowning elite.

Architecturally the churches in the countryside were relatively simple. Typically they were rectangular buildings with steep gables and roofs covered in timber shingles or thatch. Their walls were built of local stones bonded by mortar, with dressed stones framing the windows, doors and corners. They had a large window above the altar on the eastern end of the church, sometimes boasting stained glass, and a number of smaller windows with plain glass in the side walls. The doors were located towards the western end of the church, usually with a decorated baptismal font nearby. There was often a timber rood screen, with a crucifixion scene on top, separating the chancel around the altar from the nave where the congregation stood during Mass. Only one Irish rood screen survived the Reformation intact – that from St Olave's Church in Waterford – but evidence of the former existence of rood screens has been found in a surprising number of Irish churches, especially in the Pale.

There is some evidence that the internal walls of Irish churches in the sixteenth century were usually plastered. Painted on to the plaster of many churches were vivid religious images, perhaps of God and/or Jesus and some saints, or a Doom painting of Judgement Day with the just being led to heaven and the damned being carried off to hell. The windows too were sometimes decorated with religious images. Close to the altar of every church was a statue of its patron saint, and usually a statue of the Blessed Virgin also. Large wax candles were lit before the statues in displays of devotion. Parishioners with money paid generously to have their bodies, and those of their beloved, buried under the floor of the church, close to the altar and/or a statue. The shattered, roofless ruins that stand today are mere ghosts of the decorated churches that once reflected the religious fears and aspirations of our forebears.

The churches in use in the first half of the sixteenth century not only reflect the faith of the people of that time, but they also tell us about a great religious revival experienced in Ireland before the Reformation challenged long-accepted verities. That revival may have been inspired by the preaching of mendicant friars: Dominicans, Augustinians, Carmelites and especially the Franciscans. It is reflected even today in the ruins of a great number of impressive friaries built across Ireland after 1400, and in the remarkable number of parish churches and chapels built throughout the country.

The surge in church building was accompanied by the election of churchwardens in parishes across the Pale and further afield. Churchwardens took responsibility for raising money for the maintenance of their parish church and for providing the liturgical equipment and priestly accoutrements required by canon law. The churchwarden accounts for St Werburgh's Church, Dublin, show that parishioners lavished money and other gifts on their church before the Reformation. Many parishioners across Ireland joined religious societies called confraternities and committed themselves to living exemplary Christian lives. We know from the provincial synods of Cashel that choirs were established in many southern parishes in Ireland and organ music was growing increasingly popular.

With the onset of the Tudor Reformations in Ireland, the parish churches were mostly abandoned as the Mass was replaced by the Book of Common Prayer and the Catholic priest was replaced by a minister of the Church of Ireland. Not only the smaller churches in rural locations, but even many city churches like St Werburgh's in Dublin, lost their congregations as they were Protestantised and became 'ruinous'. The church ruins that we can see today stand in mute testimony to the religious commitment of a bygone age.

FURTHER READING

Jefferies, Henry A., *The Irish Church and the Tudor Reformations* (Dublin: Four Courts Press, 2010).

Pilgrimage to Rome
MÍCHEÁL MACCRAITH

D URING THE Middle Ages, it became quite popular for members of the Irish nobility to go on pilgrimage to Rome. That the religious motives of some of these pilgrims were not above reproach, however, is borne out by the following quatrain:

Teicht do Róim,
Mór saído, becc torbai;
In rí chon-daigi hi foss,
Mani-mbera latt, ní fogbai.

To go to Rome,
Much labour, little profit,
The King you seek here,
You will not find, unless you bring him with you.

Indeed the wisdom of this verse is as pertinent today as when it was first composed, and its overall message is not just confined to pilgrimages but open to universal application. Though the poet was speaking here in general terms, we do have precise details of one Irish prince who actually died in Rome while on pilgrimage. This was no other than Donnchadh mac Briain, son of Brian Bóraimhe (Boru) who died in 1064 and was buried in the church of San Stefano Rotondo. His funerary slab, surmounted by a seven-point crown, contains some interesting details. It describes Donnchadh as King of Thomond and Cashel, son of Brian Bóraimhe, King of all Ireland, and adds that he gave the royal crown as a gift to the pope.

At the beginning of the early modern period in 1511, Aodh Ó Domhnaill, lord of Tír Chonaill, landed at Carlingford on his way home from Rome via London. The fact that there was a holy well near Carlingford dedicated to St

James the Apostle, and that the nearby parish of Cooley, not to mention the church of Grange, was dedicated to the same saint, seems to indicate a link with the famous pilgrimage to Santiago de Compostela. In Ireland, churches dedicated to St James were usually found in ports, and that of Carlingford may well have been a setting-off point for pilgrims travelling abroad.

The most detailed description of an early modern pilgrimage from Ireland is found in Tadhg Ó Cianáin's account of Aodh Ó Néill and Ruaidhrí Ó Domhnaill's journey to the continent, beginning in September 1607. The Irish party visited the Marian shrine of Loreto on 22 April 1608, and the seven basilicas of Rome on 12 June. Given Turkish dominance of the eastern Mediterranean routes, a voyage to Palestine was a perilous undertaking in the sixteenth century, even after the Turks' crushing defeat at Lepanto in 1571. By substituting a visit to the shrine enclosing the house where the Blessed Virgin lived in Nazareth, as well as visiting the tombs of the apostles in Rome, the dual pilgrimage to Loreto and Rome became *the* pilgrimage *par excellence*, a virtual pilgrimage to the Holy Land.

All the evidence indicates that Ó Néill's decision to visit Loreto was most deliberate, as the fastest way to Rome from Milan was by the Via Francigena near the western coast and not in an easterly direction. Furthermore, the fact that these two days alone comprise 40 per cent of a narrative that spans over fourteen months, suggests that the author considered the visits to the Santa Casa and the Seven Basilicas as the highlights of his chronicle. He underscores the unity linking these two days by concluding the description of each one of them with the same prayer, a quite unusual prayer that is only found in medieval Irish homilies.

In 1635, Robert Corbington, an Irish-born Jesuit acting as a pentientiary in Loreto, affixed four large tablets to the walls of the basilica outlining the history of the Holy House in Irish, Welsh, Scots and English. This summary of the history of the Santa Casa and how it was transported by angels to Loreto is based on the most famous source of the tradition, Pietro di Giorgio Tolomei's *Translatio Miraculosa Ecclesiae Beatae Mariae Virginis di Loreto* (1471–3). While contemporary readers will naturally baulk at the idea of angelic transportation, it is worth noting that when, in 1294, Philip II of Anjou married Margherita, the daughter of Nikephoros Angelos, Despot of Epiros, the dowry included the stones taken from the house of the Blessed Virgin. One easily understands how the historical Angelos family morphed into the angels of legend. It is also significant that an older contemporary of Tolomei's refers to a natural seaborne transportation of the Holy House from Nazareth to Loreto.

At a time when Irish was being eliminated from public discourse at home, it is surprising to discover such a prominent public inscription in that very same language near the Adriatic. Over two metres high and one metre wide, the tablet is affixed to a pillar on the left hand of the church, nearly two metres above the ground. Robert Corbington would hardly have gone to such lengths in 1635 unless Loreto was already a popular destination for Irish pilgrims, most likely as the first step of a dual pilgrimage that carried on to Rome.

Corpus Christi in Rome, 1608

MÍCHEÁL MACCRAITH

W HILE YOUGHAL claims to have the oldest unbroken Corpus Christi Procession in Ireland, dating back to 1898, we actually have an account in Irish of such a procession that is nearly three hundred years older. This particular procession, however, did not take place in Ireland, but in Rome on 5 June 1608. The reporter is Tadhg Ó Cianáin, the learned chronicler who compiled a journal of the travels of Aodh Ó Néill, Rudhraighe Ó Domhnaill and their entourage from Ireland to the continent. In the Roman section of his narrative, from 25 April to 27 November 1608, Ó Cianáin offers many valuable insights into the world of Counter-Reformation Rome during the papacy of Paul V. His description of the Corpus Christi Procession is as follows:

> On the Thursday of Corpus Christi an order came from the Holy Father to the princes that eight of their chosen noblemen should go in person to carry the canopy which was over the Blessed Sacrament while it was being borne solemnly in the hands of the pope in procession from the great church of San Pietro in Vaticano to the church of Saint James in Borgo Vecchio, and from there back again to the church of Saint Peter. They came into the presence of His Holiness the Pope. They carried the canopy over the Blessed Sacrament and the pope, and never before did Irishmen receive a comparable honour and privilege (*ní fhuaradar Éireannaigh riamh a gcompráid sin d'onóir agus d'óirmhidin*).

> The Italians were greatly surprised that they should be shown such deference and respect, for some of them said that seldom before was any one nation in the world appointed to carry the canopy. With the ambassadors of all the Catholic kings and princes of Christendom who

happened to be in the city at that time it was an established custom that they, in succession, every year got their opportunity to carry the canopy. They were jealous, envious, and surprised, that they were not allowed to carry it on this particular day.

The procession was reverent, imposing, and beautiful, for the greater part of the regular Orders and every order and community of the great metropolitan churches of Rome were in it, and many princes, dukes, and great lords. They had no less than a thousand lighted, waxen torches. Following them there were twenty-six [bishops], both archbishops and sub-bishops. Next there were thirty-six cardinals. The pope carried the Blessed Sacrament, and the Irish lords and noblemen to the number of eight bore the canopy. His guard of Swiss soldiers were around the pope, and on either side of him and after him were his two large troops of cavalry. The streets were then filled with people. It was considered by all that they were not less than one hundred thousand [there]. When they reached Saint Peter's, the pope laid the Blessed Sacrament on the great high-altar. Then he went on his knees. He prostrated himself, invoked and prayed. Then he gave Benediction to everybody in general. He retired to his palace after that, [and] everyone who was there went to their palaces and their homes.[1]

Tadhg Ó Cianáin's account is remarkably similar to the description of the Corpus Christi procession contained in Gregory Martin's *Roma Sancta* (1581). Whereas Martin is not loath to introduce a polemical note – 'our Saviour is caried triumphantly … to the confusion of faythlesse Heretiques' – Ó Cianáin's chief concern is to emphasise the unique honour paid to the Irish. Martin unwittingly confirms Ó Cianáin's sense of pride in noting that the canopy was borne by four of the noblest persons there present, including a Polish majordomo in the papal chamber. Ó Cianáin's estimation of the crowd thronging the streets as 100,000 must be taken as an exaggeration, given that the population of Rome in 1597 was officially recorded at just over 116,000.

The Church of St James in Borgo Vecchio, better known San Giacomo a Scossacavalli, was destroyed in 1937 to make way for the Via della

---

1. See Nollaig Ó Muraíle, ed., *Turas na dTaoiseach nUltach as Éirinn: From Ráth Maoláin to Rome* (Rome: Pontifical Irish College, 2007), pp. 296–9.

〜

Conciliazione leading up to St Peter's. An eighteenth-century engraving depicts the church of San Giacomo and its piazza. The building barely visible on the right is the Palazzo dei Penitenzieri, where the Irish princes resided. The palace on the left, Palazzo Torlonia, belonged to Henry VIII who gave it to Cardinal Campeggio in 1519, the same cardinal who was to play such a vital role in the divorce proceedings between Henry and Catherine of Aragon. After England's break with Rome, the palace remained in possession of the Campeggio family until 1609.

Dr Geoffrey Keating on Transubstantiation

TADHG Ó DÚSHLÁINE

IN REFERENCE to the Eucharistic Congress of 1936, Helena Concannon, in *The Blessed Eucharist in Irish History* (1932), predicted that 'The Blessed Eucharist in Irish Poetry is likely to form a subject for discussion at the Gaelic Section of the Congress.'[1]

However, I'm not sure that it did, and although much has been done concerning aspects of native Irish spirituality since, the centrality of the Eucharist to the native tradition – from the post-Tridentine period to Vatican II – has not received the attention it merits.

The *felix culpa* that was the defeat of the native Irish at the Battle of Kinsale afforded Irish Catholic recusants accession to hands-on contemporary European learning. None more so than in the case of Dr Geoffrey Keating – priest, poet, historian, theologian – educated in the post-Tridentine continental colleges of the Catholic Counter-Reformation and rightly regarded as the father of modern Irish prose. More significant, however, is his contribution to modern Irish thought, providing in the seventeenth century some of the classics of the *ratio studiorum*, in literature, philosophy and theology. His first major work is the apologetical explanatory defence of the Mass and owes much to the work of his contempories. Despite all its Tridentine orthodoxy, however, on the substantial matter of controversy of the time, the question of transubstantiation, Keating's approach is not only illustrative of the achievement of Irish apologetics in the seventeenth century but of the Irish achievement in general, from the time of St Patrick to the time of our accession to the EU: a mutually beneficial amalgam of the native and the continental.

---

1. Helena Concannon, *The Blessed Eucharist in Irish History* (Dublin: Browne and Nolan, 1932), p. xix.

Keating's *Eochair-Sgiath an Aifrinn* (The Key-Defence of the Mass) owes much to the work of Cardinal Bellarmino and theologian Francisco de Suarez, and has much in common with the Irish Jesuit, Henry Fitzsimon's *The Justification and Exposition of the Divine Sacrifice of the Masse [sic], and of Al [sic] Rites and Ceremonies Thereto Belonging* (Douai, 1611). Chapter nine, the longest, is one 'in which is discussed and where we show, in opposition to Calvin and his followers, that not only do the words *Hoc est enim Corpus Meum* mean the image of Christ's Body, but the very body itself'.

Keating exhibits his mastery of biblical exegesis in his commentary on the sixth chapter of St John's Gospel and in his allegorical interpretation of Genesis 27, his grasp of scholastic philosophy in his discussion of Aquinas' four distinctions of metamorphosis, and his familiarity with the preaching handbooks of medieval *exempla* with versions of tales from Odo de Ceritona, Ceasarius of Heisterbach and the *Magnum Speculum Exemplorum*.

Keating appreciated that the medium is the message, and central to his methodology, both in choice of matter and form, is his mission to acculturate his teaching to his audience. His versions of the Latin *exempla* have much in common with native Fenian tales, while the apologetics and abstract theology are illustrated with homely examples. Two of these central examples still resonate.

In 'A Lough Neagh Sequence', Seamus Heaney hints at the paradoxical continuity of tradition through transformation: 'The lough will claim a victory every year./It has virtue that hardens wood to stone.'[2] Keating's use of the same example is more forensic:

The following is a wonderful example of transformation in Ireland, namely, Lough Neagh in the North. When a holly pole is left standing there for seven years, the part of it stuck in the ground is transformed into iron, the part under water into stone, and the part above water into a holly bush, as we read in Cambrensis in the book he wrote about the wonders of Ireland.

2.   Seamus Heaney, 'A Lough Neagh Sequence', *A Door Into the Dark* (London: Faber & Faber, 1969).

In the second example, Keating marvels at:

> … how blind Calvin is when he contends that God cannot transform
> the substance of bread into the substance of Christ's Body when we see
> the bread that people eat on a daily basis transformed into flesh and
> blood. This is no more difficult than seed into shoots, shoots into ears
> and ears into seeds; or the transformation of the ash of fern into glass.

In both his theological and historical works, Keating makes much of the
argument *ex traditio,* in this instance quoting from St Paul (2 Th 2). No
doubt he would have appreciated the dynamic continuity of the native
tradition in the homely explanation of the Eucharist by one of our
contemporary theologians who adverts to the eucharistic resonances of
everyday meals:

> Take any food or drink and bless God for it as part of the free gift of life;
> its necessities, supports, healings and enhancements God pours out
> to all equally and forever. Then take that food and drink in open hand
> and open chalice, the symbol of life as pure grace before it can become
> property; then first break it and pour it out to others as they must do for
> you; each prepared to sacrifice something, and if necessary in extreme
> circumstances, life itself for others.[3]

---

3. James P. Mackey, *Irish Times* (10 June 2011).

The Catholic Reformation in Seventeenth-Century Ireland: Vincent de Paul's Missionaries in Munster

ALISON FORRESTAL

You have given yourself to God to stand firm in the country in which you are now, preferring to risk death rather than fail to assist your neighbour, in the midst of dangers.

B Y THE time that the superior general of the Congregation of the Mission (Vincentians), Vincent de Paul, dispatched this message of encouragement and praise from Paris to his confrère Gerard Brin in Ireland in April 1650, King Charles I had been beheaded, an English commonwealth had been established, without a king or house of lords, and Oliver Cromwell had arrived in Ireland (August 1649). Cromwell's immediate task was to reconquer Ireland, unsettled by war since the Ulster Rising in 1641, and to secure it against future rebellion. Until his departure from Ireland in May 1650, he tackled the military resistance of royalists and the Catholic Confederate army, and implemented a policy of confiscation and resettlement of lands held by Catholic rebels. By the end of 1650, only Connaught held out against parliamentarian troops, and in April 1653 the last of the royalist forces surrendered in Cavan. War was accompanied by social and economic destruction, most notably in urban areas such as Limerick, whose population endured a dreadful outbreak of plague and a six-month siege before surrendering to the forces of Cromwell's son-in-law, Henry Ireton, in October 1651.

In the midst of this turmoil, five Irish priests and clerics, including Gerard Brin, a native of Cashel diocese, represented the Congregation of the Mission in south-west Ireland, along with two or three French colleagues. The Irish of the cohort all originated from Munster, and their familiarity with the region meant that it was there that they ministered principally after they left Paris in October 1646. In the dioceses of Limerick, Cashel and Emly, they carried out preaching and catechism, and offered sacramental care, each key elements of the ministry to which their association was dedicated. On its foundation in 1625, de Paul dedicated the Congregation of the Mission to the evangelisation of the rural Catholic poor, and it became representative of a massive recovery of Catholic institutions and piety after the Council of Trent (1545–63) as its membership grew under his stewardship. To 1660, when de Paul died, twenty-three or perhaps twenty-four Irish clerics joined the Congregation, most having left Ireland to pursue their study for the priesthood on the continent.

De Paul's decision to send five of these men to Ireland in 1646 was more pressing than a basic desire to serve the rural poor, however. In the mid-1640s, he was approached by a number of Irish bishops exiled in France who requested that he provide missionaries to serve in Ireland, where their own priests were under increasing pressure to provide pastoral services. The Congregation missionaries encountered similar troubles, and most returned to France within two years of their arrival because of the dangers they encountered, while a third died in Ireland in 1649. In one of his infrequent reports to their superior general in Paris, Brin reported that after the siege of Limerick was broken, he and his confrère, Edmond Barry, originally from the diocese of Cloyne, left the city 'with one hundred or 120 priests and monks, all disguised and mixed in with the soldiers from the town, who left the day the enemy was supposed to enter it'. Fearing for their lives, they parted in order to escape; Brin headed to his home place in Cashel before boarding a ship to France, while Barry sought refuge in the mountains. As missionaries in Ireland often did, he relied on the charity of a local Catholic woman for two months before also returning to France. Others were not so fortunate: amongst the citizens excluded by name from protection of life and property when Limerick capitulated was the bishop of Emly, Terence O'Brien, who was executed and his head exposed on Saint John's Gate in the city, after he was discovered administering to the sick.

The first Vincentian mission to Ireland thus ended in failure in 1652, and it was not until the nineteenth century that the Vincentians took up permanent residence in Ireland. Isolated from their superior in Paris, and often separated from their colleagues once they arrived in Ireland, de Paul's men were utterly reliant on the goodwill of local citizens to carry out their pastoral duties. Objectively judged, their mission had little hope of success, given the small number sent and the treacherous conditions under which they operated. De Paul appears to have been persuaded to assist the Irish because of his personal loyalty to exiled Irish clergy, notwithstanding the risks inherent in this enterprise; indeed, he was convinced that the missionaries' exposure to danger and possibly death imitated the example of a suffering Christ. In the spirit of the Catholic Reformation, there was no more 'fruitful' or 'necessary mission' than that of assisting Catholic brethren in need.

Mr Craghead Takes Communion

RAYMOND GILLESPIE

As CHRISTENDOM fragmented in the sixteenth and seventeenth centuries, the Eucharist became a source of division. Theologians devised competing explanations for what happened at the sacrament, interpreting its significance for their own communities. Outside ecclesiastical assemblies, catechisms and university theology faculties, its meaning preoccupied few people. In Ireland, Catholics, despite catechisms in English and Irish, often had a shaky view of the Eucharist. Capuchin missioners near Dublin in the 1660s were told that the Eucharist was a picture of God or the grace of God. A Mayo widow in the 1690s, when asked what the Eucharist was, replied 'I receive the Virgin Mary (God bless her) with the little Jesus in her arms.' Protestants did not know their catechism either, and one Dublin minister recorded the 'scarcely conceivable ignorance' of those who presented themselves for the Lord's Supper.[1] Most of those living in seventeenth-century Ireland were uninterested in theological controversy, but they were not unconcerned with religion. Their interest was in devotion relevant to their everyday lives rather than dry doctrine.

It is difficult to understand how early modern people understood the Eucharist, since their beliefs were so unexceptional that they did not bother to write them down. We can only explore their ideas of the Eucharist indirectly, by examining their devotional aids. In the Presbyterian tradition, advice was offered by Robert Craghead in his 1695 tract *Advice to Communicants*. There is no doubting Craghead's Presbyterian credentials. Born in Scotland in 1633, he was ordained in 1658. He ministered in Donaghmore in Donegal and later in First Derry. In 1698, he went briefly

---

1. For these examples, see Raymond Gillespie, *Devoted People: Belief and Religion in Early Modern Ireland* (Manchester: Manchester University Press, 1997), p. 25, pp. 66–7.

135

to Scotland but returned to First Derry where he remained until his death in 1711.[2] During his time in Derry, he crossed swords with the Church of Ireland bishop, William King, on forms of worship, including kneeling at the Eucharist. On these matters Craghead's position was orthodoxly Presbyterian. However his advice to communicants contains an emotional aspect that reveals another religiosity. His text prepared his readers for Communion. When it came to the liturgy, the language he used to explain what was happening was closer to the interiority often associated with the Counter Reformation:

> When thou seest the bread broken then thou art to meditate on Christ crucified and his blessed broken body and bleeding wounds and so behold him as exquisite pain crying out as being forsaken, mocked and tempted by the wicked to come out of that pain and mourn for all the deep hand we had in all his sufferings, we having pierced him, are obliged to look and mourn.[3]

Other meditations, intended to make the Eucharist applicable to the communicant in a very material way, were also provided.

How typical was Craghead of the more doctrinally austere Protestant groups in Ireland, often concerned with word over sacrament? One independent minister preaching at the Communion service at Youghal in 1681 had his words written down by a member of the congregation:

> … the ordinance you are now upon is Christ preaching to your eyes. You have heard him preached to your ears many a time but he is now in this appointment of his speaking to your eyes. Here is the flesh of the Son of God broken and the blood of God shed.

These themes appear in other sermons with the congregation being urged to 'look through the bread and wine to the blood of the holy Lamb of God'.[4] This is hardly the language of austere Calvinism that we might expect from

---

2. J. and S. G. McConnell, *Fasti of the Irish Presbyterian Church*, 12 parts (Belfast, 1937–51), I, p. 9.
3. Robert Craghead, *Advice to Communicants* (Edinburgh, 1695), pp. 84–8.
4. National Library of Ireland, MS 4201, p. 25, p. 48, p. 61, p. 202.

such a group. It shows a devotion to the Eucharist closer to what might be expected from their Catholic counterparts.

Despite the many explanations of the Eucharist in the seventeenth century, it was more than a set of ideas sometimes poorly understood. More than anything, it inspired devotion to the crucifixion of a common Christ. In this way it was both a symbol of division and of unity at the same time. As so often, the most difficult debates were between those who agreed about fundamentals.

Penal cross. © National Science Museum, Maynooth

The Penal Cross

FEARGHUS Ó FEARGHAIL

A SMALL WELL-WORN, rich-brown wooden cross with the figure of Christ carved in high relief and with symbols of the passion incised on the front and back is perhaps an unlikely Irish treasure. But this 'penal cross', as it is called, is one of those religious objects that was treasured in Irish homes down the generations. Penal crosses range in date from the early eighteenth to about the mid-nineteenth century and are so-called because they stem in the main from a time when penal laws against Catholics were in force in Ireland. They were generally carved from a heavy, close-grained timber block, often yew, and on average ranged from 20 cm to 29.4 cm in length. They are associated with the Lough Derg pilgrimage where they were used in 'devotional rounds'. The date incised on the cross probably marked the year the original owner made the pilgrimage.

The figure of Christ on the early crosses is beautifully carved, as are the symbols of the passion, which go back to the early years of Christianity and were part of a commonly recurring scheme in medieval Europe. These symbols appear in Ireland from the fifteenth century onwards on funerary monuments, and from the sixteenth century on chalices and reliquaries. The symbols that appear on penal crosses were already well known in Ireland – the ladder and spear, the title INRI, the dice, cords and stars, the jug or basin, the thirty pieces of silver, the crown of thorns, the scourges, the skull and cross bones, the veil of Veronica, the cock and pot. Other symbols of the passion were equally well-known – symbols such as the seamless robe, sword, purse, lantern, ear, hand, reed, sponge, wounds, palms, or pillar of flagellation – but these did not find their way on to the penal cross, probably because of the difficulty of fitting these symbols into a small, restricted space.

Looking more closely at the symbols, the title INRI, *Jesus Nazarenus Rex Iudaeorum*, is usually placed at the top of the shaft along with stars that may recall the sun, moon and stars of biblical stories or a legendary story associated with Adam. The dice recall the Roman soldiers casting lots for Christ's tunic woven in one piece. The image of the jug or basin recalls Pilate washing his hands; the clawed hammer, the crucifixion; the ladder and pincers, the deposition of the body of Christ; the spear, the piercing of Jesus' side by a lance. The motif of the skull and crossbones is associated with Adam. Legend has it that the body or head of Adam ended up buried on Golgotha in the place where Christ was later crucified. The eighth-century poet, Blathmac, describes how 'the flowing blood from the body of the dear Lord baptised the head of Adam'. According to another story, the wood for the cross came from the tree that grew from a seed planted in Adam's corpse. Christ is the new Adam not just in the letter to the Romans but here too. On the back of the cross the letters IHS represent a profession of faith in Jesus (*Iêsous*) as Son (*Huios*) and Saviour (*Sôtêr*). The nails are three in number – one for each hand and one for the feet – incised in fan-shaped fashion and pointing towards the date. One also finds two or three scourges incised on the cross.

One of the most common motifs on the penal cross is the cock and the pot. This motif is related to the figure of Judas and is found on tombs in Ireland. According to the ancient story, Judas, having betrayed Jesus, returned home to hang himself. His wife, who was roasting a cock on the fire, tried to allay his fears that something would befall him for what he had done. She told him that it was as unlikely that Christ would rise from the dead as it was that the cock she was roasting would come out of the pot alive –whereupon the cock flew out of the pot and crowed. The Irish version of the story has the cock, on emerging from the pot, clapping his wings and announcing Christ's resurrection with the words: 'Tá Mac na h-Óighe Slán' ('the Son of the Virgin is safe'). In Irish folklore the announcement is presented as an onomatopoeic rendering of the crowing of a cock.

For pilgrims to Lough Derg and for later generations, the penal cross provided a graphic reminder of Christ's suffering and death. The symbols of the passion may not all have been readily accessible to every pilgrim, especially the links to Adam, but most were, and provided much food for thought on the passion and death of Jesus who gave his life as a ransom 'for many' on the wood of the cross.

Lucas, A. T., *Penal Crucifixes* (Dublin: The Stationery Office, 1958).

Ó Fearghail, F., 'An Armagh Penal Cross of 1730', *Seanchas Ardmhacha* 23.1 (2010), pp. 171–84.

Ryan, Salvador, 'Weapons of Redemption: Piety, Poetry and the Instruments of the Passion in Late Medieval Ireland', Henning Laugerud and Laura Skinnebach, eds., *Instruments of Devotion: The Practices and Objects of Religious Piety from the Late Middle Ages to the Twentieth Century* (Aarhus: Aarhus University Press, 2007).

_____ '"No milkless cow": The Cross of Christ in Medieval Irish Literature', Peter Clarke and Charlotte Methuen, eds., *The Church and Literature: Studies in Church History 48* (Woodbridge: Boydell Press, 2012).

The 'Wesley' Silver

GILLIAN KINGSTON

MONG THE treasures in St Patrick's Cathedral, Dublin, are a large silver chalice and flagon: this is the 'Wesley' silver. Magnificent examples of eighteenth-century Dublin silverware, they bear silent testimony to the ministry in the city and throughout the country of the Rev. John Wesley, A.M., priest of the Church of England and evangelist extraordinaire.

Believing that his God-given mission was 'to spread Scriptural holiness through the land',[1] Wesley travelled to Ireland on twenty-one occasions, beginning in 1747 and continuing until 1789, two years before his death in 1791. His love for this country and for the people of Ireland was deep: he urged that others 'be patient with Ireland and she will repay you!'

While establishing societies for mutual spiritual support among those influenced by his ministry and training 'helpers', Wesley had no intention of setting up a new Church.[2] Rather the opposite was the case, as is revealed through journal entries. Many have compared his movement within the Church of his day to the development of religious orders within the Roman Catholic Church.

On his first afternoon in Dublin on 9 August 1747, Wesley preached in St Mary's church in Mary Street, summoned by its bells. Thereafter forbidden to preach in churches by the Archbishop of Dublin, Charles Cobbe, Wesley nevertheless continued a ministry among the people of the city; hundreds thronged to hear him and to respond to the Gospel message. He encouraged them to attend their parish churches for regular worship and the sacraments. He himself frequently worshipped at St Patrick's Cathedral.

---

1. For 'land', read both Great Britain and Ireland.
2. 'Societies' is the traditional Methodist term for a local gathering or 'congregation'. 'Helper' is Wesley's term for a trained lay preacher.

Writing in his journal for Sunday, 9 April 1775, he notes:

> The good old Dean of St Patrick's desired me to come within the rails
> and assist him at the Lord's Supper.[3] This was also a means of removing
> great prejudice from those who were zealous for the Church.

So many attended St Patrick's for Holy Communion as a result of Wesley's
ministry that more silverware was required. Thus the Wesley Silver
emerged into public view.

Some have thought that either Wesley himself or the Cathedral
authorities purchased the extra silver, but these suppositions are unlikely
on the grounds of cost. What seems more probable is that the chalice and
flagon were already in the possession of the Cathedral and were brought
out to meet the unprecedented demand.[4] Thus designation evolved
through association.

Cathedral records reveal that, due to the carelessness of the then
sexton, the original chalice and flagon were stolen in 1779. A large reward
(£100) was offered for their return, but to no avail. The Cathedral then
commissioned Richard Williams, a well-known Dublin silversmith, to
make replicas.[5] The price was not to exceed £112.[6]

Wesley continued to urge his followers in Dublin to attend worship in
their parish churches and at St Patrick's. A journal entry for Monday, 30
March 1789, reads:

> About two years ago, it was complained that few of our Society
> attended the church on Sunday, most either sitting at home or going
> on Sunday morning to some dissenting meeting. Hereby many of them
> are hurt, and inclined to separate from the Church. To prevent this, it
> was proposed to have service at the room, which I consented to, on
> condition that they would attend St Patrick's every first Sunday in the

---

3. Dean Francis Corbett, one of 'Stella's' executors, who died later that year on 25 August
   1775.
4. My thanks to Gavin Woods, Cathedral Administrator, and the Rev. Dudley Levistone
   Cooney, Methodist historian, for conversations relating to this.
5. Richard Williams worked in Church Street and Grafton Street in the mid-eighteenth
   century.
6. Check http://www.nationalarchives.gov.uk/currency/ for approximate high four-figure
   values.

month. The effect was (1) that they went no more to the meetings; (2) that three times more went to St Patrick's (perhaps six times) in six or twelve months than had done for ten or twenty years before. Observe! This is done not to prepare for, but to prevent, a separation from the Church.

A week later, on Sunday, 5 April 1789, Wesley records:

I preached in the new room at seven. At eleven I went to the cathedral. I desired those of our society who did not go to their parish churches would go with me to St Patrick's. Many of them did so. It was said the number of communicants were about five hundred; more than went there in the whole year before Methodists were known in Ireland.

Wesley's text on that spring morning was 2 Corinthians 5:19: 'God was in Christ, reconciling the world unto himself, not imputing their trespasses unto them; and hath committed unto us the word of reconciliation.'

On this last visit to Dublin, and towards the end of a long life (he was then eighty-six), Wesley continued to urge reconciliation – reconciliation with God and among the faithful. It is a message which bears repeating today. Here are motifs of witness and mission, eucharistic hospitality and response which resonate powerfully with the theme of the 2012 International Eucharistic Congress: 'Communion with Christ and with one another.' So, sometime soon, make your way up to St Patrick's Cathedral in Dublin, ask to see the Wesley silver and think on these things.

The Church in the Catacombs
DÁIRE KEOGH

THE PENAL laws (1695–1828) relating to the practice of religion in Ireland were complex. Traditionally, clerical historians have tended to see their purpose as the destruction of the 'Faith of our Fathers'.[1] In truth, the religious restrictions, like other aspects of the laws, were aimed not at the elimination of a faith community, but of Catholicism as a *political force*. With this in mind, the Banishment Act (1697), which expelled bishops and regular clergy from Ireland, was enacted not for religious reasons, but because they had been so prominent in the bloody eruptions of the seventeenth century. Similarly, the law that forbade the entry of priests to the kingdom (1704) was enacted to stem the passage of emissaries from Britain's continental enemies. Of course, whatever the intention, both measures would have ensured the extinction of the faith. Without bishops there could be no ordinations, without priests there would be no sacraments, without which there would be no Church.

As it happened, the application of the laws was uneven. Since they were rooted in the insecurity of the state, it followed that they were less rigorously enforced in tranquil times. In essence, it was the political power of Catholics and the structures of the Church which were destroyed rather than practice of the faith. The effect of the laws, then, rather than eliminating Catholicism drove it underground and, deprived of its institutional structures, the Irish Church resembled a mission rather than a Church.

Metaphorically, the Church was confined to the catacombs. Yet as historians have questioned the duration and severity of the Roman persecution, recent studies of the Irish experience have highlighted the

---

1. See Eoin Magennis et al., eds., *New Perspectives on the Penal Laws, Eighteenth Century Ireland*, special issue, no. 1 (Dublin, 2011).

creativity of Catholic survival. These point to the network of simple 'barn chapels', dotted across Ireland, the *teach an phobail* (literally, 'house of the people') which served as a Mass house on Sundays, 'hedge school' houses during the week, and meeting places throughout the year. There is evidence too of sophisticated liturgies in the Catholic chapels found in the back streets of cities, such as Dublin and Waterford, where there were merchant communities with resources to support a Tridentine Church.

The moments of dire persecution were the exception, but they existed in times of international war or potential Jacobite invasions to restore the Catholic Stuart monarchy. It is from one of these episodes that the poignant testimony of Bishop Hugh MacMahon (1660–1737) emerged in an account of his diocese sent to Rome in 1714.[2] In it, the bishop recounts the challenges Catholics faced in the Ulster diocese of Clogher, one of the poorest regions of Ireland. The context was the aftermath of a failed Jacobite invasion of Scotland and the introduction of laws (1709) which included an oath of loyalty and rewarded 'discoverers' – the priest-hunters of folklore – for information leading to the capture of illegal clergy or schoolmasters.

In this crisis, MacMahon recalled how 'the open practice of religion either ceased entirely or was considerably curtailed according as the persecution varied in intensity'. He continued:

The faithful, scattered over wide areas, can hear Mass only on alternate Sundays. To hear Mass these people must rise early and travel through frost and snow; some, many of them advanced in years, leave their homes the previous day to make sure they will arrive in time at the place where Mass is to be celebrated. In the midst of these difficulties is the great consolation that scarcely ever does a person die without the sacraments … Such fidelity even in the case of uneducated people in dire poverty is no small indication of divine assistance …

Greater danger, of course, threatened the priests, as the government persecuted them unceasingly and bitterly, with the result that priests have celebrated Mass with their faces veiled, lest they should be

---

2. Bishop Hugh MacMahon, Bishop of Clogher and administrator of Kilmore, *Relatio Status* (1714); Rev. P. J. Flanagan, 'The Diocese of Clogher in 1714', *Clogher Record*, Vol. 1, No. 2 (1954), pp. 39–42.

recognised by those present. At other times, Mass was celebrated in a closed room with only a server present, the window being left open so that those outside might hear the voice of the priest without knowing who it was, or at least without seeing him. And herein the great goodness of God was made manifest, for the greater the severity of the persecution, the greater the fervour of the people. Over the countryside the people might be seen, on meeting, signalling to each other on their fingers, the hour Mass was due to begin, in order that people might be able to kneel down and follow mentally the Mass which was celebrated at a distance. I myself have often celebrated Mass at night with only the man of the house and his wife present. They were afraid to admit even their children, so fearful were they …

Such realities, and the fidelity of the people, prompted the patriot Edmund Burke (1729–97) to compare the penal Church in Ireland to the apostolic community in Jerusalem. The scene described by MacMahon was perhaps exceptional, but no less than the devotion of his people to Christ present in the sacrament and the evocative beauty of the scene described.

Quakers and Ballitore

RACHEL BEWLEY-BATEMAN

We interpret the words and actions of Jesus near the end of his life as an invitation to recall and re-enact the self-giving nature of God's love at every meal and every meeting with others, and to allow our own lives to be broken open and poured out for the life of the world ... [We seek] unity in the life and spirit of Christ.[1]

THE RELIGIOUS Society of Friends (Quakers) was founded by George Fox in 1652 in the North of England. At the time there was religious and political upheaval in Europe. Fox and others were seeking truth and the spirit which gave forth the scriptures. Discovering that 'there is one, even Christ Jesus that can speak to thy condition' without the need of any intermediary, the word spread rapidly.[2] The first regular Meeting for Worship in Ireland was established in Lurgan in 1654. Quakers travelled to America and mainland Europe.

In 1660, Quakers presented a declaration to King Charles II stating:

We utterly deny all outward wars and strife, and fightings with outward weapons, for any end, or under any pretence whatsoever; this is our testimony to the whole world. The Spirit of Christ by which we are guided is not changeable, so as once to command us from a thing of evil, and again to move unto it; and we certainly know, and testify to the world, that the Spirit of Christ, which leads us into all truth, will

---

1. *To Lima with Love: The Response from the Religious Society of Friends in Great Britain to the World Council of Churches Document Baptism, Eucharist and Ministry* (London: Quaker Home Service, 1987), p. 10.
2. *Quaker Faith and Practice: The Book of Christian Discipline of the Yearly Meeting of the Religious Society of Friends (Quakers) in Britain* (London: Yearly Meeting of the Religious Society of Friends [Quakers] in Britain, 1995–2004), 19.02.

never move us to fight and war against any man with outward weapons, neither for the kingdom of Christ, nor for the kingdoms of the world.[3]

Ballitore, Co. Kildare, is twenty-eight miles south west of Dublin. Mary Leadbeater (1758–1826), in *The Annals of Ballitore*, describes the village as being set in a valley encompassed by gently rising hills, with a meandering river.[4] Friends John Barcroft and Abel Strettel purchased land here in the late seventeenth century. They planted trees, orchards and hedgerows and built neat dwellings. A 1792 publication described the sight of nature assisted by art, in elegant simplicity, and stated that the Quaker colony of Ballitore was industrious and happy, and seeming to prosper as if heaven smiled on its honest labours.[5]

First Day (Sunday) worship took place in the Quaker Meeting House, built in 1708. Friends attended monthly meetings in Carlow, quarterly meetings and a yearly meeting in London. Travelling ministers, men and women, came from Britain and America, while Irish Friends travelled overseas.

Abraham Shackleton (1697–1771) established a school in Ballitore in 1726. Pupils included Quaker children from various parts of Ireland, local Protestant and Catholic children, and others from Norway, France, Jamaica and England. Boys became boarders at an early age, receiving a liberal and classical education.[6] Richard, Abraham's son, also taught in the school and his daughter, Mary, became a pupil. She married William Leadbeater in 1791, becoming the first postmistress in Ballitore village. Her record of events in Ballitore and extensive correspondence give us a vivid insight into life at the time. Her great interest in people and concern for their welfare illumine the pages.

Pupils included Edmund Burke (1729–97), James Napper Tandy (1740–1803) and Cardinal Paul Cullen (1803–78). After three generations

---

3. G. Douglas, *Friends and 1798: Quaker Witness to Non-Violence in Eighteenth-Century Ireland* (Dublin: Historical Committee of the Religious Society of Friends in Ireland, 1998) p. 3.
4. M. Leadbeater, *The Annals of Ballitore,* M. Corrigan, M. Kavenagh, K. Kiely, comp. & eds. (Kildare: Kildare Collections & Research Services, the Local Studies, Genealogy & Archives Dept., Kildare Co. Library and Arts Services in association with Athy Town Heritage Centre & Museum, 2009), p. 13.
5. Ibid.
6. R. S. Harrison, *Merchants, Mystics and Philanthropists: 350 Years of Cork Quakers* (Cork: Cork Monthly Meeting, Religious Society of Friends (Quakers) 2006), pp. 90–1.

of Shackleton schoolmasters and the hardships of civil war, James White reopened the boarding school in 1806. The last boarders arrived at the school in 1836.

As part of a village community, charity, compassion, nursing the sick and hospitality were extended to pupils, neighbours and many visitors.[7] Valuable connections and friendships developed through school, Quaker and business contacts. In the 1790s Quakers in Ireland instructed members to destroy any firearms they owned.

In 1798, the horror of civil war reached Ballitore. Quakers knew people on both sides and suffered too, but their peaceable reputation saved further bloodshed. After a night of terror and carnage, Mary describes a beautiful morning 'rich with the treasures of a benign creator. It was the unbridled passion of man alone which deformed the scene.'[8] Raids continued by both hungry soldiers and United Irishmen. Leadbeater asked, 'Do men forget that their common Father is a God of love, a God of mercy?'[9] Quakers made representations on behalf of some of their neighbours.

Relief of hunger, rebuilding works and a clothing fund commenced. Friends' faith sustained them. Creating employment, prison reform and the abolition of capital punishment were on-going concerns.

Today Ballitore is again a quiet village. The Quaker Meeting House and Mary Leadbeater's house have been restored by Kildare County Council. Visitors are welcome to join Friends in Sunday meeting for worship, 'For where two or three are gathered in my name, I am there among them' (Mt 18:20):

> In silence, without rite or symbol, we have known the Spirit of Christ so convincingly present in our quiet meetings that his grace dispels our faithlessness, our unwillingness, our fears, and sets our hearts aflame … We have thus felt the power of the Spirit renewing and recreating our love and friendship for all our fellows. This is our Eucharist and our Communion.[10]

---

7. Cf. 1 Cor 13:4-8a, a passage to which the Quakers adhered strongly.
8. M. Leadbeater, *The Annals of Ballitore*, p. 132.
9. Ibid., p. 138.
10. London Yearly Meeting, 1928, as quoted in *Quaker Faith and Practice*, 26.15.

~IV
New Realities

The Pro-Cathedral Altar-Frontal

EILEEN KANE

IN THE centre of the sanctuary in the Pro-Cathedral, Dublin, stands the white marble altar table for the celebration of the Eucharist. Its frontal is an important piece of Irish art, rich with the symbolism of the Eucharist and with links to another era in the history of Christianity in Ireland.

The theme of the carving on the altar-frontal is eucharistic. In the middle is carved a monstrance, set amidst clouds that billow up around it. The monstrance contains a sacred host, stamped with the letters IHS, a monogram used since medieval times, consisting of the first two and the last letters of the Greek form of the name of Jesus. The host is represented as if contained in a round frame, encircled by a border of grapes and flowers. Around that flames blaze out, just like those that in ancient art are shown issuing from the sun, except that here the topmost flame changes shape to become a cross surmounting the monstrance. Further out are a multitude of rays of different lengths, indicating the brilliance of the glory that surrounds Christ in heaven. The host, surrounded by these rays, is held aloft between the upraised wings of a cherub.

On either side of this monstrance, an angel kneels in an attitude of reverence and adoration. One angel looks downwards reflectively, while the other kneels in a more upright position, raising his head as he looks towards the monstrance. The angels are carved in much higher relief than the monstrance, with the effect that they seem closer to us, existing in a world somewhere between heaven and our own world, in which, in the monstrance, we catch a glimpse of the glory of God.

The ends of the altar-frontal are decorated with carved festoons of grapes, vine leaves and ears of wheat, the elements from which the eucharistic bread and wine are made.

In the lower right-hand corner of the altar, at ground level, is the name of the sculptor: Peter Turnerelli, with the date 1825. It was in 1825, on Sunday, 14 November, that the Pro-Cathedral was solemnly consecrated and opened, two years after the death of its founder, Archbishop Troy.

When John Thomas Troy OP was appointed Archbishop of Dublin in November 1786, the penal laws aimed at suppressing Catholicism among the people were still in force. By the time of his death in May 1823, the 'penal era' was almost at an end. The 'Catholic Relief Acts' had been ratified in 1782 and only six years remained before Catholic emancipation would be achieved (1829).

At the beginning of Archbishop Troy's episcopate, there was no Catholic cathedral in Dublin, Christ Church and St Patrick's being in the hands of the Church of Ireland. One of the consequences of the penal laws was that Catholic chapels, where they existed at all, were small and inconspicuous. St Mary's in Liffey Street, was such a chapel. Built by Archbishop Linegar in 1729, it served (except for a break of about thirty years) until 1825 as the archbishop's parish. It was Archbishop Troy who, in the more favourable political climate at the end of the eighteenth century, took the decision to provide a large 'Metropolitan Chapel' for the diocese. In 1803 he purchased the site in Marlborough Street, and in April 1815 he blessed and laid the foundation stone. Work progressed slowly due to lack of funds, but in 1819 the building was roofed. It was not, however, ready for use when Dr Troy died in 1823.

To his successor, Archbishop Daniel Murray, fell the task of completing the new church. Archbishop Murray's first task was to provide an altar and tabernacle. As the building was in the neo-classical 'Grecian' style, he chose pure white marble as the material most appropriate for the architectural setting. In February 1824, he wrote to Peter Turnerelli (1774–1839), inviting him to do the work. Turnerelli was then at the height of a successful career. Born in Belfast into an Italian Catholic family, he had been educated in Dublin. In 1793, his family had moved to London and it was there that he trained as a sculptor and spent most of the rest of his life.

No doubt it was Archbishop Murray's idea that the new altar-frontal should have a eucharistic theme. When, today, we see the Blessed Sacrament exposed on that altar, in the silver-gilt monstrance which so closely resembles the monstrance carved in marble, we may reflect on how the Eucharist was present for the people in the penal days when Archbishop Troy first came to Dublin, and how, through his actions and those of his successors throughout the nineteenth and twentieth centuries, it is still there for us today, gathering, no longer only the Dubliners, but now a cosmopolitan population, into one community of faith.

John Steiner: Margaret Aylward's 'Venerable Worker for the Cause of Poor Children'

ETHNA REGAN

I N THE cemetery of the Holy Faith Sisters in Glasnevin, Dublin, is the grave of a German layman who came to Ireland in 1856. Born into a Lutheran family in Württemberg, John Steiner (1832–1916) lived a pilgrim's life. He made a personal Christian journey from Protestantism to Catholicism and then spent decades walking the roads of Ireland as a collector for St Brigid's Orphanage, the non-institutional childcare system founded by Margaret Aylward (1810–89), founder of the Holy Faith congregation. His lifelong devotion to the cause of poor children can be traced to his own experience of being orphaned at the age of twelve.

On his travels as a young man, Steiner experienced an 'unaccountable attraction' towards Catholicism, particularly to the liturgy, for example, Christmas Midnight Mass. His faith journey was also marked by times of doubt 'akin to despair', when he felt no religious attraction to either Christian tradition. His Protestant upbringing gave him a great familiarity with the scriptures and he searched these, particularly the Gospel of John, as he struggled with doubt and faith: 'I would give the whole world if only I could believe.'[1] Steiner became a 'Catholic in spirit' on his first visit to Ireland and was formally received into the Church in London in 1856.

In Dublin, Steiner was employed by a shoemaker, Mr Reynolds of North King Street, who was himself a member of one of the men's guilds established by Margaret Aylward to support the mission of St Brigid's Orphanage, not just through fundraising but also through personal

---

1. Holy Faith Congregational Archive, Glasnevin (GA): JS/BC/09.

example of practical faith, prayer and advocacy for poor children at risk of proselytism. Steiner joined the guild and gradually became convinced that God was calling him to devote his entire life to this work. In 1872, he formally requested to be permitted 'to give all my life to St Brigid's institution … without any recompense whatsoever … entirely for the Glory of God, for the salvation of poor children and my own sanctification'.[2] A supporter of 'the great and heroic Miss Margaret Aylward', Steiner was an important link between the founding figures of Holy Faith and the later leadership of the congregation. He emphasised the centrality of the poor in their mission: 'with the Sisters of Faith, the poor, and the poorest of the poor have first claim on their sympathy'.[3]

His collector's notebooks show Steiner to be a model of transparency in fundraising. His integrity was recognised by all sections of society. He writes of his astonishment at 'the generosity of people and the large subscriptions they entrusted to my care, [especially] the very poorest who are so willing to give even their last penny and find it hard to accept my refusing to take it from them.'[4] Like Margaret Aylward, he adopted an unpatronising approach to the poor, respecting their dignity and engaging with the details of their lives. However he also understood the danger of societal neglect of the poor and their faith: 'The poor may be compared to the foundation of the edifice; where the foundation is insecure, all else is in danger of destruction.'[5]

When Steiner was arrested in 1914 as a German alien, an article in the *Ulster Evening Herald* of 18 October came to the defence of 'this venerable worker for the cause of poor children'. It gives us an insight into the public perception of Steiner towards the end of his life:

The well-to-do gave liberally to his orphan's exchequer, the poor would give him 'the last copper in the house' and the children regarded him with inexpressible reverence.

2.   GA: JS/BC/09, no. 4.
3.   GA: JS/BC/09, nos. 16, 19.
4.   GA: JS/BC/09.
5.   GA: JS/BC/09, no. 19.

On his journeys, he wrote numerous letters back to Holy Faith headquarters containing interesting observations on Irish life and culture across the decades of nineteenth-century land struggles and early twentieth-century war and revolution. Steiner's written accounts of his life reveal a man who was in touch with his own emotions, self-critical without being scrupulous, deeply sensitive to God working in human lives and to the responsibility of the laity in the work of faith.

When Steiner was becoming a Catholic, the priests at the church in Warwick Street, London, asked him to become a member both of the Confraternity of the Blessed Sacrament and of the Society of St Vincent de Paul. Steiner describes these as 'two beautiful devotions'. A glimpse of his theological depth is evident as he writes:

> ... in the first we get the bread that comes down from Heaven, in the second we give him the Bread come up from the earth in the persons of the Poor.[6]

Steiner thus offers us a way of understanding the Eucharist in terms of what we call *orthodoxy* (right belief) and *orthopraxis* (right practice). The challenge to recognise Christ both in the bread of heaven and in the bread of the earth in the persons of the poor is an enduring one. John Steiner's life offers us an insight into that challenge.

---

6. GA: JS/BC/09, no. 10, pp. 9–10.

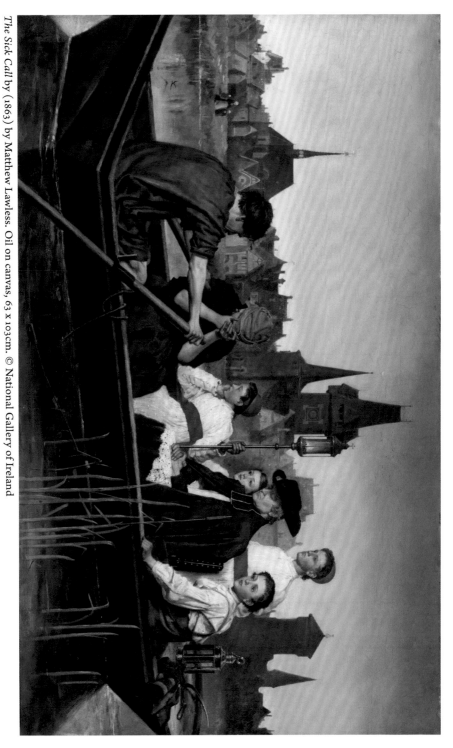

The Sick Call by (1863) by Matthew Lawless. Oil on canvas, 63 x 103cm. © National Gallery of Ireland

The Sick Call

BRENDAN MCCONVERY

'SICK CALL' for Irish Catholics normally means a pastoral visit to the home or hospital ward of a sick person by a priest, for the purpose of conferring the sacraments of confession, anointing of the sick, and Holy Communion. The care of the sick is one of the most important pastoral tasks of priests in parish ministry. In most parishes in Ireland, Holy Communion is brought to the long-term sick and housebound each month, usually on the First Friday or the day before. Many parishes now use lay eucharistic ministers to bring Communion to the sick on a more regular basis, e.g. after the parish Sunday Mass. The *Pastoral Care of the Sick* (1983) is the manual currently in use in Ireland. It contains an important theological introduction on the pastoral care of the sick and housebound. Its three major sections provide texts for celebrating the sacraments and other liturgies with the sick and their families, namely the sacraments of reconciliation, anointing and Holy Communion, as well as prayers for the dying and for use with the family immediately after death.

The importance Irish people have traditionally attached to receiving the sacrament of the sick is well conveyed by William Butler Yeats's poem, 'The Ballad of Father Gilligan'. The poet may have drawn on a traditional folk story that describes how, during the Great Famine (1847–48), an elderly priest was called to the sick bed of a dying parishioner. He was so worn out from attending his dying flock that he fell asleep in his chair before he had time to visit the house. On waking, he hurried to the home but the family members were surprised to see him return so soon. Father Gilligan then realises that an angel had taken his place, for 'He who hath made the night of stars,/For souls who tire and bleed,/Sent one of His great angels down/To help me in my need.'

The painting, *The Sick Call* in the National Gallery of Ireland, was painted by the Irish artist Matthew James Lawless (1837–64). The picture depicts a priest being brought by boat to attend a sick person. He wears a black cloak over his white surplice and sits with eyes cast down, solemnly intent on the task that lies before him. He is accompanied by three acolytes, wearing white albs and carrying a liturgical lantern. Another boy sits near the priest, with another lantern beside him and a sickle. A strong, able-bodied man rows the boat and the final person in the composition is a woman weeping with her face in her hands, probably a relative of the person to whom the sacraments are to be brought. The picture is not set in Ireland, but more likely in Belgium with its canals and medieval walled towns, where Holy Communion was brought to the sick with a certain amount of ceremony.

Matthew Lawless was already in the advanced stages of consumption when he painted this picture, which was exhibited in the Royal Academy in London in 1860.[1] He was then just twenty-three years of age. He was known by his contemporaries as a devout young Catholic, and it is not unlikely that the painting expresses a personal faith in the meaning of the last sacraments and his hope to receive them before his own death. It is likely that the figures in the painting are based on people he knew. It has been suggested, for example, that the face of the priest is modelled on that of the doctor who treated him in his final illness. The artist may have chosen to set this scene outside of Ireland as it enabled him to call on some of the ceremonies associated with bringing Holy Communion to the sick in traditionally Catholic countries. Much of the imagery in the picture suggests that death is close at hand. The colour of the sky suggests that evening is coming. The reaping hook on the stern of the boat suggests that the harvest of life is at hand, while the boat itself is a common symbol for death. The lantern beside the reaping hook does not contain a candle – another indication that life has run its course. Despite the sadness of the subject, the mood the painting conveys is one of grave serenity, and trust that in the final journey into death the believer will be strengthened for the journey by the Bread of Life.

---

1. Christopher Baily, 'James Matthew Lawless', *Irish Arts Review* Vol. 4, No. 2 (Summer, 1987), pp. 20–4.

The Station Mass

BRENDAN MCCONVERY

THE STATION Mass is an Irish tradition, especially in rural parishes, of celebrating the Eucharist for the households of a particular area in one of the homes in that area, once or several times a year. It should not be confused with the 'stational Masses' of the Roman Missal, where each day during the season of Lent the daily liturgy was celebrated in a different church in the city. The custom of the Station Mass probably grew up in the penal times when churches were few and Mass was celebrated wherever the priest could find a quiet place that was accessible to the congregation. Although efforts were made in the course of nineteenth-century Irish Church reform under Cardinal Cullen to end the practice, the people remained deeply attached to it.

In the past, the Station Mass was celebrated early in the morning. The parish priest and curate would arrive at the home, be available to hear the confessions of the people and then to celebrate Mass in the largest room of the house. After the Mass, the priests and neighbours were served breakfast. However, following the reforms of the Second Vatican Council, the Station Mass was usually celebrated in the evening. The Station Mass meant a great deal of work for the host family. They often redecorated the house, sent out invitations to the neighbours and catered the meal that followed the celebration. Theologically, the Station Mass was a way of emphasising the bond between the liturgy of the Eucharist and fostering a sense of local community that is essential to its understanding.

Mass in a Connemara Cabin was painted by the Irish artist Aloysius O'Kelly (1853–1941), who received his early art training in Paris.[1] He

---

1. Niamh O'Sullivan, 'The Priest and the People: *Mass in a Connemara Cabin*', *From the Edge: Art and Design in Twentieth Century Ireland*, a CIRCA special (Summer 2000), pp. 16–18.

Mass in a Connemara Cabin by Alonsius O'Kelly (1853–1941). Oil on canvas, 134.5 x 180cm. © National Gallery of Ireland. On loan to the NGI from the people of St Patrick's, Edinburgh and the trustees of the Archdiocese of St Andrews and Edinburgh exhibited this picture in the Paris Salon in 1884 and in London in 1888. It attracted much favourable comment for its style, particularly its artistic realism and attention to detail. *The Freeman's Journal* (2 June 1888) described it as 'most notable for drawing, both as to beauty of facial form and drapery and for the infinitude of detail sedulously followed. The shawl on the back of one of the women nearest the priest is a marvel in this latter respect in itself. As a composition it certainly must take exceptionally high rank.' Despite this high praise, it disappeared from view for more than one hundred years until it was rediscovered hanging on the wall of the presbytery of the Catholic Church of St Patrick in Edinburgh. It is now on long-term loan to the collection of the National Gallery of Ireland.

The painting represents a typical Station Mass. The congregation, numbering some twenty people of varying ages, is gathered around the young priest celebrating the Mass on an ordinary kitchen table spread with a white cloth. He appears to be speaking to the people, perhaps delivering the homily at the Mass. The priest's top hat and overcoat lie on a wooden chair beside the altar. The various representations of the people's devotion are striking. An elderly woman in red in the second row of worshippers raises her hands in the ancient *orante* position of prayer, known from figures in the art of the catacombs; another prostrates herself, her face towards the ground in adoration; while the rest kneel devoutly with bowed heads. The clothing is typical of Irish country people of the period, with heavy patterned shawls or scarves for the women and girls. The man kneeling on one knee at the front wears typical work clothes with heavy boots. The house is clean but simply furnished. The dresser against the wall on the right-hand side probably contains the family's best collection of coloured dishes. Against it rests a churn for making butter and a small tin bathtub hangs from a hook at the end of the dresser. On the rear wall, there is a simple unframed picture of the Sacred Heart, the standard religious image in an Irish home. The ceiling of the room is formed by wooden-beamed rafters, through which can be seen the remainder of the annual supply of hay or straw, while a simple lamp hanging from the ceiling provides the only source of light apart from the windows.

O'Kelly, the artist, was known as a political radical. The Land League had been founded in Castlebar in 1879, not long before this picture was painted. Critics have speculated that he may have intended his picture to mirror the close egalitarian relationship between priest and people that was key to any profound social change in nineteenth-century Ireland. The setting of the Station Mass allows him to do this in a vivid manner. The priest is on the same level as the people, not raised above them on an altar or in a pulpit. The setting for the celebration of the Eucharist is the everyday world of work and family life. While this may be interpreted as a political statement, it is also one that has a profound theological truth: priest and people form a community through celebrating the Mass together and sharing in the Body of Christ: 'because there is one bread, we who are many are one body, for we all partake of the one bread' (1 Cor 10:17).

Catherine McAuley (1778–1841)

MOIRA BERGIN

CATHERINE ELIZABETH McAuley was born on 29 September 1778 in Drumcondra, Dublin, to James and Elinor McAuley. As a young woman she would begin a mission of Mercy that grew and spread over the years and is still relevant today. Catherine had a sister, Mary, and a brother, James. Her father died in 1783 and, as a result, life for the children changed dramatically, both economically and socially. During her late teenage years her mother became seriously ill, necessitating Catherine to nurse her until she died in 1798. Catherine, together with her brother and sister, were cared for by their relatives.

In 1799, Catherine met William Callaghan, a wealthy Protestant, and his wife Catherine, a Quaker who had recently returned from India. They took an immediate liking to Catherine and adopted her. She went to live with them at Coolock House, north Dublin, as household manager, companion and nurse to Mrs Callaghan until her death in 1819. She also nursed William Callaghan until his death in 1822. Both William and Catherine Callaghan were received into full communion with the Catholic Church before they died. Catherine was named the sole beneficiary of the Callaghan estate.

Catherine first began her mission of Mercy from Coolock House. Living out her Gospel values, she worked among the poor, the sick and the dying but she knew that this work required schools, hostels, orphanages and opportunities for employment to provide the underprivileged with the skills to help themselves, a sense of dignity and a belief in their own self-worth.

Catherine set about realising her great dream of establishing a centre in Dublin by purchasing a piece of land in the city's fashionable and residential Baggot Street. Along with her two assistants, Anna Maria Doyle and Catherine Byrne, she had classrooms built, as well as a dormitory for

Catherine McAuley (1886) by Sr M. Raphael Nelson. © 2003 Mercy International Association

unemployed and homeless girls. It also had a chapel where she and those who might wish to work with her could pray. On 24 September 1827, the House of Mercy was blessed and opened.

Though she enjoyed the support of Archbishop Daniel Murray, her new ministry was looked on with suspicion by many. At first, seeing the restrictions that would be placed on her work, Catherine did not intend to found a religious congregation, but she then decided that a new congregation could be founded while remaining faithful to her purposes. On 8 September 1830, Catherine and two co-workers, Anna Maria Doyle and Elizabeth Harley, entered the Presentation Convent, George's Hill, Dublin, to begin their training in religious life.

On 12 December 1831, the first three Sisters of Mercy took their vows and the congregation was born. Over the next ten years the Sisters of Mercy spread throughout Ireland and England: Tullamore (1836); Charleville (1836); Carlow (1837); Cork (1837); Limerick (1838); Bermondsey, London (1839); Galway (1840); Birr (1840); and Birmingham (1841); together with two houses near Dublin – Dún Laoghaire (1835) and Booterstown (1838). The congregation became one of the largest of women, both in Ireland and throughout the world. Today some 2,324 members in nine countries, belonging to the Irish congregation, follow in the footsteps of Catherine McAuley.

Catherine McAuley was a woman of great vision. The care of the sick, the homeless and the care of women were close to her heart. In her own time she was regarded as 'holy, eminently holy', in a way that had not been seen 'in Ireland since the days of St Brigid'. In 1990, she was declared 'Venerable' by decree of Pope John Paul II. She died in 1841, just ten years a Sister of Mercy, yet her life and vision still contribute, not only to Irish society today, but throughout the world.

Today, Sisters of Mercy continue her legacy by teaching, nursing, visiting the sick and helping those in need. The mission of mercy from Irish sisters continues across the world in England, Brazil, Nigeria, the United States of America, Zambia, Peru, Kenya and South Africa. In Nigeria, for example, that work includes education, catechesis, and home, hospital and prison visitation – highlighting still Catherine's passion for reaching out to the poor. In Kenya, two-thirds of the congregation's sisters are Kenyan-born. In Peru, they promote human rights and peace-making. In Ireland, where once Sisters of Mercy were involved in schools and education, hospitals and care of the sick, now they are engaged in a diversity of ministries, but still reaching out to the needy and marginalised in our time.

A Mission Re-imagined: All Hallows College

THOMAS G. DALZELL

THE EUCHARIST has an obvious missionary dimension. The missionary college of All Hallows was founded by Fr John Hand in Dublin in 1842. It has been in the care of the Congregation of the Mission, the Vincentians, since 1892. The lands originally belonged to the priory of All Saints where Trinity College now stands.[1] Father Hand had left Maynooth in 1835, as a deacon, to join a small group of former Maynooth priests and students who intended to form a missionary community. The group initially opened a school on Usher's Quay in Dublin and later secured a property in Castleknock, in the chapel of which John Hand was ordained a priest in 1835.[2] The Castleknock group had decided on becoming Vincentians. By the time they had made formal approaches to Paris, Fr Hand had come up with a new idea. He had been greatly impressed by M. Choiselat-Gallien, who had come to Dublin to establish the Propagation of the Faith in the country, and he became convinced that a college for the foreign missions was sure to succeed. With the support of the Archbishop of Dublin and the Bishop of Meath, he set off to France in 1841 in search of a model for his missionary college.[3] He had already consulted the Marist Fathers and the Paris College for Foreign Missions, but found their rules of life and mission policies unsuitable to his purpose.[4]

1. Caroline Guihan and Colm McQuinn, eds., *An Historical Guide to All Hallows College Lands and Buildings* (Dublin: All Hallows College, 2011), p. 2.
2. John MacDevitt, *Father Hand: Founder of All Hallows Catholic College for the Foreign Missions. The Story of a Great Servant of God* (Dublin: M. H. Gill and Son, 1885), pp. 84–7.
3. Kevin Condon, *The Missionary College of All Hallows 1842–1891* (Dublin: All Hallows College, 1986), pp. 14–18.
4. Alois Greiler, 'Studying Colin, the Marists, the Catholic Church and Western Oceania', *Catholic Beginnings in Oceania: Marist Missionary Perspectives*, Alois Greiler, ed. (Hindmarsh: ATF Press, 2009), pp. 14–15.

A long stay at Saint Sulpice in Paris allowed him to investigate a number of institutes, and he found the Sulpician formation system of training priests, as well as the College of the Holy Spirit's practice of sending priests to the French colonies, more promising. In fact, the All Hallows rule would turn out to be almost identical to the Sulpician one, although it would not be applied so formally.[5] Since the tragedy of the Great Famine began in Ireland only three years after Fr Hand had received approval for his college, All Hallows priests would be sent mainly to Catholics who had been dispersed by the famine throughout the English-speaking world.

More than 4,000 priests have been sent to the English-speaking missions since those early days.[6] A good number of them became bishops, and John Joseph Glennon, Archbishop of St Louis from 1903–46, was made a cardinal. Most recently, in 2011, Fr John Sherrington was appointed an Auxiliary Bishop of Westminster. The photographs of hundreds of All Hallows ordinands still hang on the long corridor that leads to Senior House, but these photographs also demonstrate that classes began to decrease in size after the Second Vatican Council. In the 1980s, it seemed that the well was running dry. But a new president of the College, Fr Kevin Rafftery CM, came up with a fresh vision for All Hallows. It would still be Fr Hand's missionary college, but its doors would now be open, not only to candidates for the priesthood and to religious, but laymen and laywomen seeking formation in pastoral ministry for the contemporary world. Today, the majority of All Hallows' students are lay, but they are still sent out on mission to all nations.

Under Fr Mark Noonan CM, president from 1998–2011, All Hallows became a linked college of Dublin City University. A whole suite of Masters degrees was launched for further training in community service and the John Hand Library was built. And so that theology could hold its own in the university, research by staff and students was promoted to an unprecedented degree. In line with an emphasis on adult education in the college since the 1980s, All Hallows has established its own adult learning school which offers degrees in personal and professional development so as to meet new needs in the Church and in society. In 2011, the college welcomed a new president, Fr Patrick McDevitt CM, an American

5. Condon, pp. 38–9; p. 215.
6. James Murphy, 'All Hallows Looks Forward', *The Furrow* Vol. 43, no. 8 (1992), p. 445.

Vincentian priest. All Hallows will continue to re-invent itself. It remains committed to its mission, but the possibilities are exciting.

Catholic University Church

CIARÁN O'CARROLL

FROM THE outset of his discussions in 1851, regarding the establishment of the Catholic University of Ireland, John Henry Newman planned the construction of University Church, which was incorporated into his vision of a Catholic University. Such a church, according to Newman, would have both a symbolic and practical value. For Newman, the church represented a theological statement in stone, marble and paint. It would, in his own words, symbolise 'the great principle of the university, the indissoluble union of philosophy with religion'. An important role was the provision of a setting for university sermons. Furthermore, it would provide a suitable location for the formal and public acts of the university – ceremonies of conferral, addresses on important occasions and solemn lectures.

Identification of a suitable site for University Church proved to be challenging. Eventually Newman settled on the garden at the rear of 87 St Stephen's Green. Newman turned to John Hungerford Pollen (1820–1902) for the design of the church, outlining to him his vision for a university church in the following terms: 'My idea was to build a large barn and decorate it in the style of a basilica, with Irish marbles and copies of standard pictures.' With the view that it would be used as a lecture theatre and graduation hall as well as a place of worship, Newman instructed that the church should be large. He also entrusted Pollen with its decoration.

Work commenced on the church in May 1855. It opened a year later on Ascension Day under the patronage of 'Our Lady, Seat of Wisdom'. The interior decoration was completed some months later.

The Church is distinctive in its architectural style and exceptional in its decoration. It has a special place in the heart and the heritage of Dublin city. Artistically and architecturally, University Church embraces both the

Catholic University Church, high altar and *baldacchino*, Stephen's Green, Dublin. © John McElroy

TREASURES
OF IRISH
CHRISTIANITY

Eastern and Western traditions of Christianity. Although an Irish church, it is designed in the style of a continental basilica. The cost of building University Church, at £5,600, was almost double its original estimate. A substantial donation from Newman himself helped defray most of the costs.

In a short article such as this, a full description of the church is impossible. A few features, nevertheless, can be mentioned. The sanctuary is raised above the level of the nave and is approached by a flight of five steps. A short alabaster communion rail marks the division between the sanctuary and the nave. The original alabaster altar-frontal boasts twelve discs of Derbyshire fluorspar crystal set in two groups of six. Between them, inset into the outline of a cross, are nine compartments. Each compartment has an inset panel painted on a gold background. Christ in majesty is depicted at the centre of the cross, and the evangelists surround him – John to the right, Matthew to the left, Mark above and Luke below. In the corners above, on the right and left, are two doctors of the Latin Church, Augustine and Ambrose; on the two corners below are two saints from the Eastern tradition, Gregory and Jerome.

On the altar, along with a cross made of brass, stand six tall Byzantine-shaped candlesticks carved to Pollen's design by carpenters employed by the contractor J. P. Beardwood and Son, of Westland Row. The canopy or *baldacchino* is made of deal, with five small domes and decorative carving.

The semi dome above the sanctuary was inspired by the apse of San Clemente Church in Rome. In the centre of the semi dome, Pollen depicted Our Lady enthroned as *Sedes Sapientiae* – Seat of Wisdom. Newman featured it as the principal article in every edition of the *Catholic University Gazette*, with the words *Sedes Sapientiae, ora pro nobis*. Above the image of Our Lady, wings outstretched, is a dove, representing the Holy Spirit. Above the dove is a cross representing Christ. At the summit, rays in brilliant colours emanate from the hand of God.

From the centre of the base rises the depiction of a vine which sends its branches coiling outwards in a series of circles. In each of the circles, saints stand, many bearing palm branches. A variety of birds and insects inhabit the branches of the vine. At the foot of the vine, various animals, such as deer and rabbits, are depicted. At the base of the semi dome there is a broad border, depicting other birds among the vine branches, some of which are laden with grapes. Newman described the apse to Pollen as 'magnificent'.

Blessed John Henry Newman
and the Holy Eucharist

THOMAS NORRIS

T HE FATHERS of the Oratory in Birmingham relate an anecdote well over a century old. It tells of an Irish woman who immigrated to England shortly after the Famine. She was always particularly happy when it was Fr Newman's turn to celebrate Mass in the Oratory Church. When asked why this was so, she replied, 'Oh Fr Newman! How he used to lift our hearts!'

Blessed John Henry Newman, who lived for various periods in Ireland, from 1851–58, crossing the Irish Sea some fifty-five times, established the Catholic University of Ireland in Dublin and wrote much about the Eucharist. He did so in both the Anglican and Catholic phases of his long life (1801–90). The purpose of this short piece is to look briefly at the Eucharist in a few of his sermons and meditations.

Human beings are prey to a deep restlessness. This disposition stands out in a particular way in their search for happiness. If the way to happiness is not discovered, then a void opens up in the human heart. God's response to that void consists in his own coming among us. This is a principal purpose of the incarnation of the eternal Son of the Father and his redemption of humanity in the fullness of time.

Just as the Son came to Mary in the incarnation, so he desires to enter each person that believes and welcomes him. As he did to Mary, so he wishes to do to us. He fills the void in us through the eucharistic gift of himself. Commenting on St Luke's story about the Road to Emmaus, John Henry Newman writes:

Only by faith is he known to be present; he is not recognised by sight. When he opened his disciples' eyes, he at once vanished … He vanished from sight that he might be present in a sacrament.[1]

To each communicant Christ's Real Presence is given. It is given in a most personal and transforming fashion. In order to explain this, Newman goes into Christology, and specifically the fact that the eternal Son took on our human flesh, our very humanity, in order to take it through life, through suffering, and all the way to the Cross and into the glory of resurrection:

> Christ took on our nature when he would redeem it; he redeemed it by making it suffer in his own person; he purified it by making it pure in his own person. He first sanctified it in himself, made it righteous, made it acceptable to God, submitted it to an expiatory passion, and then he imparted it to us. He took it, consecrated it, broke it, and said, 'Take, and divide it among yourselves.'[2]

The fact is that the Body which he received from the Virgin Mary and in which he suffered the cross, and then took up in glory to the very right hand of the Father, *is the Body which we receive in Holy Communion*. He fills in the void created by the fall and deepened by the malice of our sins. This is the higher gift than grace, 'God's presence and his very self and essence all divine.'[3]

Those who lived 2,000 years ago in Palestine saw Christ, but it is a greater thing to live in him now, and this is precisely what the Eucharist enables! Through the sacrament we enter into his dying and rising. Newman explains, 'In the holy Mass, that one Sacrifice on the Cross is renewed, continued, applied for our benefit.' In order to drive home this truth, he puts these words on the lips of Our Lord:

> My Cross was raised up 1,800 years ago, and only for a few hours – and very few of my servants were present there – but I intend to

---

1. John Henry Newman, *Parochial and Plain Sermons*, 8 vols. (London and New York: Longman, Green and Company, 1891–94), VI.132.
2. Ibid., V.117.
3. These verses from the *Dream of Gerontius* can be found in John Henry Newman, *Prayers, Verses and Devotions* (San Francisco: Ignatius Press, 1989), p. 721.

bring millions into my Church. For their sakes I will perpetuate my Sacrifice, that each of them may be as though they had … been present on Calvary. I will offer myself up day by day to the Father, that every one of my followers may have the opportunity to offer his petitions to Him, sanctified and recommended by the all-meritorious virtue of my Passion … My priests will stand at the Altar – but not they, but I rather will offer.[4]

For Newman, the unique act of Our Saviour's sacrifice is the centre of all religion and the axis of time.

---

4. John Henry Newman, *Meditations and Devotions,* William Paine Neville, ed. (London and New York: Longmans, Green and Company, 1923), p. 203.

177

College Chapel interior, St Patrick's College, Maynooth. © Dominic McNamara

The College Chapel in Maynooth
DOMINIC MCNAMARA

EVERY TIME I take a group on the tour of the College Chapel, on first entering the recurring reaction is 'Oh my God!' There is an overwhelming sense of beauty, of art from floor to ceiling, of the history of thousands of men being ordained to the priesthood, and of peace.

Built in the French fourteenth-century Gothic style during the neo-Gothic revival of the nineteenth century, and officially opened for worship on 24 June 1891, everything is designed to raise ones thoughts to heaven. The carved stalls rise in tiers from the floor and the columns and windows culminate in points on the ceiling, which itself has seventy-two paintings of the heavenly host. The theme of the chapel is *Laus Deo* (Praise God) and all of God's creation is portrayed praising him. The mosaic floor has the Latin text inviting young men to praise God:

Laudate pueri Dominum,	Young men praise the Lord,
Psallite Deo, Psallite	Sing praise to God, Praise him
Quoniam rex omnis terrae Deus,	For God is King of all the earth,
Psallite sapienter	Praise him wisely

As a seminary chapel it is designed to facilitate the prayer life of the seminarians. There are no typical pews, only 454 individually carved choir stalls, making it the largest choir stall chapel in the world. Carved in American Oak and seasoned with a century of incense and prayer, one can feel the history of the place. Behind the stalls are carvings of the coats of arms of the Irish dioceses, and at the end of each set of stalls the finials represent the wild plants of Ireland, each one reaching heavenward in an expression of praise.

The Stations of the Cross are life-size, painted with oil on canvas by Nathaniel Westlake (1833–1921), and adhered to the wall. As well as the fourteen stations, there are two additional panels, one dedicated to Saints Peter and Paul, and the other to the four prophets – Daniel, Jeremiah, Isaiah and Ezekiel – each of whom were considered to have prophesised the passion of Christ.

Above the stations are the corbels and string course. Each corbel portrays an angel holding a symbol of the various orders that led to the priesthood – porter, lector, acolyte and deacon. Those who reach the fullness of priesthood as bishops are also reflected in the two angels nearest the altar, who hold the mitre and crosier. Between the corbels the string course shows the animal kingdom of birds and animals, all praising God.

The stained-glass windows tell the story of the life of Christ. Starting near the sacristy, the south windows portray moments from his childhood and private life, while the north windows illustrate some of his miracles. The rose window over the entrance illustrates Christ the King holding the orb of the universe in the centre. This is surrounded by windows depicting Saint Michael the archangel and the other archangels, followed by the Blessed Virgin, St Joseph, St John the Baptist and the four Evangelists. The apostles and prophets are in the outer ring.

The ceiling has seventy-two medallions showing the heavenly host praising God. These were also painted by Westlake, using oil on canvas. Among them are fifteen of the early Irish saints, including the patrons of Ireland, Patrick and Brigid. It also includes those that left Ireland as missionaries and who would later give Ireland the accolade of the 'Island of Saints and Scholars'. These include Saints Columba and Columbanus, Feargal, Gaul and Killian, who are sometimes better known in Europe than they are in Ireland. There is a large collection of angels holding the symbols of the passion, and near the sanctuary are the Blessed Virgin, St Joseph, St John the Baptist and St Michael.

The sanctuary is richly endowed with a high altar of marble and alabaster, with the Last Supper on the centre panel. Beneath the surrounding windows are six paintings of outstanding incidents in the lives of the Irish saints. The sequence from left to right is as follows:

Saint Laurence O'Toole appeals to the Norman soldiers at the gates of Dublin not to sack the city; Saint Brigid and her companions pronounce their religious vows (*Brigida ejusque sociae vota religiosa emittunt*); Saint Bernard greets Saint Malachy on his way to Rome (*Malachiam salutat Bernardus Roman pergentem*); Saint Patrick preaches in the presence of the High King of Ireland (*Patricius coram summo Rege Hiberniae praedirat*); Saint Columbanus oversees the foundation of the Monastery of Bobbio (*Columbanus monast Bobien stabiliendum curat*); and Saint Columba sets sail from the port of Derry (*Columba navem a portu Derriensi soluit*).

Five side chapels surround the main altar, with the Lady Chapel in the centre the most beautiful, adorned with Venetian glass mosaics of scenes from the life of the Blessed Virgin.

The restoration of the College Chapel was started in the 1990s in anticipation of the college's bicentenary in 1995. Through the generous support of Friends of Maynooth in Ireland, the United States and several countries around the world, €10 million has been spent preserving this magnificent national treasure for future generations. All in the college are indebted to those who have made the restoration possible.

Ag Críost an Síol
(To Christ be the Seed)

NÓIRÍN NÍ RIAIN

Ag Críost an síol,
Ag Críost an fómhar,
In iothlann Dé go dtugtar sinn.

Ag Críost an mhuir,
Ag Críost an t-iasc,
I líontaibh Dé go dtugtar sinn.

Ó fhás go haois
Is ó aois go bás
Do dhá láimh, a Chríost anall tharainn.

Ó bhás go críoch
Nach críoch ach athfhás,
I bParthas na ngrás go rabhaimíd.

To Christ be the seed,
To Christ be the autumn,
May we too be gathered into that harvesting shelter.

To Christ be the sea teeming with fish,
May we be caught in the fish pot.

From growth to wisdom
And from old age to death
May your two hands, O Christ, envelop and uphold us.

From death to the end
Not end but re-birth,
May we all be on our way to Grace-filled Paradise.

THIS BEAUTIFUL hymn composed by the Archbishop of Sydney, Michael Sheehan (1870–1945), set to music in a traditional air by Seán Ó Riada (1931–71) and sung so often at eucharistic celebrations in recent decades in Ireland, always creates a harmony between my heart, my life and my God. An entire book could come alive about this prayer-poem, but here I want to highlight two completely different but obvious resonances: firstly, a point on the architecture, the structure of this deep yearning for Divine blessing; secondly, that this Christ-centred poem of trust echoes back to one source of the Christian story – the psalter, the book of psalms, in the Hebrew scriptures.

Ag Críost an Síol is a verbal icon that was a primal heart-cry – a *crie de coeur* – to the Son of God by someone in dire straits, and it has all of that healing consolation and compassion even in its very make-up.

A dozen short lines symbolise the twelve apostles and the twelve days of Christmas. Four verses and the four syllables of the first two lines of each verse remind us of the quartet of evangelists or storytellers of the Christ story. Three lines in each verse represent the beautiful Trinity of God the Divine Source and Creator, God the healing and redemptive Christ, and God the guiding and guarding Holy Spirit. Then, subconsciously, but surely guided by that Holy Spirit, each of these three-line verses follows the outline of the greatest prayer of prayers given to us by Christ, the Our Father. Both prayers are perfectly symmetrical; praise is first due to God through our Lord Jesus Christ and this then prepares the perfect way for our begging of a dignified personal blessing – may we live and have our being in you. In both prayers (and indeed the Hail Mary follows suit), when human longing for blessing ensues, 'we' (not 'I') are calling – we pray in the plural, not the singular. The secret message of Christian prayer is therefore communal: we are not alone – the prayers of others are ours and vice versa.

Praying the *Ag Críost an Síol* prayer beautifully unravels the loving, prophetic message of the Judaeo-Christian, age-old psalms. Christ, the incarnated one of God, is the invisible energy of the earth which 'has yielded its fruit for God', and through this visible world 'our God has blessed us' (Ps 66). The germ, framed and called forth at harvest-time, is a graceful cosmic model that inspires humanity to break free of the bonds of loneliness and imbalance which will propel us into the dynamic intimate spiritual belonging with the Triune God: 'Do not fret – it leads only to evil' (Ps 37); 'For with you is the fountain of life: in your light we see light' (Ps 36).

Furthermore, Christ, the chosen one of God, continues to walk again invisibly on all waters of the world, gathering us in, along with the 'fish that make their way through the water' (Ps 8). The anonymous writer of Psalm 103 begins and ends with advice to all the residents of this earth to continually call for blessing from the Lord – the underlying message of *Ag Críost an Síol*: 'The sea, vast and wide, with its moving swarms past counting ... living creatures great and small ... Bless the Lord, my soul.'

And from the womb to the tomb, there is of course no death, because your two hands, O Jesus, are all around us, sustaining us, and in Grace-filled Paradise, we will reside with you forever and ever. 'But those who wait for the Lord shall inherit the land ... and delight themselves in abundant prosperity'(Ps 37).

In praying this hymn, three things stand out: firstly, its words invite us to be obsessed with the incarnated Son of God, tipsy with the living and redeeming Christ, who knows for certain that 'through him, and with him, and in him, O God, Almighty Father, in the unity of the Holy Spirit, is all honour and glory, for ever and ever.' Secondly, it tells us we must begin crossing the bridge to Paradise, the ultimate home of the Triune God, with our respectful friendship, relationship and belonging to one another and to nature's rhythm and time. Finally, it brings us to meditate upon the new heavenly Jerusalem, the third heaven, our ultimate 'happy home', in the realm of the Grace of God and we, as Christians, are offered a residency – a mansion in our Father's House.

The Bible in Ireland
FEARGHUS Ó FEARGHAIL

FOR NEARLY sixteen centuries the Bible has been an integral part of the religious and cultural landscape of Ireland. Saint Patrick's authentic works reveal how important the Bible was to his writing, preaching and spirituality. The version which he used freely was the Old Latin version, replaced (and then not completely) only in the sixth century when St Finnian of Moville is said to have introduced Jerome's Vulgate into Ireland. The Bible was the chief subject of study in the monasteries of early Christian Ireland. St Comhgall (d.c. 605), founder of the monastery of Bangor, was said to have been 'learned in the scriptures'. The writings of Adamnán (c. 627–704), abbot of Iona and biographer of Colm Cille, are characterised by biblical quotations and allusions as well as by biblical vocabulary and phraseology. For abbot, monk and bishop it was essential to be well versed in the sacred writings. Medieval authors made widespread use of their biblical learning in writing lives of the saints.

In the scriptorium, the most copied books of the Bible were the Gospels and psalms. The psalter associated with Colm Cille, the *Cathach* (c. 600), is the earliest surviving biblical manuscript in Ireland. The Gospel book *Codex Usserianus Primus* is also a very early manuscript. The ninth-century Book of Armagh is the only surviving manuscript containing a complete version of the New Testament. Sadly many manuscripts did not survive due to conflict and the ravages of time, but occasionally new finds enrich our knowledge of the manuscript tradition, as did the eighth-century psalter found in Faddan More bog in 2006.[1]

The best known product of the scriptorium is the illuminated manuscript. Skilled illuminators from the seventh to the ninth centuries

---

1. See John Gillis, 'Treasure from the Bog: The Faddan More Psalter', an essay in this book, pp. 257–61.

lavished their art on biblical manuscripts such as the seventh-century Book of Durrow and the exquisitely decorated ninth-century Book of Kells. Outside the scriptorium, sculptors lavished their art on biblical scenes sculpted on High Crosses in Monasterboise, Kells, Arboe, Durrow and Clonmacnoise, and elsewhere.

Many manuscripts copied in Ireland were carried by Irish missionaries and scholars to Britain and the Continent, some of which still survive in libraries and museums throughout Europe. Irish scribes also produced commentaries on biblical books, particularly the psalms. The missionaries brought with them their distinctive exegesis, whose influence may be seen in many continental manuscripts.

By the eleventh century, Jerome's Vulgate was the version of the Bible that was read in Ireland, but the vernacular eventually made its presence felt in works found in manuscripts such as the fifteenth-century *Leabhar Breac*, with its biblical citations and its poems and sermons suffused with biblical themes and images. The sixteenth and early seventeenth centuries saw a spate of Protestant translations of the Bible in English culminating in the King James Bible (1611) and a Catholic translation, the Douai-Rheims (1582, 1609). These versions probably also circulated in Ireland.

A translation of the New Testament into Irish was begun in 1571/72 and published in 1602/3 by Uilliam Ó Domhnail. Ó Domhnail also translated a number of psalms and Old Testament readings for his Irish translation of the *Book of Common Prayer* (1608/9). The impetus for the translation of the Old Testament into Irish came from William Bedell, provost of Trinity College Dublin (1627) and Bishop of Kilmore and Ardagh (1629). It was complete by the time of his death in 1642 but was not printed until 1685.

The eighteenth century saw Cornelius Nary's revised translation of the Douai New Testament (1718, 1719) and Walter O'Kelly's history of the Bible in Irish (c. 1726), as well as printings of Catholic and Protestant versions of the Bible in Dublin and Belfast. The number of printings increased in the first half of the nineteenth century. The advent of the 'Bible Societies' in the early years of the nineteenth century led to interconfessional controversy surrounding the Bible. In the years 1810 to 1830 it is estimated that 67,000 Irish New Testaments and 25,000 Irish Bibles were printed in Ireland for distribution among Irish speakers.

In the nineteenth and twentieth centuries a steady stream of commentaries and other studies on books of the Bible emanated from Irish scholars. While parts of the Bible were translated into Irish over the years, it was only in the third quarter of the twentieth century that a Catholic edition of the Bible in Irish finally appeared, the Bíobla Naofa, mainly through the efforts of Rev. Prof. Pádraig Ó Fiannachta, then professor of Irish at Maynooth, and Cardinal Tomás Ó Fiaich.

Biblical associations and various study groups have contributed greatly to the ecumenical study of the Bible in Ireland in recent years. The liturgical reforms that followed Vatican II opened up the scriptures as never before to the laity. These and many other initiatives ensure that the word of God will not return 'empty' from Irish soil (Is 55:11).

FURTHER READING

Kenny, James F., *The Sources for the Early History of Ireland: An Introduction and Guide* (1929) (Dublin: Four Courts Press, 1993).

Mac Conmara, Máirtín, ed., *An Léann Eaglasta in Éirinn 1000–1200* (Dublin: An Clóchomhar, 1982).

_____ *An Léann Eaglasta 1200–1900* (Dublin: An Clóchomhar in Éirinn, 1988).

McCaughey, Terence, *Dr Bedell and Mr King: The Making of the Irish Bible* (Dublin: Dublin Institute for Advanced Studies, 2001, repr. 2009).

Matt Talbot and the Eucharist: The Conquest of Freedom in the Face of Addiction

JOSEPH MCCARROLL

D UBLIN WAS home to a remarkable man who overcame the determinism of family wounds and dysfunction by a lifestyle centred on the Eucharist. For Matt Talbot, son of an alcoholic and an alcoholic himself, the Eucharist was the key to his conquest of his inner freedom.

On 7 December 1931, *Time* magazine ran an article on Matt under the headline 'Saintly Lumberman'. It began with the story of Fr F. X. Talbot SJ, associate editor of the Jesuit magazine *America*, disembarking at Kingstown (Dún Laoghaire) in 1927. A porter, noticing the name on his baggage, asked him if he was related to 'the new saint'. The Jesuit had never heard of Matt Talbot. He learned that, although only dead a few years, Matt was already popularly regarded as a saint and that an account of his life had been 'translated into a dozen languages and sold 60,000 copies'.

Matt Talbot, the *Time* article said, 'was a thin, small man with a high forehead and big eyes'. He was born on Saturday, 3 May 1856. His father, Charles Talbot, was a small man with a violent temper, an unskilled labourer who drank his wages, with the result that the family lived in poverty and had to move home nearly a dozen times. Matt was the second of twelve children – all but one of the boys inherited their father's vulnerability to alcohol abuse, and they suffered at his hands as he tried to punish them as a result.

Matt left school at the age of twelve, in 1868. His father found him his first job as a messenger boy in Burke's, a wine and beer company and then in a whiskey warehouse – both places where Matt had the opportunity to drink.

Today we would speak of substance abuse, addiction and alcoholism and recommend the Alcoholics Anonymous' twelve-step programme and meetings, but this was before all that. Matt was just a drunk. For sixteen years he drank, wasting his wages and getting into debt. Once he stole a fiddle from a busker and sold it for drinking money.

In 1884 he was twenty-eight. He had been unemployed for a week and had no money, so he waited outside his local expecting his friends to stand him a drink. They didn't. With this, he hit rock bottom. He went home and told his mother he was going to 'take the pledge', introduced by Fr Theobald Matthew in 1838, whose statue stands to this day in O'Connell Street. He took the pledge first for three months – and he went through hell. Yet he had to go through it on his own, without anyone to support him, explain what would happen to him or how best to cope with it. And he kept that pledge for the rest of his life, some forty years.

Around 1909, he went to work at T. & C. Martin's timber yard. Everyone who knew him was aware that religion was at the heart of the change he had made in his life, so it was no surprise that on Sunday, 7 June 1925, when he collapsed with a heart attack on Granby Lane, he had been on his way to Mass in Dominick Street. It was only when his body was examined, however, that it was discovered that he had been wearing penitential chains and the mysterious details of his austere inner life began to emerge.

President Seán T. Ó Ceallaigh (1882–1966), who knew Matt, described him at prayer: 'I would say he was as close as possible to a person in ecstasy as I imagined that state. His fervour, his recollection, was extraordinary.'

Looking at Matt's life and the harsh practices he undertook to come to terms with his addictive condition, his is the story of an astonishing conquest of freedom. By an ascetic lifestyle centred on the Eucharist, his higher power, Matt Talbot freed himself from a sixteen-year lifestyle of alcohol abuse.

But there was more to his life than this negative fight. On the way, he discovered asceticism as a path to higher experience. Matt's asceticism was as tough as any Irish monk's or Indian fakir's, but had a eucharistic focus and led him to rapt eucharistic contemplation.

Venerable Matt Talbot is an icon of hope in the struggle for inner freedom in the face of addiction, and an icon of love, the eucharistic encounter with Jesus opened up to him by his practice of asceticism in early twentieth-century Dublin.

The 1932 Congress and the Irish Diaspora

RORY O'DWYER

THE 1932 Eucharistic Congress, held in Dublin, highlighted the remarkable number and status of Irish ecclesiastics serving both the Irish diaspora and countless others in many different parts of the world. Among those who participated in the congress was the Waterford-born Archbishop of Sydney, Michael Kelly, who had sponsored an international Eucharistic Congress in his adopted city in 1928. Many Irish people would have been aware of other Irish ecclesiastics prominent in the Catholic Church hierarchy in Australia at this time (Daniel Mannix, Patrick Clune, James Duhig, Robert Spence etc.). Similarly, many prominent figures in the Catholic Church in the United States were either Irish-born or of immediate Irish descent. The Archbishop of New York, Cardinal Hayes, was one of those to have visited for the congress. Like others, he travelled around the country creating much interest and excitement. He received a tumultuous welcome when he visited his mother's native place near Killarney. Unprecedented crowds filled the cathedral and grounds at Killarney when he said Mass there, stirring the crowd when he spoke emotionally of his pride in his Kerry roots. The Archbishop of Boston, Cardinal O'Connell, both of whose parents were Irish emigrants, and the Archbishop of Philadelphia, Cardinal Dougherty, whose parents had emigrated from Mayo, were two other 'princes of the Church' who travelled to Ireland for the congress and participated in the events. The celebrant of the Pontifical High Mass in the Phoenix Park (attended by approximately one million people and the highlight of the congress) was the Archbishop of Baltimore, Michael Curley, a native of Athlone and a former school friend of the great Irish tenor John McCormack, who himself contributed so memorably to the High Mass. It was a source of great pride to Curley to have been chosen by the Papal Legate, Cardinal Lauri, to celebrate the Mass. As most of the vast throng in the park were aware due to the wide media coverage, it was a particularly poignant choice as Curley's ninety-two-year old mother was gravely ill in Athlone. In the Ireland of the time no mother could have had a greater honour bestowed upon one of her sons.

A significant number of Irish missionary priests and bishops serving in Africa, India, China, the Philippines and elsewhere also participated in the congress. The Bishop of Abila, Joseph Shanahan (CSSp), who had directed the building of schools, hospitals, mission stations and teachers' colleges in Western Nigeria for thirty years, attended the Congress. Another inspirational missionary figure was Thomas Broderick (SMA), Bishop of Western Nigeria. Irish missionary institutions had been assigned vicariates in many parts of Africa in particular. Father John Heffernan travelled to Ireland from Africa to be consecrated Bishop of Uzzpari and Vicar Apostolic of Zanzibar (Tanzania) just three days before the Congress officially began. The consecration took place in the chapel at Blackrock College, where both he and one of his former school friends, Eamon de Valera, had been students. The consecration was attended by many state dignitaries, including de Valera.

Among the more colourful churchmen visiting Dublin for the congress was Fulton Sheen, a priest of Irish descent who was attracting considerable attention for his work on American radio. Sheen was then presenting a very popular weekly radio broadcast in the US, *The Catholic Hour*, which would soon have a weekly listening audience of four million people. He would later present the first religious service broadcast on the new medium of television, drawing as many as thirty million people on a weekly basis. In Dublin, in 1932, Sheen gave an address, 'Calvary on Irish Altars', at a meeting of the American group in the Mansion House and was very well received.

The Eucharistic Congress provided the setting for the creation of international contacts between two related families – the O'Rourkes of Ireland and Poland. Present at the Congress was Bishop Edward O'Rourke of Danzig (now Gdansk). O'Rourke had been nominated by the Pope as Bishop of Danzig in 1925, following the creation of the diocese around the Free City of Danzig (split between Germany and Poland). His family were of Irish ancestry, descended from exiles that had left Ireland in the 1690s after the Battle of the Boyne. In Russia they became an aristocratic family, holding high office under the Tsars, retaining the hereditary title of 'count'. Born in Minsk, in present-day Belarus, Bishop O'Rourke was conscious of his Irish roots and visited Ireland in the early years of the century. At the congress he met with Senator Bernard O'Rourke and the two established a strong relationship, enjoying their shared family heritage. After the congress, Senator O'Rourke visited Bishop O'Rourke in Danzig. Later, following Bishop O'Rourke's flight from Poland, Senator O'Rourke lobbied the Irish government to have the bishop admitted to Ireland as a refugee, but was unsuccessful. And at the end of the Second World War, members of Bishop O'Rourke's family came to Britain and Ireland from Poland as refugees (some having experienced the concentration camps), and contact was renewed with the Irish O'Rourkes.

During the congress, University College Dublin (then situated mainly in Earlsfort Terrace) served as a meeting place for the many sectional groups of congress pilgrims (including groups from Portugal, Mexico, Uruguay, France, Malta, Poland, Holland, Belgium, Czechoslovakia, Spain, Italy, Lithuania, Australia, New Zealand, Canada, and the 'oriental group'). These meetings included addresses that frequently focussed on Irish connections with a particular country and the work of Irish missionaries there. There was an exhibition in the college on Irish Catholic education, directed towards the visiting pilgrims. The old UCD building in St Stephen's Green featured another very significant exhibition intended to further stimulate public interest in mission work – especially that of contemporary Irish missions. Overall, there was undoubtedly a demonstration of pride in the 'Irish spiritual empire' during the congress.

Frank Duff

FINOLA KENNEDY

F RANK DUFF was born in Dublin in 1889. His family roots were in County Meath, where his father and mother, John Duff and Susan Freehill, had been educated in the Model School in Trim, an interdenominational school under public management. Susan's father, Michael Freehill, was headmaster at the school. Both John and Susan entered the civil service, as would their two sons, Frank and John. John became Secretary of the Department of Justice. When Frank started work, his father had already been forced to retire on health grounds. Frank became the family breadwinner, spending twenty-six years as a civil servant in the Land Commission and the Department of Finance from 1908 until his resignation in 1934. His most important work in the civil service was in relation to the Land Act, 1923.

As a young man, Duff was not particularly religious. A critical event in his life occurred in 1913, when he joined the St Vincent de Paul Society (SVP), having been invited to do so by a colleague. There he was confronted with the grinding poverty of Dublin tenement life. Soon afterwards, Duff started to attend mass daily. In 1914, he decided to pray the whole of the Divine Office daily. Always a thinker, he extended his reading to include John Henry Newman and, critically, Louis Marie Grignon de Montfort. At a certain point, he grasped the ideas of the Mystical Body of Christ and of Mary's motherhood of that Body – ideas which would become the twin pillars of the Legion of Mary.

One evening in 1921, in Myra House on Francis Street in the Dublin Liberties, a few members of the SVP (then confined to men) and of the Pioneer Total Abstinence Association, together with the local curate, Fr Michael Toher, were discussing visitation of the cancer wards in a Dublin hospital. Some young women asked if they could do similar work. Their question was the catalyst that led to the formation of the Legion of Mary.

In 1922, Duff opened the Sancta Maria Hostel in Harcourt Street as a refuge for prostitutes. In 1927, he opened the Morning Star Hostel for homeless men; and in 1930, the Regina Coeli for homeless women. Soon he made provision for unmarried mothers to rear their children themselves rather than forcing them to place their children in orphanages, something revolutionary at the time.

At the same time as the hostels were taking root in Dublin, the Legion started to spread outside Ireland. In 1928, the Legion began in Scotland; the following year in England and in India in 1931. The spread of the Legion across the world intensified following the Eucharistic Congress in Dublin in 1932, which Duff described as the 'Epiphany' of the Legion. Many of those who visited Dublin learned about the Legion and brought it back with them on their return. Today the Legion exists in close to 200 countries and counts an estimated four million active members.

In every work that Duff undertook there were obstacles. If Duff's hallmark in confronting these obstacles was courage, it was a courage rooted in faith. He compared presence at Mass with presence at the Last Supper and Calvary, but without its sight and sound, for an essential idea of the Mass is that it is 'an exercise in faith'.

'Real faith', Duff wrote, 'does not mean an empty sentiment, but an action.' Real faith requires that one is prepared 'to lay down one's life, or be destroyed or ruined in some way or other, in the search of the interests of God'. True faith demands service of one's fellowman. In a letter to Fr Aedan McGrath in China in 1948, he held that where the laity did not fulfil its role, the Church would fail, saying 'an inert laity is only two generations removed from non-practice. Non-practice is only two generations from non-belief.'

It is significant that the final chapter of the *Handbook* of the Legion of Mary, which was written by Duff, is a reflection on the relevance for the Legion of Mary of St Paul's great letter to the Corinthians on the character of love. In that reflection Duff insists that there shall be no social, racial, national or colour discrimination in the Legion ranks and that the Legion apostolate will accomplish even more by indirect action, that is, as 'the leaven in the community', than directly by the works in hand.

The Legion represents ordinary Christianity for ordinary people. It was Duff's genius to recognise the role of the ordinary layperson in the Body of Christ and to create a mechanism for its expression decades before such a role was endorsed by the Second Vatican Council, where Duff was recognised as 'the pioneer of the lay apostolate'.

Duff died in his home beside the Legion hostels on Dublin's northside on 7 November 1980. He had attended two Masses that morning.

FURTHER READING

Kennedy, Finola, *Frank Duff: A Life Story* (London: Continuum, 2011).

The Legacy of Two Remarkable Missionary Women: Marie Martin (1892–1975) and Edel Quinn (1907–44)

ISABELLE SMYTH

FOR MANY years St Patrick's parish church in Monkstown, Co. Dublin, was a place of regular prayer for two women who have left their mark on the missionary outreach of the Church in Ireland – Marie Martin (1892–1975) and Edel Quinn (1907–44). With the serenity that only faith can bring, both women overcame enormous obstacles to achieve the work to which they felt called.

Their lives intertwined from time to time. Edel left the home in Monkstown where her family had eventually settled and sailed for East Africa on 30 October 1936. Two months later, Marie Martin and her first companions left the basement 'convent' at her family home at Greenbank, Monkstown, and sailed for Nigeria, where she had already worked as a lay missionary from 1921–24. While there, she had seen clearly that to meet such wide medical needs, a congregation of religious sisters committed to healthcare was required.

On 4 April 1937, Marie Martin, while very ill in the government hospital in Port Harcourt, made her profession of vows, and so the Congregation of the Medical Missionaries of Mary was founded. From then on she was known as Mother Mary Martin. On that very same day in Nairobi, Edel Quinn founded the Legion's first African Curia – the council which federates and governs a number of Praesidia of the Legion of Mary.

For both Edel Quinn and Mother Mary Martin, devotion to the Eucharist was a key source of energy. Following her profession on Low

Sunday 1937, the foundress wrote to her first novices: 'Just before receiving Holy Communion I took my vows, and what a Holy Communion.' In later correspondence to her sisters, she made many references to this source of grace and energy:

> Take all God sends you with love, in a spirit of sacrifice, united to his Sacrifice on Calvary, and culminated at Holy Communion when he gives us himself whole and entire. This is what he asks of us, a total offering of ourselves, no reserve, no self, but all for him.

A close friend of Edel, who later became a Carthusian nun, Mother Mary Celestine Walls, wrote: 'Edel understood in a very spiritual way the mystery of the Blessed Eucharist and the Sacrifice of the Mass.'

It is known that in her extensive travels in East Africa, Edel would fast from midnight, obligatory at the time, in order to receive Holy Communion, which for her was the source of deepest joy. 'I could assist at Mass all day,' she wrote to her friend.

Both women also shared a deep devotion to Mary, Mother of God. For Edel, Mary was truly her mother, to whom she turned in any difficulty, and to whom she consecrated herself according to the teaching of St Louis Marie de Montfort. Mother Mary Martin was known to say 'the load is great, but not too great or hard with Jesus and Mary'. Both women also shared a common interest in the writings of Dom Columba Marmion, and both drew great inspiration from the writings of St Thérèse of Lisieux, co-patron of the Missions.

By 1940, Edel Quinn was travelling widely in East and Central Africa establishing the Legion of Mary. On 28 December that year, from the mission at Likuni in Malawi, she sat down and wrote a three-page letter to Mother Mary asking for sisters for maternity work, as it meant 'such a lot for the African women', as well as helping to reduce the infant mortality.

At that time, there were only three professed members of the Medical Missionaries of Mary in Ireland, and it was not possible to take up this request. But twenty-one years later a foundation was made in Malawi, where the sisters continue to provide health services today.

Though both women were of frail health, they lived the rough and tumble of missionary life to an amazing degree. Not only did Mother

Mary Martin return to Africa, but she completed visitation and hospital inspection in the many missions where her sisters worked in East and West Africa. She crossed the entire continent of the United States by land in search of vocations and financial support, as well as visiting many countries in Asia in response to requests for personnel.

The TB from which Edel suffered gradually depleted her strength. The story of her heroism as an envoy of the Legion of Mary in East and Central Africa is well known. She died in Nairobi on 12 May 1944, to the great sorrow of her fellow Legionaries and the many missionaries who valued her work for the Church. Her grave in the Missionaries' Plot at St Austin's Cemetery, Nairobi, is visited by many Irish missionaries to this day, as is the grave of Mother Mary Martin in St Peter's Cemetery in Drogheda.

Mother Mary Martin. © Medical Missionaries of Mary

Blessed Nicholas Charnetskyi

BRENDAN MCCONVERY

BISHOP NICHOLAS Charnetskyi was a bishop of the Ukrainian Catholic Church who attended the Eucharistic Congress in Dublin in 1932. As part of the official congress programme, Bishop Nicholas celebrated the Pontifical Divine Liturgy according to the Byzantine (Greek Catholic) Rite in the Jesuit Church of St Francis Xavier, Gardiner Street, Dublin. This was probably the first public celebration of the Byzantine Rite in Ireland. Over recent decades, many Christians, both Catholic and Orthodox, have made their home in Ireland and use that venerable and beautiful form of the Divine Liturgy in their ordinary Sunday worship. The Greek-Rite Catholic community of Dublin commemorates him by using his name in its title, the Community of Hieromartyr [martyred bishop] Nicholas the Wonderworker.

Nicholas Charnetskyi was born on 14 December 1884 in the Western Ukraine, the eldest of nine children. He was ordained to the priesthood in 1909 and continued his postgraduate studies in Rome. In October, 1919, he entered the novitiate of the Greek Rite Redemptorists and the following year made his religious profession. He spent his early years as a Redemptorist preaching parish missions in Ukraine.

In 1931, he was appointed bishop and apostolic visitor for Ukrainian Catholics in the Volyn and Polissia regions. At the outbreak of the Second World War, Ukraine was overrun, first by the Germans and then by the Russians. After the war, Ukraine came under Soviet control. The Greek Catholic Church was suppressed by the state and its bishops and priests were rounded up for interrogation. Bishop Nicholas was arrested on 11 April 1945. After prolonged interrogation and torture, he was sentenced to ten years' imprisonment as a 'Vatican agent'. He served his term in the gulags of Siberia, often working in coalmines. It has been estimated that he spent 600 hours under torture and interrogation and was imprisoned in thirty different camps and forced-labour prisons.

When his health began to fail, the Soviet authorities feared that his death in prison might attract international attention to the fate of other religious prisoners of conscience. He was released in 1956 and permitted to return to the city of Lviv in Ukraine. There he lived in a poor apartment with a Redemptorist brother to care for him. Although seriously ill and almost blind, Bishop Nicholas continued to work quietly as a priest. He prepared candidates for the priesthood and ordained at least ten of them secretly before his death in 1959. His grave became a place of pilgrimage for Roman and Greek Rite Catholics and many cures were attributed to his intercession. When the Greek Catholic Church emerged from the shadows in the 1980s, Bishop Nicholas's cause for canonisation as a martyr was introduced. He was beatified by Pope John Paul II on 24 April 2001 along with twenty-five companion martyrs, including three from his own Redemptorist Congregation.

St Patrick's Purgatory, Lough Derg: Keeping 'An Ancient Vow'

EAMONN CONWAY

PATRICK'S PURGATORY, Lough Derg, is a little island on a lake in the north west of Ireland, with Christian remains that may go back to the fifth century and even to St Patrick himself. It has had an unbroken history of pilgrimage for almost a millennium. If you want to know about Celtic Christianity, you have to 'do Lough Derg'.

A three-day pilgrimage, involving a twenty-four-hour vigil while fasting and walking barefoot around the jagged stones of the long-ruined monastic cells, often in inclement weather, Lough Derg offers a most embodied kind of prayer.

'The twentieth century blows across it now./But deeply it has kept an ancient vow,' wrote Patrick Kavanagh in his poem about the pilgrimage.[1] While numbers visiting the island have fallen in recent decades, several thousand still undertake the arduous pilgrimage during the summer months, among them many young people.

Despite the wounds that secularisation has inflicted upon traditional forms of religiosity, the more physically demanding pilgrimages generally escape unscathed. This is because today's culture drives us to achieve and to 'invent' ourselves. Self-realisation is 'in'. Interestingly, research shows that more people today tend to believe in their own immortality than believe in God. This is because they cannot entertain the possibility that having invested so much in personal development and fulfilment, they would or could, in death, simply cease to be.

---

1. The lines from 'Lough Derg' by Patrick Kavanagh are reprinted from *Collected Poems*, edited by Antoinette Quinn (Allen Lane, 2004), by kind permission of the Trustees of the Estate of the late Katherine B. Kavanagh, through the Jonathan Williams Literary Agency.

This perspective can also have an impact on our faith. As self-made men and women, we can also desire to earn our eternal keep, and an arduous pilgrimage can offer the means (the heresy of Pelagius is not quite gone away). Poet and philosopher John Moriarty used to comment that generally we tend to be generous givers but 'damn mean receivers'. In our fallen state, the idea of being generous receivers of God's mercy and love is too humbling and disempowering for us and we are suspicious of anyone, even God, who appears as a free and generous giver.

Pilgrimages such as Lough Derg also enjoy contemporary appeal because they provide a sense of belongingness with deep roots in a tradition going back centuries, yet the belongingness can be transient and it does not necessarily involve any long-term commitment. Many pilgrims to Lough Derg, for instance, would not consider themselves practising Catholics, and have no connection with institutional religion apart from their annual pilgrimage.

However, the main reason pilgrimages remain popular despite secularisation is because they provide privileged moments of sacred encounter. Fasting and keeping vigil are exercises which deliberately wear down our defences, confronting us with our limitations, fragility and creaturely dependence. Faced with the reality of ourselves and the truth of our all-too-human condition, genuine penitential acts open us to a profound encounter with the living God.

Interestingly, both devout pilgrims who come with their 'shopping lists' of petitions, and the more suspicious self-realising searcher, have to learn the same thing: to 'self-empty' and to let go. A rigid 'shopping list' of demands to which God is firmly requested to respond, and indeed expected to, in view of the arduous penitential exercises undertaken, can prove just as much an obstacle to an experience of God's surprising grace as doubts about God's existence.

The journey of pilgrimage is always itself the destination. True pilgrims come to know their own smallness, and this includes the pettiness of their petitions and the fragility of their knowledge and understanding of God and God's will for them. They develop a disposition of trust in God's love and mercy and of utter humility to receive the gift of God's self in the circumstances of the day to day, however difficult. The ability to let go, and to trust more in God, are the authentic fruits of pilgrimage, as is the ability to give thanks no matter what one's circumstances.

Giving and receiving, journey and destination, food for the journey and fruit of the journey all come together in the Eucharist. There is something special about celebrating Eucharist on Lough Derg. Being barefoot is humbling. It is a great leveller, and it somehow signals that we all come before God in the same vulnerable state. The vigil, though physically draining, prepares pilgrims for the Eucharist: pilgrims are like the wise virgins described in the parable who wait for the bridegroom to arrive so the wedding feast can begin (Mt 25:1-13). The nagging physical hunger becomes a very real reminder of hunger for the bread that nourishes soul as well as body. Barefoot and deprived of food and sleep, the body and blood of Christ are experienced as nourishing in a profoundly physical way.

St Patrick's Purgatory, Lough Derg, and pilgrimages like it, continue to keep their 'ancient vow' and remain important sources of renewal and strength for the Irish Church at this challenging time in its history.

God's Truth is Life: Patrick Kavanagh's 'The Great Hunger'[1]

KEVIN O'GORMAN

S EAMUS HEANEY's depiction of Patrick Kavanagh's 'The Great Hunger' as 'a poem that throws up language as dark-webbed and cold-breathed as the clay the potato-digger kicks up in its opening lines', at first sight and sound seems an unlikely place to look for an expression of the Eucharist which engenders both light and life, to say nothing of love.[2] Reprising the opening line, the long poem (its fourteen sections perhaps reminiscent of the Stations of the Cross) ends with a loud announcement of 'the apocalypse of clay/In every corner of this land'. However, the sense of darkness, defeat and death which pervades is pierced by a 'tiny light in Oriental Darkness/Looking out chance windows of poetry or prayer'. The combination of light and sight through these 'chance windows' move the reader beyond John Keats' 'magic casements' to the threshold of mystery.[3] The romantic poet's forlorn imagination yields to the realism of faith-seeking imagination. This becomes concrete in the following exposition of the Eucharist.

Section six sees the hero (or anti-hero) sitting on a railway slope watching children plucking primroses and daisies, 'picking up life's truth singly'. His metaphysical musing leads him to contemplate the implication of the incarnation and the intertwining of the *mysterium salutis et fidei* in the merging of salvation and faith: 'O Christ, this is what you have done

---

1. The lines from 'The Great Hunger' by Patrick Kavanagh are reprinted from *Collected Poems*, edited by Antoinette Quinn (Allen Lane, 2004), by kind permission of the Trustees of the Estate of the late Katherine B. Kavanagh, through the Jonathan Williams Literary Agency. References are to the poem unless otherwise specified.
2. Seamus Heaney, 'Strangeness and Beauty', review of *Collected Poems of Patrick Kavanagh*, ed. Antoinette Quinn, in the *Guardian* (1 January 2005).
3. John Keats, 'Ode To A Nightingale', *Selected Poems* (London: Penguin, 2007), pp. 193–4.

for us./In a crumb of bread the whole mystery is.' Like the Mass, these
lines are divided into a liturgy of the Word and a liturgy of the Eucharist.
The vocative 'O Christ' announces the history of salvation, a summary of
what the Word made flesh has achieved 'for us', these final words an echo
of the Creed, 'for us and for our salvation'. The post-consecration mystery
of faith is acclaimed in the paradox of the presence of 'the whole mystery'
in a fragment which the disciples would probably have missed in their
gathering of the 'broken pieces' (Mk 6:43) after the miracle of the loaves.
William Blake's perception of the 'world in a grain of sand' gives way to the
wonder of the Godhead present 'in a crumb of bread'.[4] Poetry and prayer
dovetail in a memorial formula of the faithful imagination.

Reverence for the mystery of the sacrament of the Eucharist is
reinforced by reference to turning 'To the door whose combination lock
has puzzled/Philosopher and priest and common dunce'. Placing the
'common dunce' with the philosopher and priest in this collection is not
so much a putdown (something Kavanagh did not shy away from) as a
pronouncement about the universal puzzlement that all people ultimately
experience before the mystery. All stand equally before the threshold of
truth and wait for the door to be disclosed. The poet's intent is mystical and
points to the transcendence of reason, to the truth of theology articulated
by Augustine: *Si comprehendis non est Deus* – if you have understood then
it is not [of] God. Revelation is a reminder of what God has given us in
creation and what Christ has 'done for us' through the paschal mystery.

The poet's sacramental imagination sees 'God in the bits and pieces
of Everyday/A kiss here and a laugh again, and sometimes tears,/A pearl
necklace round the neck of poverty.' The whole of life – love, laughter
and tears, pleasure and pain, wealth and poverty – is included in this
incarnational perspective. As an elucidation of George Herbert's 'Heaven
in ordinarie', it embraces and expresses the range of human experience and
its encounter with grace.[5] Vatican II taught 'the things of the world and the
things of faith derive from the same God' and the Church's task, in and for
the world, is to show how the whole of life, sin notwithstanding, is taken

---

4. William Blake, 'Auguries of Innocence', *Selected Poems* (London: Penguin, 2006), p. 295.
5. George Herbert, 'Prayer', *The Complete English Poems* (London: Penguin, 2005), p. 45.

up and transformed in 'the whole mystery'.[6] The poet's task is to enable us to imagine this eucharistic theology, to believe that God's truth and human life are in communion and to hope that 'the pregnant Tabernacle lift[s] a moment to Prophecy/Out of the clayey hours'.

'The Great Hunger' operates on many levels, the personal and polemical, the poetic as anti-pastoral, the prophetic and philosophical. Reading it as a metaphor for the hunger(s) of the heart, one intuits the desire for communion – both human and divine – and is invited to share the poet's own journey in search of that communion which my own poem, 'Kavanagh's Second Chance', tries to capture:

> To see grace again
> Not as in earlier,
> Earthier forms of
> Fields and flowers,
> Seeping from trees,
> Springing from ditches
>
> But in children,
> Canals and courtship,
> The city sounds of
> Summer's symphony,
> Incarnation echoing
> Relationally the human
> Crescendo of creation.

---

6. *Gaudium et Spes: The Church in the Modern World*, Vatican Council II, Austin Flannery, ed. (Dublin: Dominican Publications, 2007), 36, p. 201.

St Kevin's Way: A One-Day Camino to Glendalough

KEVIN DORAN

STANDING IN the car park at Glendalough, Co. Wicklow, it is easy to forget that in times past, most people came to this place on foot. The ancient pilgrim route into Glendalough came over the Wicklow Gap from Hollywood. Pilgrimage on foot is an opportunity to 'seek the Lord where he may be found' (Is 55) and, in the process, to rediscover ourselves. On my pilgrim walk I carry a tiny wooden cross in the pocket of my jacket. It represents whatever or whoever I carry with me in my prayer.

While St Kevin's Way follows roughly the same route as the N756, most of it is on country lanes or forest track. The second half, starting from Ballinagee Bridge, is a three-hour walk, not counting breaks. On the Glendalough side of the bridge, we enter a forest track to the left. Shortly after the stile we turn right, up a narrow track, towards Teampall Tighnáin. Yellow arrows indicate the remains of a pilgrim hostel to the left above the path. St Benedict, a contemporary of St Kevin, wrote: 'In the reception of the poor and of pilgrims the greatest care and solicitude should be shown, because it is especially in them that Christ is received.'[1]

A few steps take us back down to the road. Crossing with care, because drivers rarely travel at the pace of the pilgrim, we follow the road for 100 metres. We cross another stile and follow the track across open ground towards a rocky escarpment ten minutes away. Just after the second of two wooden bridges, we turn to the left into a clearing among the trees overlooking a deep rock pool. Here, the Gospel account of the baptism of Jesus reminds us that we too are beloved sons and daughters, entrusted with a mission, and empowered by his Spirit.

---

1. *The Rule of St Benedict*, 53.

≈

Returning to the track, we climb steadily for a few hundred metres before passing through a clearing, after which the path levels off. This section can be boggy because drainage is poor. As in daily life, good discernment and a careful choice of path are required if we are to make progress without sinking into the mire. Another wooden bridge appears to lead to a dead end, but the path continues in the same direction, just a few metres to the left, taking us through some trees and uphill towards the main road. Just below the road, I sit on a rock looking back over the track we have climbed and think of another gathering on another hill. Blessed are the gentle; blessed are those who hunger and thirst for what is right. The kingdom of heaven is theirs.

We follow the track to the right for about fifteen minutes before scrambling up a steep bank to the road side and on to the car park at the top of the Wicklow Gap. Turning left across the car park, we rejoin the track at the far side. Just below the crest of the hill lies an enormous flat rock which makes a great table. A reflection on the feeding of the five thousand will serve as 'grace before meals'. We break bread and share it. The 'twelve baskets' gathered up speak of God's abundant goodness. They also remind us to 'leave no trace'.

Continuing on downhill, we cross the small road leading to Turlough Hill power station and follow the track along the edge of the forest, keeping the trees on our left. Leaving the trees behind us, we continue downhill and bear left, crossing the stream on stepping stones, and return briefly to the N756. Ten minutes later, we turn off across a wooden bridge, towards the old mining village above Glenmacnass.

This downhill part of the track has been renewed using rock and old railway sleepers. It takes us down past the old mine, alongside the river and onto the forest track which, after a further half hour, arrives in Glendalough. A left turn at the road takes us down to the ninth-century stone archway leading into the monastery. Listening to the words of Jesus: 'I am the gate of the sheepfold, all who enter through me will be safe' (Jn 10), we enter into the peace experienced by generations of pilgrims after a weary and dangerous journey over the mountains, in the face of bandits, wolves and weather. We pray for wisdom to enter through Jesus into all that we are and all that we do.

Inside the monastery, just below the remains of the cathedral, stands a simple granite high cross, a reminder to all of the presence of Christ at the heart of the community. I take my little wooden cross from my pocket and, in silence, touch it against the old granite cross as a small gesture of communion.

Memory and Nostalgia: The Feast of Corpus Christi

MARTIN HENRY

I T HAS often been remarked that the worst thing that can happen to a religion is for it to become successful. Yet if one thinks back to penal times, when people had to gather secretly for Mass at isolated 'Mass rocks' – in remote spots like Craigagh Wood in Innispollan near Cushendun, Co. Antrim, or Killoughcarron, Creeslough, Co. Donegal, to name just two – and compare such times with our own, it is at one level understandable to speak of 'success'.

It is, nevertheless, hard to suppress a kind of nostalgia for what were in many respects the 'bad old days', when the Catholic faith was outlawed. In those former times, Mass rocks were still a living reality, and not quasi-mythical places memorialising the countless men, women and children of the past, who, by their largely anonymous witness, preserved the Catholic faith in and through their lives and ensured it could be passed on to their descendants. Nostalgia, of course, can often just be a kind of sentimental regret for what are regarded as simpler times, free of the perceived complexity and bewildering confusion of our own.

Perhaps, therefore, the word 'envy' might be closer to the mark. Our attachment to the period of the Mass rocks might have more to do with a kind of envy of the centrality in their lives of the 'faith of our fathers' than with nostalgia for an earlier age. For in retrospect our forebears' faith does seem to have been tougher than ours. They had lost practically everything in terms of worldly security and success, but they had retained the *unum necessarium*, the one thing necessary our faith talks about, the one thing the world itself cannot give for the simple reason that it is not of this world, and yet without which everything else is finally worthless.

Since the time of Christ, we believe that God is no longer to be worshipped in the temple in Jerusalem alone or in any other specific city or place, but 'in spirit and in truth' anywhere in the world. Perhaps it was providential then that the testing period of the Mass rocks should have occurred in our history, because that period can probably bring out this fundamental truth of the Catholic faith more starkly and unambiguously than the splendour of even any of the great churches of Christendom can ever do.

For that matter, the small hills and woods where people formerly gathered at Mass rocks bear perhaps more similarity to the hill of Calvary on which our faith was founded than do the traditional famous sites associated with the practice of the Catholic faith. And that may be one of the secrets of the grip such sites can still have on the religious imagination.

To speak of the hill of Calvary is to approach the heart of the feast of Corpus Christi, the feast of the Body and Blood of Christ, which recalls the sacrifice Christ made for the redemption of the world. It is interesting to notice how many ancient peoples conceived of the world itself as having come into existence as the result of a divine sacrifice. The Christian faith also believes that the world, while not being created by the sacrifice of the Son of God, was nevertheless recreated or redeemed by this sacrifice. In Christianity, too, the body of God is destroyed in a sacrifice that brings about the recreation or the redemption of the world.

The similarity or closeness in outlook between ancient creation stories and Christianity seems to imply a shared human insight into a truth embedded in the very fabric of reality. This is that nothing of real value or truth or beauty can ever be attained without struggle or suffering or sacrifice, but also that what is finally reached in this way is worth having and can, with God's grace, last forever.

What is involved here, however, is not a glorification of suffering and sacrifice for its own sake. Sacrifice for its own sake, sustained religiously, will only create a stubborn but ultimately idolatrous sense of security. God is the 'rock of ages', not to be confused with the human capacity for sacrifice. It is, therefore, crucial to see that for the Catholic faith only God can make the sacrifice that takes away the sins of the world, not any ordinary human mortal.

The feast of Corpus Christi celebrates the awesome and humbling mystery at the centre of Christianity: that God sees in humanity the pearl of great price for which he was willing to sacrifice his life in Jesus Christ. It is that divine, saving death and resurrection that our ancestors celebrated and gave thanks for in the past, just as we in our turn can continue to give thanks to God for the reality recalled so vividly in the feast of Corpus Christi.

In Communion with the 'King of Sunday'

DAVID KELLY

A PAINTING BY James Humbert Craig, in the Crawford Art Gallery in Cork, depicts people going to Mass. Indeed the painting (c. 1935) is entitled *Going to Mass* and shows a scene from Connemara. It is a traditional rural scene from yesteryear, but on reflection it may offer food for thought even in our time. It has been suggested that the line of people walking to Mass 'has a kind of liturgical character: it can be likened to a procession.'[1] This links the procession with people's preparation for Mass, the high point of the celebration of Sunday. In traditional Irish prayers we find Sunday, the Christian Sabbath, welcomed and personified ('we bid you welcome, blessed Sunday/*Dé bheatha chugainn, A Dhomhnaigh bheannaithe*').[2] The welcoming of Sunday is, in turn, a welcoming of the King of Sunday (*Rí an Domhnaigh*), Christ himself.

This king is not meant to be seen as some secular monarch of the past, an absolute ruler, remote and detached from the lives of his people. Rather, more along the lines of a local Irish king, Christ as king of Sunday is known to his people in a relationship of kinship and familiarity. At the same time, Christ's kingship is understood as *kurios* (the risen Lord) in the New Testament (Rm 14:4). 'Christ is both "High King of heaven" and "King of my heart".'[3] We find this familiar reverence for Christ in the depiction of Sunday in the prayer referred to above, as 'a fine lovely day to speak to

---

1. Vincent Ryan, *The Shaping of Sunday: Sunday and Eucharist in Irish Tradition* (Dublin: Veritas, 1997), p. 72. A detail from the painting forms the cover of this book.
2. Ibid., p. 68. English/Irish version as in *Saltair: Urnaithe Dúchais (Prayers from the Irish Tradition)*, Pádraig Ó Fiannachta and Desmond Forristal, eds. (Dublin: Columba Press, 2000), pp. 28–9. See also Diarmuid Ó Laoghaire, *Ár bPaidreacha Dúchais* (BÁC: Foilseacháin Ábhair Spioradálta, 1990), p. 26.
3. *The Shaping of Sunday*, p. 70.

Christ'/*Lá breá aoibhinn chun Críost a agallamh*. We can discern a sense of communion being expressed here, a sense of fellowship and oneness with Christ, among the people walking together to Mass.

There is also among the people a sense of purpose and vitality of spirit. Each person is exhorted, in welcoming Sunday, to 'stir your feet and make your way to Mass'/*Corraigh do chos is téire chun an Aifrinn*. Each person's heart must be right for this task: 'stir your heart and drive from it all spite'/*Corraigh do chroí agus díbir an ghangaid as*. There is a strong exhortation here to open one's heart in conversion and that this is essential for encountering both Christ and neighbour in communion.

The sense of communion with Christ and one's neighbour as expressed in traditional Irish prayers is rooted in the New Testament notion of *koinonia* – shared life, fellowship and communion with God as Father, Son and Spirit (cf. 1 Jn 1:3;2 Cor 13:13). The same sense of communion defines the inner nature of the Church. Saint Augustine expresses this eloquently and succinctly in one of his sermons:

> You see on God's altar bread and a cup. That is what the evidence of your eyes tells you, but your faith requires you to believe that the bread is the body of Christ, the cup the blood of Christ … If then you want to know what the body of Christ is, you must listen to what the apostle tells the faithful: *Now you are the body of Christ, and individually you are members of it.* If that is so, it is the sacrament of yourselves that is placed on the altar, and it is the sacrament of yourselves that you receive … You hear the words 'The body of Christ' and you reply 'Amen'… Be, then, what you see, and receive what you are.[4]

Augustine here is drawing on St Paul's understanding of the Church as the body of Christ, an expression that also defines the Eucharist.

There is a richness of theology and spirituality springing from a vibrant faith, both personal and communal, to be discerned in our native Irish tradition. If we could but connect, even reconnect with this tradition, perhaps our sometimes negative contemporary experiences of Church

---

4. Sermon 272, as cited in Henry Ashworth, *Christ Our Light: Patristic Readings on Gospel Themes* (Maryland: Exordium Books, 1981), pp. 279–80. The Pauline quotation in italics is 1 Cor 12:27.

and Eucharist would be enriched as communion with Christ and with one another. The prayer we have been quoting throughout ends with the hope that 'we may be his in life and death'/ *Gur leis a bhuafar beo agus marbh sinn.* A wish that echoes the words of St Paul:

> We do not live to ourselves, and we do not die to ourselves. If we live, we live to the Lord, and if we die, we die to the Lord; so then, whether we live or whether we die, we are the Lord's. (Rm 14:7-8)

Seán Ó Leocháin's *An Chéad Aoine* ('The First Friday')[1]

MÍCHEÁL MACCRAITH

Nuair a tháinig an sagart	When the priest came
ag m'athair inniu,	to my father yesterday,
mar a thagann de ghnáth	as he normally comes
ag tús na míosa,	at the beginning of the month,
le lón na beatha	with the food of life
a roinnt ar fhear	to give to a man
nach bhfágann an chlúid	who doesn't leave the fireside
In aon chor le tamall,	at all these days,
ní hé an gnás	it wasn't the ritual
ab ait liom féin.	that I found most strange.
Ní hé ba mhó	It wasn't my greatest
ba bhun le m'iontas	source of wonder
fear dá chlú,	that a man of his fame,
dá chleacht, dá éirim	experience and intelligence
ar cuairt na sean	should visit the old
i dtús na míosa	at the beginning of the month
le comhairle a leasa	with the best of advice
a chur ar dhream	to give to people
nach bhfágfadh clúid	who would never leave
na haithrí choíche,	the corner of repentance
ach Críost a theacht	but that Christ would come
i gcarr athláimhe	in a second-hand car
a cheannaigh an sagart	that the priest had bought
ó fhear i Ros Comáin.	from a man in Roscommon

---

1. This has recently been republished in Seán Ó Leocháin, *Cloch Nirt Rogha Dánta agus Dánta Nua* (Indreabhán, Conamara: Cló Iar-Chonnacht, 2011), p. 53. Reprinted by permission of Cló Iar-Chonnacht, 2011.

Having recently published his twelfth volume, Seán Ó Leocháin, author of the above poem, is one of the most prolific poets writing in Ireland today. Though permeated with deeply held religious values, some of his early poetry is racked with anguish and doubt, expressing a hard-won faith that is constantly tested, allowing little or no respite to the tortured believer. At its most optimistic, however, Ó Leocháin's verse depicts a world where immanence and transcendence converge. His distinctive vision enables him to invest every object, no matter how trivial, with symbolic value rooted in its immanence but pointing beyond itself to the transcendent. The image contained in the last four lines of *An Chéad Aoine* is both stunning in its ordinariness and overwhelming in its implications, and all the more effective for coming so unexpectedly in the wake of the nonchalant approach of the previous lines. This is not merely a religious poem, but one that unveils a precious insight into the mystery of the incarnation with all its consequences, not least the gift of the Eucharist.

Evie Hone and the Manresa House Stained-Glass Windows

MICHAEL SHORTALL

FIVE STAINED-GLASS windows line the small oratory in the Manresa retreat house in Dollymount, Dublin, greeting those who gather with an array of images. The central pane is of the Last Supper. Immediately the eye is drawn to Jesus, dressed in red, sitting at table with his disciples. His hand, raised in blessing, consecrates the bread and wine and those present with him in the scene. It is only then that the viewer notices the event unfolding in the lower half of the windowpane: Jesus washing the feet of Peter.

The artist's name is Eva Sydney (Evie) Hone (1894–1955), a foremost exponent of an Irish flourishing in the artistry of stained glass during the first half of the twentieth century. Born in Mount Merrion, Dublin, to a relatively affluent Anglican family, she overcame partial paralysis due to a childhood accident to spend time in Europe and be exposed to the exciting developments that art was undergoing at that time. While there she developed a lifelong friendship with Mainie Jellett (1897–1944) and, on returning, they forged new ground for abstract painting in Ireland. A late arrival to the skill of stained glass, she joined the studio *An Túr Gloine* (The Glass Tower), adding a new expressionist intensity.

Her early art always showed a religious sensibility but her turn towards stained glass provided a medium for a more explicit expression of theological themes. In 1937, she was received into the Catholic Church by the Archbishop of Dublin, John Charles McQuaid. Her extensive work reaches back into a tradition of strong colours and symbols, while at the same time exhibiting a creativity and vibrancy not often associated with the religious expression of that era in Ireland.

Evie Hone stained-glass window. Manresa, Jesuit Centre of Spirituality, Dublin. © Manresa, Jesuit Centre of
Spirituality

Three years before she died her most internationally renowned piece was completed – the replacement of the east window of Eton College Chapel, England, earlier destroyed during the Second World War. Dominated by the crucifixion scene, it also includes the Last Supper. However not all her stained glass is religiously themed. One of her most celebrated pieces now welcomes guests in the foyer of the Irish Government buildings. Originally commissioned for the New York World Fair in 1939, *My Four Green Fields* symbolically represents the four provinces of Ireland.

To return to that small oratory: it is housed in Manresa, the Jesuit Centre for Spirituality, Dollymount, Dublin. Completed in 1946, it graced the novitiate of the Irish Jesuit province in Tullabeg, Rahan, Co. Offaly. The stained-glass window at the centre of the room frames two scriptural accounts of the Last Supper. The upper part depicts the breaking of bread and sharing of wine recounted in the Synoptic Gospels (Mt 26:17-30; Mk 14:12-26; Lk 22:7-39) and by St Paul (1 Cor 11:23-26); the lower part illustrates the washing of feet as told in the Gospel of John (Jn 13:1–17:26). Taken as a whole, it is a wonderful arrangement of scriptural and theological understandings of the Eucharist.

In the upper part, Jesus, sitting at table, dominates the image. He is noticeably larger than the huddled disciples assembled around him, asserting the centrality of Christ as the consecrator. He blesses the gifts of bread and wine. The table fare also includes two fish, referencing the feeding of the multitude (Mt 14:13-21; Mk 6:31-44; Lk 9:10-17; Jn 6:5-15). Although an imposing figure, the face of Jesus has a gentle demeanour. On his shoulder, John the beloved disciple rests affectionately if somewhat sorrowfully. At the front of the table, another disciple points to himself with a pleading look. He is responding to Jesus' acknowledgement of a betrayer. Judas turns away knowingly, while clutching a small brown sack (Mt 26:14-16; Jn 12:4-6). Between them is a space at the table, as if it is for the onlooker – an open invitation to join the meal.

In the lower part, Jesus kneels before Peter, a towel wrapped around his waist and over his arm. As a figure, it is smaller than that of the upper part. If the former asserts the divinity of Christ, this latter image signifies the Jesus who humbled himself to become human (Phil 2:6-11) and, as a servant, to become an exemplar of true love (Jn 13:15). Peter humbly submits. By contrast, in a dark corner of the window, thirty pieces of silver are strewn on the ground and a body hangs from a tree. Rather cryptically, in the foreground there appear to be two shoes lying on the ground. Perhaps they indicate that this is holy ground, referencing the event on Mount Sinai, when God, by way of the burning bush, asked Moses to remove his shoes (Ex 3:5).

Hone weaves a variety of motifs. Yet by portraying the washing of feet she emphasises the centrality of service in the meaning of Eucharist. In particular, it is Jesus who serves in the Eucharist and 'So if I, your Lord and Teacher, have washed your feet, you ought to wash one another's feet' (Jn 13:14).

Poignantly, it was while attending Mass on 13 March 1955 in her local church that Evie Hone died.

St Mary's Church of Ireland, Julianstown, Co. Meath[1]

JANET E. RUTHERFORD

NESTLING ON the edge of Julianstown, just south of Drogheda and about a mile from the sea, is a small neo-Gothic church dedicated to St Mary. It is a pearl produced, as it were, by the oyster of Meath's long and rich Christian history and its relationship with Wales through Hugh de Lacey. In 1108, he founded an Augustinian abbey in Llanthony in Wales, and monasteries under the authority of its prior were later established at Duleek and Colpe. It was to Colpe that de Lacey gave, as part of its endowment, the church of Ainge – named after the Nanny River, which runs through Julianstown. When the monasteries were dissolved, Llanthony Abbey's Irish possessions came into the hands of the Moores, who became earls of Drogheda and patrons of the parish of Julianstown.

The original church was most likely made of wood, and no trace of it remains. However, we know that by the time of the bishop's visitation in 1685, the civil upheavals of the seventeenth century had left a later stone church without chancel roof or bells. In the record of this visitation we encounter an early reference to the Pepper family, who were to prove loyal patrons of the church into the twentieth century. In 1770, this first stone church was replaced with what would become the basis of the present one. From what little is known of its initial form, it was a rectangular 'shoe box' with plain glass windows, a small porch and bell tower at the west end, and no chancel. But from this unprepossessing start, a marvellous transformation evolved.

---

1. This essay is indebted for many of its historical details to Bernie Daly's guide book to the church, *St Mary's Church Julianstown* (Dublin, 1995).

St Mary's Church of Ireland, Julianstown, Co. Meath. Photo courtesy of Janet E. Rutherford

In the early nineteenth century, local architects were employed to add rock-faced limestone with ashlar trim to the walls, a spire, leaded windows and a chancel. By 1906, renovations were being led, and endowed, by another Pepper, Colonel Charles. When the nineteenth-century tower became unsafe and had to be replaced, he took the opportunity to make the extensive alterations and renovations that have resulted in the present church. All the alterations were parts of an overarching neo-Gothic design. The beautifully proportioned new tower at the west end contributes to the Gothic asymmetry of the whole. The 'shoe box' acquired a steeply pitched roof and a gabled porch on the south wall, where a plaque bears the engraved names of all the vicars (and later, rectors) since 1615 (the names of five earlier vicars from 1341, 1396, 1426, 1470 and 1576 are also known).

An extension was made to the nineteenth-century chancel, including a new sanctuary. These additions to the east end of the 'shoe box' create a dramatic view down the nave to a beautifully tiled chancel with ribbed Gothic arches, forming a frame for the jewel-like sanctuary of marble and alabaster and three Gothic stained-glass east windows created by Clayton and Bell in 1884, retained from the previous sanctuary. There is a brass rail with delicate tracery, and the wooden altar is gilded and painted with the four evangelists and an Alpha and Omega, all in the Art Deco style appropriate to Gothic Revival architecture (as are all the windows). The view towards the west end is hardly less beautiful, and as worshippers turn to depart they encounter over the ancient stone font three Gothic windows depicting the ascension, surmounted by a star-shaped window of angels.

The windows along the nave enhance the jewel-like quality of the whole interior. One is a remarkably beautiful memorial window created by the artist Michael Healy. In addition to the many generous gifts of the Pepper family, Charles Pepper presented a new bell to the church in 1907. The old bell, cast in 1736, is still in the possession of the parish. The head of a high cross that was found in the churchyard of Colpe is now displayed in the porch. Just outside the porch, at the edge of the churchyard, is a row of ancient stone carvings of the twelve disciples, which was brought to St Mary's in 1908, and may date from the dissolution of monasteries. Casualties of Ireland's troubled past have thus been lovingly preserved as part of a living, worshipping community today.

St Mary's Julianstown has been the focus of the continuous devotional and sacramental life of generations of local families as well as new arrivals, and continues to be much loved by its present parishioners. It is appropriate to conclude with the final statement from Bernie Daly's 1995 guide to the church, which remains true today:

> The architecture, the windows, the warmth, the light, the sound of the bell on Sunday morning, the high standard of worship, and the people who come to worship, all serve to maintain St Mary's as a continuing oasis of peace and prayer.[2]

---

2.   Ibid., p. 26.

The Ancient Pilgrim Path Between Ballintubber Abbey and Croagh Patrick

FRANK FAHEY

JULY WAS a hungry month for our pagan Celtic ancestors as they eagerly anticipated the ripening of autumn. But before they satisfied their hunger, they sacrificed the first fruits of nature to the pagan god on the harvest festival of Lughnasa. Only then, when they had acknowledged their indebtedness to the god Lugh for these gifts, would they feel free to eat and celebrate the abundance of harvest. This celebration on County Mayo's Croagh Patrick, then known as Cruachán Aille, took place in other places around Ireland and indeed in many cultures around the world. And the smoke from the immolations billowed to the heavens like incense. Perhaps these celebrations, in some aspects, prefigured the Eucharist.

Even thousands of years before the druids offered the sacrifice of the first fruits, our Neolithic farming ancestors celebrated the festival of the Corn King at the autumn equinox on the same mountain. The sacrifice was accompanied with a community meal and celebrations. In times of great hardship, the sacrifice might even be that of a human being. The Corn King, as he was called, would be a person of noble origin, specially chosen. His willing sacrifice for the sake of the community earned him the right to become a demi-god in the 'other world'. After a seven-day wake or celebration, he would be ritually buried with great honour under a *cromleac* or dolmen. The cairn of stones that marked his burial chamber grew in volume each subsequent year, as his tribe celebrated the successful gathering of the harvest on the autumn equinox.

Patrick must have seen the significance of these places and festivals as foreshadowing things to come. At the very spot of druidic sacrifice on

Cruachán Aille, tradition relates that he dispelled the demons through the ringing of his Mass bell (now in the National Museum). Further back on Tóchar Phádraig, the ancient pilgrim path between Ballintubber Abbey and Croagh Patrick, is the Rock of Boheh. The cup and circled marks that cover it date to the Neolithic or Early Bronze Age (4000–2000 BC). But an incised cross among circled hollows confirms the tradition that Patrick celebrated Mass there. This tradition is continued today on the Tóchar pilgrim walks.

This Rock of Boheh was also a 'food stone' on which our ancestors placed a *struán* cake, made from the first sheaf of corn, as an offering to the god. In Christian times that cake, made from the first sheaf of wheat, was made into loaf for the harvest Mass. This festival is still celebrated today as the Lammas (Loaf-Mass) Fair.

Further back along Tóchar Phádraig, the Mass rocks in Lankill and Log na hAltóra, the Patrician church at Teampaileen, the bare altars in the now ruined churches in Aghagower and the hallowed sanctuary of Ballintubber Abbey indicate that the pilgrim journey of our people was nourished by the Eucharist. In that ancient 'abbey that refused to die', Mass has been celebrated without interruption since it was founded in 1216, in spite of burnings, famine and penal laws.

In that abbey, the east windows behind the altar powerfully depict the *parousia*, that dimension of the Eucharist that proclaims that 'Christ will come again in glory'. The morning sunrise, filtering through the exquisite stained glass executed by de Loire from Chartres, fills the sanctuary with shades of that mystery. And around the abbey, on the outside, the dead lie sleeping in their graves since Patrick's time. They face the east and the rising sun, awaiting their awakening in hope, to celebrate the eternal liturgy of the Lamb. And on that day of judgement, all graves – whether in consecrated grounds, in famine plots or under dolmens and cairns – will stand empty.

On the last Sunday of July, as the dawn Eucharist is celebrated on the top of Croagh Patrick in the presence of 20,000 pilgrims, one is struck with wonder and awe as a magnificent panorama reveals itself, and one is left pondering on the breadth and height and depth of the eucharistic mystery, with its promise that 'Creation will itself be set free from its bondage to decay to obtain the glorious liberty of the children of God' (Rm 8:21).

Ó Riada's *Ár nAthair* (Our Father)

JOHN O'KEEFFE

SOME TWENTY-FIVE years after the liturgical reforms of Vatican II, at a farewell meal for the outgoing pastor of a community in the south-west of the country, various contributors voiced their appreciation of all that had been achieved during his time amongst them. Two principal themes emerged. The first related to the provision of a new parish church, a new place to pray, the opening of which was keenly anticipated. Coming a surprisingly close second was the community's sense of gratitude for the fact that the priest had taught them to sing Seán Ó Riada's *Ár nAthair* at Mass.[1]

A new way to pray – this was a theme very close to the hearts of the Vatican II reformers as they welcomed vernacular languages and increased community involvement in the liturgy. Attention had also been focused from the outset on the musical heritage of individual peoples, with a view to identifying elements of worship which could be adapted to their native genius. In the spring of 1968, a number of Irish church musicians gathered in Glenstal Abbey to discuss the implications of the recently promulgated *Musicam Sacram*, 'Instruction on Music in the Liturgy', which included the following reflections on the challenges ahead:

> Adapting sacred music for those regions which possess a musical tradition of their own … will require a very specialised preparation … It will be a question in fact of how to harmonise the sense of the sacred with the spirit, traditions and characteristic expressions proper to each of these peoples. Those who work in this field should have a sufficient knowledge both of the liturgy and musical tradition of the Church, and

---

1. The 'Our Father' in Irish, published as part of the composer's *Ceol an Aifrinn* (Baile Átha Cliath: An Chlóchomhar Teo, 1971).

Copy of Ó Riada's original setting of the *Ár nAthair*, which was sent on a postcard to Tomás Ó Canainn

of the language, popular songs and other characteristic expressions of the people for whose benefit they are working.[2]

As one of the panelists of the Glenstal symposium, Seán Ó Riada would have noted this paragraph with particular interest. In 1963, the year of the Liturgy Constitution, he had obtained a music lectureship at University College Cork and taken the decision to fully embrace all aspects of native Irish culture by moving his family to the west Cork Gaeltacht (Irish-speaking area) of Cúil Aodha. The following year he had formed a church choir of local men, many of them accomplished traditional singers, and together they had been working on a combination of traditional Latin chants and a growing body of native vernacular religious texts for which Ó Riada provided musical settings.[3] These settings drew increasingly on the vibrant tradition of (largely secular) song for which the area was renowned and which provided the composer with a working, living language.

In his essay 'Ó Riada at Glenstal Abbey', the Benedictine monk Dom Paul McDonnell recounts how, in Christmas of 1968, he sent a greeting card to Seán Ó Riada, the main illustration on which was the plainchant melody of a Gospel acclamation long in use in the monastic liturgy. 'By return of post,' he recalls, 'he sent a plain postcard on which he had scribbled the Our Father in Irish, set to his own music.'[4] The handwritten setting, marked *go mall, oscailte, sean-nósach* ('slowly, freely and in the traditional manner'), is quite clearly in traditional Irish song style.[5] The significance of this exchange between the monk and the musician is difficult to overstate. McDonnell sends, from the heart of the Latin tradition, a hallowed chant from the Church's universal canon, and in response Ó Riada sends, from the heart of the Gaeltacht, his own musical setting of the Lord's Prayer, as realised in the distinctive rhythms of Irish prose. The nature of Ó Riada's reply certainly bespoke a confidence, perhaps not so much in his own abilities as in the artistic richness and potential of the native tradition. The

2. MS 61, *Vatican Council II: The Conciliar and Post-Conciliar Documents* (revised edition), Austin Flannery, ed. (New York: Costello Publishing Company, 1988), p. 95.
3. This choir constituted the beginnings of what would later come to be known as *Cór Chúil Aodha*.
4. Paul McDonnell, 'Ó Riada at Glenstal Abbey', *The Achievement of Seán Ó Riada*, Bernard Harris and Grattan Freyer, eds. (Ballina: The Irish Humanities Centre, 1981), p. 111.
5. See illustration as reproduced in Harris and Freyer, p. 171. Our thanks to Tomás Ó Canainn for permission to reproduce this here.

composition itself, comprising living musical gestures expertly woven into the unique textual structure of this pre-eminent Christian prayer, managed to distil within a few bars the essence of what might be possible in the future interplay of two rich traditions.

As things turned out, this setting, which McDonnell reckoned to be Ó Riada's 'first essay in liturgical music', was to mark the beginning of a process initiated by the composer and continued to this day in the work of his son Peadar Ó Riada, an organic development which has already produced a significant body of Irish vernacular settings for the liturgy. For its own part, over four decades later, the confident, uplifting strains of Seán Ó Riada's *Ár nAthair* continue to resound in parishes throughout Ireland, fostering an ever-strengthening unity between prayer and song, music and liturgy, earth and heaven.

Naomh Íde and the Heart of the Eucharist

MÍCHEÁL DE LIOSTÚN

THE RELATIONSHIP between two women, Íde and Áine, in the landscape of Ireland has held a constant fascination for me. Within human perspectives we can accept separations and even hostilities as the full story. At the heart of the Eucharist there is a proclamation that invites all to be one family, perhaps expressed best in Irish as one *muintearas*:

> For in him all the fullness of God was pleased to dwell, and through him to reconcile to himself all things, whether on earth or in heaven, making peace by the blood of the cross. (Col 1:20)

Naomh Íde, or St Ita, is patron of the diocese of Limerick and a living presence around much of west Limerick, not just in Cill Íde (Kileedy), or the neighbouring parish of Cill Míde (Kilmeedy). I find it intriguing that her name is also part of the landscape of County Dublin, with signposts proclaiming her name in Mullach Íde (Mallahide) and Domhnach Míde (Donaghmede). There, traditional story goes that she received her name because of her thirst for God. The question of what to do with the human thirst that never seems to be satisfied with what human life is offering is as fresh today as it was among the young women of ancient Ireland. Íde was called the foster mother of the saints because she fostered St Brendan and so many others. This was not enough. To her great delight she was finally given the privilege of nursing the child Jesus, known affectionately in Irish as *Íosagán*. Today Jesus seems to be a very fragile child in the hearts of so many, a child that cries out to be nursed. The loving word of God found a secure place in the heart of Íde and she trusted in the affection and nourishment that her friendship with Jesus would bring.

Another female presence that lives on in the rural landscape and poetry of Ireland is Áine. Cnoc Áine is a low hill in the neighbourhood of Lough Gur and the great stone circle of Grange, Co. Limerick. Áine represents the land in its glory, its beauty and its fertility. In the following poem I see Áine as mother of what the earth gives us and Íde as the grateful daughter who recognises in her heart a place that hungers for more than human life can give. As Jesus gave thanks and praise to God and then gave himself for the life of those he loved, even those who betrayed him, Íde expressed her gratitude in self-giving to those in need. Íde leaves home but recognises that her lover is the giver of the life and death and resurrection of all, *Rí na nUile* ('King of All'). We are all called to the Supper of the Lamb.

Áine agus Íde

Cad tá ort, a chailín, cén fáth an mí-shuaimhneas?
Tá tart orm , a mháithrín, sin fáth mo uaignis.

Nár thugas duit bainne, is ná fuil tuilleadh ar fáil?
Thugais, a mháithrín, is bhíos buíoch é a fháil.

Tá uisce úr an tsléibhe anseo faoi do láimh!
Ní beag liom an t-uisce, a ghlaine is a cháil.

An mian leat fíon, a chailín chiúin óig?
Níl agat aon fhíon don íota seo am'dhó.

Cá raghair, a chailín, ní fhágfair an baile?
Tá leanbh am' iarraidh is téim dá altrom.

Nach dána an mhaise dhuit a leithéid d'iontaoibh!
Briathar an teachtaire a chuaigh fám'chroí.

Cad faoi do shláinte is an freastal gan seó?
Gealladh dom dáimh is uisce bithbheo.

An mbeidh aon trá, a iníon, ar fhlaithiúlacht do dhé bhig?
'Sé bhronn orainn ár nginiúin, ár mbás, is ár n-aiséirí.

Áine and Íde

What is on you, girl, and why are you so uneasy?
I am thirsty, mother, and that is why I am lonely.

Didn't I give you milk and isn't there more?
You did, mother, and I was grateful to receive it.

There is water from the mountain here at hand!
I love water, so clear and fresh.

Do you want some wine, quiet young girl?
You have no wine for the thirst that burns me.

Where are you going, girl, will you leave the house?
A child is looking for me and I go to nurse him.

Isn't that bold of you, such confidence!
The word of the messenger went straight to my heart.

What of your health and the service without show?
I was promised affection and living water.

Will the generosity of your little hero ever run dry?
It is he who gifted us all with our life, with our death and with our
resurrection.

Knock – A Sacred Place in the West of Ireland Where Heaven and Earth Meet

JOSEPH QUINN

PILGRIMAGE AND devotion to Mary, the Mother of the Lord, has deep roots in Irish Christianity across fifteen centuries. 'Mother of God, will you look at the state that I'm in,' cried a young Cork mother many years ago while here at Knock. She had come on pilgrimage with her small son who had a serious and painful skin disease. During the day the boy was in distress; he was restless and uncomfortable and needed his mother's total attention. It was time in the evening to begin the journey home and the young woman thought to herself: 'I haven't said a prayer all day.' She went with her tired and distressed son to the Apparition Gable and cried out. When the young boy woke up at home the following morning his skin was clear. He was cured: his mother's faith, and Our Lady's intercession. Healing occurs at Knock every day.

Knock is Ireland's National Marian Shrine and the Shrine of the Lamb. The apparition of Our Lady occurred at Knock on 21 August, 1879. It was seen by fifteen people of all ages. Two Church commissions concluded that the evidence of the fifteen was 'trustworthy and satisfactory'. They saw Our Lady, St Joseph, St John the Evangelist with Book in hand, and an altar on which stood a Lamb with a Cross. They saw angels too. The apparition lasted for two hours at the gable wall of the parish church on a wet and windy August evening. Pope John Paul II gave Knock the ultimate recognition when he came as a pilgrim for the centenary in 1979. He called his visit 'the goal of my journey to Ireland'. He blessed the statues depicting the apparition, presented a Golden Rose to the shrine and raised the then new church to the status of a basilica. Included in the new Roman Missal is the Feast of Our Lady of Knock.

In no other recorded apparition did the Lamb of God appear. Knock is thus unique. During the Knock apparition, no word was spoken, no message was given. In its silence it speaks eloquently about the truths of our faith. The Knock apparition is rich in eucharistic symbolism. And at Knock there is eucharistic spirituality in abundance as it is a sacred place of communion with Christ and one another. Pilgrims are not tourists. They support each other, pray together and bond.

Knock is a special place of pilgrimage and prayer – a place of evangelisation, devotion and spirituality. Today, people search for ways to reach out to God and connect with him. At Knock, people can experience peace, freedom, reconciliation and healing as they search. At Knock, heaven and earth meet in a unique way.

The one hundred acres of the shrine domain, with its landscaped grounds and myriad of colour, speaks in itself of the wonder, beauty and majesty of the Creator God and helps us raise our hearts and minds to that God. At Knock, 'the world is charged with the grandeur of God'. The liturgy is always solemn and beautiful – Masses and ceremonies, anointing, rosaries and processions. The pilgrims 'contemplate the face of Christ at the school of Mary'. And then too there's the Knock holy water.

The Apparition Chapel, with its pristine white marble tableau of the apparition itself, is a haven of peace and a source of wonder and renewal for the tired and weary pilgrim. The Reconciliation Chapel, with its sixty rooms, provides an opportunity to celebrate the sacrament of reconciliation and experience God's forgiveness, mercy, healing and peace. There are many books in the shrine book centre for when 'faith seeking understanding' and prayer needs support and nourishment, as it does.

The museum reminds us of our heritage and roots. To lose your sense of history and heritage is to quickly lose your identity. In the prayer guidance centre, trained prayer guides help people pray with sacred scripture. The Family Life Centre provides resources and support for the family. There is a counselling service at the Reconciliation Chapel and a spiritual direction service too. In the Blessed Sacrament Chapel one can spend quality time with the Lord in prayer and adoration and deep communion with him. Knock shrine provides for its pilgrim visitors.

The shrine staff at Knock includes hundreds of volunteers. They are generous with their time, loyal and committed, friendly and helpful. At

Knock there is a warm welcome for people of all faiths and none, and for people of every race and culture. And in keeping with Irish hospitality there are always refreshments in the Rest and Care Centre and at the shrine's café at the museum. Knock is a unique place of pilgrimage and prayer, devotion and spirituality, welcome and hospitality for the 1.5 million pilgrims – many of whom are sick, disabled and elderly – who come every year.

Gile mo Chroí do Chroí-se: The Light of My Heart is Your Heart

BRÍD LISTON

Gile mo chroí do chroí-se, a Shlánaitheoir,
Is ciste mo chroí do chroí-se d'fháil am chomhair;
Ós follas gur líon do chroí dem ghrá-sa, a stór,
I gcochall mo chroí do chroí-se fág i gcomhad.[1]

The light of my heart is your heart, O Saviour,
The treasure of my heart is your heart poured out for me;
Since it is clear that your heart is filled with my love, O beloved,
In my innermost heart leave your heart for safe keeping.

GILE MO *chroí do chroí-se* is a confessional poem written by the Irish poet, Tadhg Gaelach Ó Súilleabháin in the eighteenth century, when the penal laws forbidding the practice of the Christian religion were enforced in Ireland. During this time, the Eucharist which was central to people's lives was celebrated on 'Mass rocks' in country valleys or in the 'Mass houses' of safe communities.[2] The poet expresses how Christ's presence in the Eucharist clothed people with the dignity of being beloved daughters and sons of God: 'Since it is clear that your heart is filled with my love, O beloved.'

In the Eucharist today, these same sentiments are expressed in a short Trinitarian prayer said quietly by the presider after the 'Lamb of God' and before the 'Lord, I am not worthy' as we prepare for communion:

---

1. Tadhg Gaelach Ó Súilleabháin, *Gile mo chroí do chroí-se*, Máire B. de Paor (Kildare: Mainistir Eibhín, 2005).
2. Peter O'Dwyer, *Towards a History of Irish Spirituality* (Dublin: Columba, 1995), p. 206.

Lord Jesus Christ, Son of the living God,
who, by the will of the Father
and the work of the Holy Spirit,
through your Death gave life to the world,
free me by this, your most holy Body and Blood,
from all my sins and from every evil;
keep me always faithful to your commandments,
and never let me be parted from you.

The generous and saving love of Christ that is expressed in Tadhg Gaelach's poem is echoed in the words: 'your death gave life to the world, free me by this, your most holy Body and Blood'. Christ, sent by the Father, incorporates us into God. The prayer affirms our baptismal identity, freeing us 'from every evil', never letting us 'be parted' from Christ and placing us in the heart of the Christian community. Through this communion with the Trinity and our union as living members of the body of Christ, the Church, we are God's healing presence in the world.

The theme of the 2012 Eucharistic Congress – 'The Eucharist: Communion with Christ and with one another' – affirms this sense of oneness with Christ and the community. In the Eucharist, we remember, give thanks and celebrate the divine–human encounter, signified in the Word, and bread and wine. In this eucharistic community, individual believers united in the Spirit become a 'we'. As a community of disciples in companionship with Jesus and with each other, we are called to proclaim, serve and witness to God's reign of justice, love and peace. Today, the oppressive power of the 'penal laws' could perhaps be seen in the deceptive lure of busyness, individuality and a lack of ethical living. The question for each of us as individuals and as families is to ask 'How can I/we live as Eucharist in a broken Church at a time of world recession? How can I/ we respond to the needs of people who hunger and thirst for belonging, people who are exploited or displaced from their homes?' In the Eucharist, Christ offers us courage, confidence and nourishment to live this mission together.

Gile mo chroí do chroí-se later expresses Christ's oneness with all humanity in its suffering because he was himself 'astray … from heaven'. Tadhg Gaelach closes his poem with a reminder of God's unconditional

love which Christ bore silently "til the lance tore open a haven in [his]
heart for the whole world':

> Ar fán cé bhíse, a Rí ghil naofa ó neamh,
> Go cráite trínne, i slí nach léir a mheas.
> Do ghrá-sa, a Chríost, níor mhaís gur réab ab tslea
> Áras-dín ad chroí don saol ar fad.

Even though you were astray, O fair Holy King from heaven,
Tormented in our midst in a way that cannot be estimated,
You made no boast of your love for us, O Christ, 'til the lance
   tore open
A haven in your heart for the whole world.

Corpus Christi in Bandon

GEARÓID DULLEA

I T IS one of the great paradoxes of our faith that we believe in a God who is a hidden God (Is 45:15) but yet a God whose nature is in Jesus Christ (Phil 2:6). Our faith in God-with-us stands alongside our faith in a God who is wholly Other. Perhaps our belief in the closeness of God is shown very vividly and evocatively in our belief in the Eucharist, our participation in the Body and Blood of Christ. Is it any wonder that the expression 'Holy Communion' lies at the centre of the meaning of this great sacrament? One expression of devotion to the Eucharist that loomed large in my parish was the annual eucharistic procession for Corpus Christi. From the inception of this procession in Bandon in the 1930s, it has remained a colourful and important feature of the life of our community.

I remember as a child staring in wonderment as the verger, in his oddly shaped hat, walked with his staff and led off the assembled group. There were different sections in the procession, including First Holy Communion children with their unconscious gravity; women wearing the traditional hooded cloak of west Cork, bringing a sense of tradition and continuity to what was happening; the marshals and banner bearers in white gloves, wearing sashes and carrying staffs; the scouts and guides in serried rows; and so forth. The silence of the participants, punctuated only by the responses to the prayers which were transmitted by loudspeaker around the town, was a striking feature of this event.

The choir in choral dress wound its way around the town and eventually made its way from South Main Street into Market Street; it was followed by the Blessed Sacrament section of the procession. This section was led by an altar server carrying a cross and a long line of altar servers carrying thurible and incense boat and baskets of petals. The altar servers strewing the petals walked backwards as a mark of respect in front of the canopy with the Blessed Sacrament. Lighted lanterns flanked the canopy and guards of honour were provided by the FCA (Irish Reserve Defence Forces) and the Garda Síochána. The priest carried the monstrance with the host. As the canopy approached the people gathered in the street and on the church steps, men and women dropped to their knees out of reverence for what was happening. The choir struck up the *Lauda Jerusalem* ('Praise the Lord, Jerusalem') and began the ascent to the top of the steps, from where benediction was given at a temporary altar.

There were two moments in particular that are indelibly etched in my mind and they have always fed my imagination. The first was when the Blessed Sacrament left the church building. The bugler sounded the salute, the church bell tolled out and the entire procession stopped walking. Here we were being reminded that Jesus Christ, the divine Son of God, under the appearance of bread in the sacrament of the most blessed Eucharist, had left the tabernacle in the church in order to come into our town, past our shops, pubs, cinema, banks, restaurants, homes and offices, into the streets that we walked on and talked in, past the premises where we did our business, right by the places we met our friends. For the duration of the afternoon the town became, as it were, a church. Here was a God who was intimately interested in all that went on in my life, a God who was reaching out in friendship to come to the places I knew and loved, a God meeting people I cared about and cherished and meeting many more besides, a God who was walking with us.

The second striking memory that I have is of when the canopy approached the gathered assembly in Market Street and on the church steps. The people knelt down, as if they instinctively knew that the Son of God was approaching and they perceived their own unworthiness as he came by. As a child I felt the hair stand on the back of my neck, because something so sacred that it was beyond words was happening before my eyes – Jesus Christ was passing by and I was there. There were shades of the account in the scriptures of the blind man in Jericho (Lk 18:35-43) and what the presence of the Lord could do to transform lives. Or again, we became the assembled crowd on the first Palm Sunday who welcomed Jesus into Jerusalem (Jn 12:12-19). Here Jerusalem was located at the end of Market Street and we acclaimed the arrival of the Lord.

Earthing the Eucharist

KEN NEWELL

I FELT CHURNED up inside with anger and despair when I got the news. On Wednesday afternoon, 5 February 1992, two UFF gunmen walked into Sean Graham's Bookmakers on Belfast's Ormeau Road and shot dead five innocent Catholics, four men and a fifteen-year-old boy. My church was close by.

The next evening I visited the five families with some of our church leaders and prayed with them. We were welcomed with extraordinary warmth. As Sunday approached I found it difficult to concentrate on preparing the liturgy for the Lord's Supper. I kept asking myself, 'What is the link between the sacrament and the murders?' Slowly it dawned on me that the grace of the Eucharist sacrament lies in its being earthed in my locality just as the cross was sunk deep into the soil of Golgotha.

As the congregation was gathering on Sunday morning, I placed 150 photocopied sheets with the addresses of the bereaved families on the Communion table, between the chalice and the bread. On leaving church, each person was given a sheet and urged to visit the families.

I witnessed remarkable scenes: Presbyterians and Catholics embracing each other in homes darkened by grief but lit up with love. Those images convinced me that the Eucharist is organically inseparable from reconciliation.

The eucharistic project undertaken in Geneva by the Reformer John Calvin (1541–64) was shaped by his conviction that the Lord's Supper should be 'set before the church at least once a week'. As we encounter Christ, he writes, 'our souls are fed by his flesh and blood. He pours his life into us, as if it penetrated into the marrow of our bones.'

Exposing worshippers to such a Niagara of grace raises hope that our churches might become centres of reconciliation. In the last decade,

≈

remarkable steps in that direction have been taken. But another reality screams back at us.

Two thirds of young people aged between sixteen and twenty-five have never had a meaningful conversation with someone from the other community in Northern Ireland. Only 10 per cent of Protestant ministers and Catholic priests have attempted to build bridges towards each other. Spiritual estrangement still scars Northern Ireland.

Peace-building initiatives have been sustained by a few courageous individuals, while noble ecclesiastical declarations have evaporated into the ether of moral evasion. Churches backed away from becoming a reconciling influence during the Troubles and now display minimal interest in post-violence reconstruction. If Christ *pours his life into us,* why doesn't it show up locally?

In what ways, then, does our risen Lord impact us at Communion?

He makes our lifestyles more inclusive
On every page of the Gospels, Jesus models for us the choice to become inclusive. In a society fractured by cultural, political, religious and ethnic animosities, he welcomes into his friendship a motley crew of followers and moulds them into one family. They reverence God as Father and embrace each other as brothers and sisters (Mk 3:31-35). If we shrink our circle of relationships to people like ourselves, grace will attempt to prise it open.

He fosters within us a vocation to peacemaking
In every child birthed by the Spirit of God, the Father nurtures a passion for peacemaking. The first lessons Jesus gave his followers in kingdom living spelt out this new self-understanding: 'Happy are those who work for peace; God will call them his children!' (Mt 5:9; 21-24). Reconciliation soars like Everest as a discipleship priority in his teaching, and ranges from the kitchen to the cosmos.

He releases into us a breathtaking vision
The vision that motivated Jesus (Mt 8:5-13; Lk 13:28-29) is not deeply rooted in Northern Irish Christians. Yet it is immense, both in the confidence with which Jesus espoused it and also the tenacity with which he took it into the darkness of Calvary:

Many outsiders will soon be coming from all directions – streaming in from the east and west, pouring in from the north and south, sitting down at God's kingdom banquet alongside Abraham, Isaac, and Jacob!

When we take into ourselves the Body of Christ, his Messianic dream is also gifted and planted within us. We are captured by his vision and set ourselves to challenge the barriers around us, as Paul reminds us: 'Christ brought us together through his death on the Cross. He got us to embrace each other and that was the end of the hostility' (Eph 2:14-18).

Earthing the Eucharist, therefore, in the soil of divided communities allows the new realities of unifying grace to blossom. The Sean Graham murders clarified this for me, just as the death of Jesus did for the early Church.

From Segregation to Community in Christ

GESA ELSBETH THIESSEN

ON A visit to the Baroque section in the National Gallery of Ireland, one will come across a painting that might be easily passed by but which, in fact, presents in one striking image a summary of Counter-Reformation theology. The Baroque not only constitutes one of the culturally richest epochs in history, but during this time art emerged as an instrument of ecclesiastical propaganda.

The Veneration of the Eucharist or *The Triumph of the Eucharist* was painted by Jacob Jordaens (1593–1678) circa 1630. Among Antwerp's most famous sons, Jordaens and Rubens epitomise the Baroque in their sumptuous rendering of Christian, mythological and other themes.

Jordaens, a Catholic who became a Calvinist, continued to work on Catholic commissions. This large image concerns 'the true Eucharist'. The viewer's gaze is immediately directed to the woman, symbolising the Church, on the lion, a symbol of power, who carries the sacred host in the monstrance. She is surrounded by the Church's founders, Saints Peter and Paul, the four Latin doctors (Augustine, Jerome, Gregory, Ambrose), and Saints Catherine of Siena, Rosalia [?] and Sebastian. Underneath her/the Church, much smaller, sits the Christ Child. He holds the flaming heart and cross, triumphing over death, symbolised by the skull. Perhaps the most striking and, for us today, offensive aspect of this work is the fact that Jesus is placed *beneath* and not above the Church and that he is physically smaller than it. Further, the Church is symbolised by a woman – bride of Christ – something that today strikes one as sad irony, given the fact that through the centuries women have endured oppression in all mainline Churches. Another interesting facet is the expression on the lion's face – not triumphant but sad.

The Veneration of the Eucharist (early 1630s) by Jacob Jordaens. Oil on canvas, 283.6 x 233.9cm. © National Gallery of Ireland

Put simply, what centrally matters in this work is the power of the Church, not the power of the love of Christ – even though its power seems ultimately tinged with sadness.

One wonders, does Jordaens' depiction of the lion convey his own and his fellow Christians' sadness at the unintentional schism that the Reformation and its aftermath had brought about?

From our perspective today, after a century of ecumenism, this image is a reminder of how the universal Church of Christ has changed – indeed, has changed profoundly for the better. It is safe to say that in the twenty-first century we will not find any Church that would dream of commissioning an artist to depict the veneration of the Eucharist in this manner.

The Eucharist communicates the love of Christ to his Church and reconciles us with Christ and one another. It is the sacrament which is celebrated by most Christians as an essential element of their lived faith, an act of memorial of the Last Supper and Christ's life, death and resurrection. Holy Communion means sharing, community, *koinonia* – in which, we believe, Christ becomes truly present to us. Like baptism, this sacrament not only embraces the founders and doctors of the Church, the martyrs and saints, but, instituted by Christ, it has been given to *all* God's people through history.

We are only too aware that the people of God – the Church – is not a perfect society. Indeed, through the ages the Church has been prone to the starkest sins, to unspeakable failure, to schism, hate and sectarian segregation – all in the name of Christ and Church institutions.

But, at times, the people of God have also been heroic, i.e. truly Christian – heroic to the point of laying down one's life for one's friends, as Jesus commanded his disciples. Such heroism has rarely been manifested in the Churches' structures, but in the women and men who have led exemplary lives of faith, people whom we admire for having lived what they preached; Christians who have not been afraid of risk nor to speak out for a faith that does justice, a faith that dares to be counter-cultural and subversive to those who arrange themselves unquestioningly with unjust utilitarian economies and societies, where personal gain and success rank more highly than solidarity, civility and respect for the other. People like Dietrich Bonhoeffer and Oscar Romero, Hildegard of Bingen and Edith Stein, outspoken theologians, mission workers who spent their lives bringing the love of Christ to people wherever they went, Christians who work with and for the poor and marginalised; all those have shown through their commitment, thought and action, how community in Christ is authentically lived and realised.

In an age in which the churches in Europe attract low attendance, it seems to me that an authentic faith that is not afraid to admit its own doubts and failures and takes risks is something which may still attract even those who have become disengaged from the Church, especially young people. Their future is also the future of the Church, i.e. life in community with Christ and one another, where all share in worship and sacrament, word and deed, faith, hope and love.

A Community of Communities
Together for Europe

BRENDAN LEAHY

T HOUGH THERE may be different eucharistic theologies, Christians of different Churches and ecclesial communities on the island of Ireland find much that can unite them. One example is an event that occurred on 12 May 2007. The eyes of the world looked towards Belfast during the first days of that month. Following decades of sectarian hatred and suspicion between opposing sides, so often labelled 'Catholics' and 'Protestants', a power-sharing government comprising politicians from both sides was coming to life on 8 May, almost 'miraculously'. Celebrations all round. A few days later, however, Belfast was also the location for another new beginning. On 12 May, over one hundred representatives from eighteen Christian movements and seven different Churches met together for the first time ever in Northern Ireland as part of the Together for Europe project – a network of communities and movements that want to contribute to giving a soul to Europe.

The participants at the event, linking up with a major European-wide initiative, came from such new movements and communities as Corrymeela, Cornerstone, L'Arche, Cursillo, Focolare, Koinonia, Charis and Restoration Ministry, all of which have come to life or found a home in Ireland in recent years. They spent a remarkable day together in the Church of the Resurrection, Elmwood Avenue, Belfast, speaking 'a new language', as one veteran of inter-Church relations, Dr John Morrow, put it. Not only did they link up via satellite with the central events taking place in Stuttgart but they also got the opportunity to worship together and get to know each other's movement, each a window onto the Gospel and a gift for the healing of wounds in the surrounding society. Young people from

Youth Initiatives and Youth with a Mission provided an upbeat injection of enthusiasm into the day.

Particularly moving was the L'Arche contribution, as the co-ordinator Maria Garvey, together with Jillian and other companions, opened up their window onto the Gospel: 'God made all things good. There is no such thing as disabilities. We have all been created in the image of God. Jillian is a gift, no one is a mistake.'

The words of the founder of Focolare, Chiara Lubich, relayed from Stuttgart, also resonated as she invited participants to recognise the face of Jesus forsaken, who cries out 'why?' in every division, darkness and trial. Yes, as someone commented afterwards in agreement, it's a time for 're-abandoning ourselves to the Father' like Jesus on the cross, 'and going outside ourselves to love'.

How? In each present moment and each person we meet, building up a culture of the resurrection, a culture of communion and fellowship. The Rev. Ruth Patterson indicated ways of doing so. Particularly inspiring was her invitation not to forget all who had worked so diligently over many years to bring about peace and to make sure we expressed our gratitude.

Joyce Williams from the Corrymeela community – which since its foundation in 1965 by Dr Ray Davey has been a beacon of reconciliation in Northern Ireland and beyond – witnessed to her community's multi-layered, honest and inspiring commitment to reconciliation that involves constantly renewed 'inner-' and 'inter-' community relations.

Isabel Hunter from Cornerstone shared the story of how this peace-line community came to life. From Focolare, Kevin McKeague, principal of St James Primary School, Newtownabbey, and David McConkey, principal of Whitehouse Primary School, shared their experience of fraternity in building bridges between two schools linked to a further seven schools in Europe.

This meeting was the beginning of what has grown to become a network of points of interaction. Not that everything ran perfectly that day! But there was something about the atmosphere. It was as if the Lord himself enveloped everyone in freedom, joy and peace. As one person commented, it was as if we were taken into an ocean wave, turned upside down and then found ourselves now on the same shore ready to be together living words of a common message.

And the project has gone ahead. Members of these communities have come together to get to know each other better. Young people from the communities have also met up. There's a growing appreciation for this emerging 'community of communities', as the late David Stevens called it.

Treasures Old and New Within One Cover

RICHARD CLARKE

WITHIN THE span of my own time within the ordained ministry, I think I would point to the introduction of a new Book of Common Prayer for the Church of Ireland in 2004 as a moment of immense significance within the overall theme of 'The Eucharist: Communion with Christ and with one another'.

The 2004 Book of Common Prayer broke new ground in a number of ways. Now, included within the covers of a single book, are not only liturgies in modern idiom and language, but also services in the traditional language of the original Anglican Book of Common Prayer. Each mode of worship is given precisely the same place, dignity and significance in the life of the Church of Ireland. This was an adventurous new departure for a number of reasons, in that it certainly appears to have prevented an institutionalised polarisation between traditionalist and contemporary ways of worship.

In parallel with the Latin Missal in the Roman Catholic Church, there was, to all intents and purposes, a single liturgy throughout world Anglicanism until the 1960s. The Old Prayer Book (as it is now known) dated back to 1662 but it was, in effect, the Book of Common Prayer devised by the Anglican Reformers of the sixteenth century, Archbishop Thomas Cranmer in particular. There were, it is true, local translations of the Old Prayer Book, including an Irish version, and a few minor modificatons to suit local contexts (for example, prayers for the legislature in the Republic of Ireland, in the case of the Church of Ireland), but the original Book of Common Prayer in English was recognised as the universal liturgy and a common thread within Anglicanism.

When the movement to modernise liturgy and provide worship in more vernacular languages gathered pace throughout western Christendom, Anglicanism lost this bond of unity, and it would not be going too far to suggest that this had a fragmenting effect on any specific Anglican 'identity'. Within easy reach of these shores, the English, Scottish and Welsh provinces of the Anglican Communion all produced their own modernised liturgies, as of course did the Church of Ireland itself. One now had to follow the script far more closely when attending worship in other countries. Even within Ireland, the production of new liturgies was a lengthy process (with experimentation of variable success) before a particular modern liturgy became settled, ending a rather uneasy period for the Church of Ireland during which there was a tendency for parishes to divide into those which used only the old services and those which were prepared to experiment with the modern services.

But there has been ecumenical advantage also. Not only was the language of the 'new services' more accessible, but the structures were based very closely on the earliest Christian liturgies known to scholars. In the case of the Eucharist, the similarities between the eucharistic liturgies of different Christian traditions (including the Roman Catholic tradition) became glaringly obvious, as all the western traditions were returning to the same sources. There is no doubt that this has had a remarkable ecumenical impact. Visitors to churches of another tradition – whether it be one of the reformed traditions or the Roman Catholic tradition – will often emerge from worship noting how extraordinarily alike the worship has been to that of their own tradition. Subliminally at least, this creates a new understanding of how much the traditions have in common, not least in the way we offer worship to God.

The placing of the old and the new within the covers of a single book has, it is hoped, created other encouragements for good. One of the glories of the Old Prayer Book was that, within its language, it created real *spiritual space* where one might encounter the transcendence and beauty of God. This was not simply because the language is now archaic but rather because it was written at a highpoint for the English language, a period – within a few years, we should recall, of the production of the King James Bible or the plays of Shakespeare – when imagery, poetry, rhythm and metaphor might be appreciated, not as high-flown affectation

255

but as a natural encouragement to deep thought and spiritual reflection for anyone and everyone, regardless of background or education. And so, many Church of Ireland people, certainly until this generation, would have known the prayers of the Old Prayer Book by heart (and they can be memorised without difficulty), able to recall them instantly at times of joy or sorrow in their own lives. One of the hopes of those responsible for the compilation of the 2004 Book of Common Prayer is that people will again make the prayers of public worship their own, within their own private devotions, and that 'common prayer' may therefore be – in part at least –spirituality that we hold in common, and not simply in church on Sundays. Our communion with Christ and with one another must surely take us outside the walls of the church building.

Treasure from the Bog:
The Faddan More Psalter

JOHN GILLIS

O N 20 July 2006, a medieval manuscript was unearthed during the working of a peat bog in the townland of Faddan More, North County Tipperary. The very next morning, staff from the National Museum of Ireland were on site and it was quickly identified as a psalter from a fragment of one folio peaking out of the wet bog material, which had been wisely placed on top of the book by the Leonard brothers (owners of the bog) in order to maintain moisture and prevent the drying out of the delicate vellum. The very poor state of preservation and the unique nature of the find would set a challenge for the next four years, which would include the trial and development of a system to de-water the saturated folios. Other aspects of the project involved the difficult and complicated removal of clumps of vellum fragments before separating out and cleaning, accompanied by painstaking and detailed recording in order to establish the foliation and allow collation analysis to take place. Much of the methodology was developed as work progressed, due to the unique nature of the project in conservation terms. The tanned leather cover, which in itself is of significant importance in relation to early medieval binding structures, was also de-watered and fully recorded. This in turn led to some exciting additional discoveries.

Boglands, of which there is a high percentage in Ireland, are often rich in archaeological finds as organic material typically survives better here than in soil. Research suggests that sphagnum moss, a component part of a peat bog, plays a major role in this process; it has the ability to immobilise micro-organisms by producing an antibiotic substance called sphagnan, which bind with proteins on the surface and at the same time have a kind

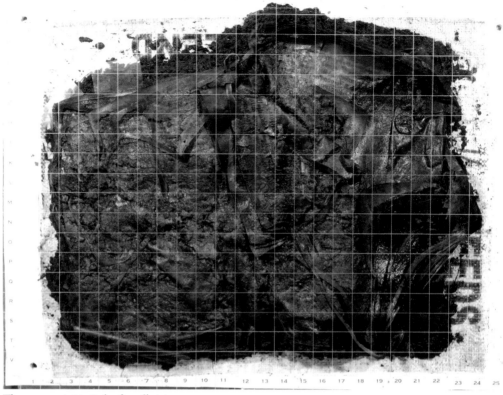

The manuscript in its 'as-found' state

Some folios of the manuscript after restoration

s leather cover showing flap and buttons. Photographs provided by John Gillis

of tanning effect on the organic material, thus helping it to survive for long periods buried below ground.

After three years of intense work at the Conservation Department of the National Museum, there was success in drying all the major fragments of the vellum text block and indeed all the minor ones. The tanned leather cover is also now dry and stable.

The text of the Faddan More Psalter is laid out in single column and may well have been the labour of more than one scribe, although with so little surviving it is difficult to be certain.[1] It is a reasonably competent and confident hand but sometimes erratic in quality, with plenty of scribal errors and typical variants to the psalms; interestingly it displays no marginalia or glosses. The hand is best described as a form of insular or Irish majuscule. There is little in the way of decoration or illumination when one compares this manuscript to other insular manuscripts of the period, such as Kells or Durrow. But during the four-year conservation process, modest, well-executed display lettering and the remains of what was once a fully illuminated folio at the beginning of the manuscript, completed to a high standard, was discovered.

The version of the psalms in Faddan More is the Gallican, based on Jerome's revision from the Old Latin, the same version found in Ireland's oldest psalter, the *Cathach*. However, Faddan More is divided into the 'three 50s' – a tradition found in many insular psalters but not the Cathach.

The Faddan More Psalter is, in many ways, a unique find and has excited experts from a number of disciplines, including art historians, palaeographers, historians and of course conservators. This is no surprise, as it is the first Irish or insular manuscript to be discovered in over two hundred years. In addition, it has spent over a millennium buried deep in a bog and thus contains many original features usually lost to manuscripts above ground as a result of direct intervention, such as re-binding and other changes made to the structure due to repair or changing fashion. One of these features is its binding or, to be more accurate, its cover. It is a single piece of skin, creased at appropriate points to form a wallet-

---

1. It is estimated that approximately 15 per cent of the text of the psalter has survived, the majority of the vellum substrate having gelatinised in the fluid conditions of the bog and dissolved away.

type structure.[2] Although we were aware of this kind of simple binding, all examples from the early period of book production come from areas such as Egypt and the eastern Mediterranean.[3] To our knowledge then, the Faddan More is the only extant example in Western Europe. When we add to this the discovery of papyrus fragments adhered to the inside, the story becomes even more intriguing.

During the early medieval period, the Church in Ireland was monastic. When we look at the archaeology of the area around the find spot, we can identify a number of monasteries, the most prominent and closest being at Birr in neighbouring County Offaly. Its founder was St Brendan (d. 573), and although no physical evidence of this monastery remains and its exact location is unclear, we do have an extant manuscript from here, namely the Mac Regol Gospels (named after its scribe who was abbot of the monastery for a period), dating from sometime before 822 – positive proof of a scriptorium in existence at that location.[4] There were other prominent monasteries associated with early medieval manuscript production within a fifteen-kilometre radius of the find spot – at locations in Lorrha, Terryglass, Roscrea and Kinnity – and any of these may have also been responsible for the production of the Faddan More Psalter.

The Faddan More Psalter is now on permanent display in the National Museum, where everyone can experience this unique discovery. There is much for us to learn from this rare treasure and, given the time and resources, we can unlock a little more history from Ireland's Golden Age.

---

2. Roy Thomson identified the species as young cattle stock based on common historical animal husbandry practice, and that the animal had been born in the spring and slaughtered in the autumn of the same year. He also concluded, on examination, that the leather had been tanned with a vegetable tanning material and had been properly prepared by experienced craftsmen.
3. This relates primarily to the Nag Hammadi Gospels, a fourth-century collection of manuscripts discovered north of Cairo in the late 1940s.
4. Bodleian MS D.2.19.

In Communion with the Irish Saints

PATRICK JONES

THE NEW edition of the Roman Missal (2011) includes a very full National Calendar and Proper, that is, the prayer texts and, in some cases, the readings that are used at Mass on the saints' days. Though the Calendar has been included in the annual Liturgical Calendar since 1999, following approval in October 1998, and the Proper was published in booklet form in 2009, their publication within the new edition of the Missal makes them completely available to all congregations in Ireland.

Revisions of National Calendars following the Universal Norms on the Liturgical Year and the Calendar (1969) tended to reduce the number of observances, leaving most to diocesan or local celebration. The National Calendar, as revised in 1972, had only five observances: the solemnity of St Patrick and the feasts of St Brigid, St Columba (Colm Cille), All the Saints of Ireland and St Columban, with a sixth, St Oliver Plunkett, added in 1976. Previously, diocesan patrons had been included. However, the further revision approved in 1998 offers a very full Calendar, with its one solemnity (St Patrick), three feasts (St Brigid, St Columba, All the Saints of Ireland) and fifty-eight memorials. In April 2011, three additional memorials were included: Our Lady of Knock, Blessed Columba Marmion and Blessed John Henry Newman. Eight of the memorials are classed as obligatory: St Ita, St Kevin, the Blessed Irish Martyrs, St Oliver Plunkett, Our Lady of Knock, St Ciaran, St Malachy and St Columban. Diocesan patrons are again included, though mostly as optional memorials. The revision, however, allows for a greater Irish identity in the Calendar.

A few examples of the prayer texts composed for the Irish saints conveys the richness of our spiritual tradition:

Lord God, it was through the power of your Spirit,
that Saint Ita was tireless in caring for the afflicted
and in guiding the young towards holiness,
and so we pray:
prepare in our hearts, as you prepared in hers,
a home where you will dwell.

This collect for St Ita, the first obligatory memorial that we celebrate in the year, on 15 January, recalls the saint's nurturing of the young and her great success in leading many to holiness as well as her kindness to those in need. The second part of the prayer echoes a ninth-century poem, reflecting St Ita's deep prayer life.

The collect for Our Lady of Knock (17 August) is the newest composition:

O God, who give hope to your people in a time of distress,
grant that we who keep the memorial
of the Blessed Virgin, Our Lady of Knock
may, through her intercession,
be steadfast in the faith during our earthly pilgrimage to heaven,
and so come to eternal glory with all the Angels and the Saints.

The first line, adapted from the Knock novena prayer, notes the sign of hope that the apparition was to the Irish people in a time of distress, but also applies this to our own times. Pilgrims go to Knock, imploring the intercession of Our Lady, praying that we may be steadfast in the faith. 'With all the Angels and Saints' reminds us of their presence at the apparition.

The National Proper gives us four additional prefaces for St Patrick, St Brigid, St Columba and All the Saints of Ireland. The preface highlights the element of thanksgiving to God in the Eucharistic Prayer. On the feast of St Brigid (1 February) it is specified in the following words:

For your wonderful love is seen in Saint Brigid:
you taught her to open her heart and hands to the poor
and to seek the image of your Son in every welcomed guest.

Through her you showed a people
the way of Mary, the Mother of your Son,
in dedicated service and holiness of life.

On this feast you fill our hearts with joy
for you continue to bless the Church
you planted by her labours.

The reference to Mary is included in the Solemn Blessing with St Brigid called Mary of the Gael. The final lines of that blessing are taken from her *Vita* in the Book of Lismore:

May God fill you with his love,
as you honour Saint Brigid,
whose heart and mind became
a throne of rest for the Holy Spirit.

On the memorial of St Kevin (3 June) we ask that our lives, like the life of the saint, may be inspired by the desire for God, since our hearts can only find true rest in God:

In the solitude of Glendalough, O Lord,
you spoke to the heart of Saint Kevin
and taught him to find through prayer
the life that he desired;
by his intercession,
turn our hearts from all that would betray us,
for you alone are our goal and our reward.

St Laurence O'Toole was abbot of Glendalough when, in 1162, he was chosen as the first native archbishop of Dublin. The collect (14 November) reflects the contrast in his life between the retreat of Glendalough and the tensions of the city of Dublin but it also highlights him as a shepherd of the people, a teacher of the clergy and a friend of the poor. He died on a peace mission at Eu in Normandy in 1180. All of this is reflected in the Collect as we pray to follow his example of perseverance and, through his intercession, arrive at the peace of God's kingdom:

God of all holiness, who called Saint Laurence O'Toole from a life of quiet and solitude to be a shepherd of your people, a teacher of the clergy and friend of the poor; grant, we pray, that we may follow his example of perseverance and through his intercession arrive at the peace of your kingdom.

Indeed, it is a Great Sacrament …

TOMÁS O'SULLIVAN

ONE OF the new translations of our Eucharistic Prayers contains the following moving plea to God our Father:

Look kindly, most compassionate Father, on those you unite to yourself by the Sacrifice of your Son, and grant that, by the power of the Holy Spirit, as they partake of this one Bread and one Chalice, they may be gathered into one Body in Christ, who heals every division. (Eucharistic Prayer for Reconciliation I)

In this short prayer, we entreat and praise the Trinity for drawing us, as a united community, into an ever-more intimate union with God, redeemed and re-united with our Creator through 'a new bond of love so tight that it can never be undone' (to quote words found earlier in that same Eucharistic Prayer).

This vision of the Eucharist – as a Trinitarian sacrament in which God himself reaches out to us and embraces us tightly in communion – has ancient roots, and two ninth-century manuscripts, now housed in the Vatican Library, preserve a short but powerful eucharistic reflection which reveals a similar understanding of the sacrament from the early Middle Ages.[1] Although these manuscripts were written on the Continent (probably in France and Germany), this eucharistic meditation is closely associated with Irish or Irish-influenced material in both, suggesting that this piece may well have circulated in early Christian Ireland and may even have originated amongst the Irish. This reflection reads as follows:

---

1. The two Vatican manuscripts which contain this piece are Reg. lat. 1050 and Pal. lat. 556. My translation is based upon the Latin edition from the latter manuscript by Graziano di S. Teresa, 'Il florilegio pseudagostiniano palatino', *Ephemerides carmeliticae* 14 (1963), pp. 195–241, p. 220 (no. 5).

266

Indeed, it is a great sacrament, which has been granted to us by God through Christ, who not only came down from heaven, sent by the Father, he redeemed us through his holy blood; and, furthermore, we are daily renewed to a better state through the water of rebirth, and – what is better and more sublime than all of these – in the holy mystery of this table we prepare for the kingdom of heaven, that is, in taking up the body and blood of our Lord Jesus Christ, coming from heaven through the Holy Spirit (who is the pledge of our inheritance); until we may come to that inheritance and will be like him.

The language of this reflection echoes the scriptures, evoking Christ as the living bread which 'came down from heaven' (Jn 6:33; compare Jn 6:38 and 3:13), the Holy Spirit as 'the pledge of our inheritance' (Eph 1:14), and the sacrament of baptism as 'the water of rebirth' (Ti 3:5); it also reiterates the Johannine conviction that, when the world is made new, we will be like Christ for we shall see him as he is (1 Jn 3:2).

While it presents the Eucharist as the best and most sublime of sacraments, this medieval meditation also understands its graces as intimately related to the entire mystery of our salvation. Thus, it aligns the Eucharist with both Christ's incarnation (his descent from heaven) and our redemption 'through his holy blood', and stresses the baptismal foundations of our communion. Significantly, this washing in 'the water of rebirth' is not conceived of as a one-off event in the distant past, but rather as a daily renewal through which we progress and improve on our on-going journey with Christ.

The presentation of the Eucharist as a gift of the entire Trinity (also seen above in our contemporary Eucharistic Prayer) is another noteworthy element. Although the Body and Blood of the Incarnate Son is, rightly, placed front and centre, this reflection reminds us that Christ's coming down from heaven – both in his birth from the Virgin Mary and his entry into our own lives 'in the holy mystery of this table' – was ordained by the Father and enabled by the Holy Spirit. Therefore, our communion is not – indeed, it could not – simply be with Christ alone; rather, Father, Son, and Spirit reach out to draw us into the perfect union of the Triune God.

This leads us to the final insight offered by this medieval reflection on the Eucharist: communion in Christ's Body and Blood is an encounter in which we ourselves are transformed. Christ descends from heaven to our table and to our hearts, so that we might return to heaven with and through him. In the Eucharist, we are reminded, 'we prepare for the kingdom of heaven': Christ descends, 'coming from heaven through the Holy Spirit', so that we may ascend and come to our heavenly inheritance, transformed and renewed, daily becoming more and more 'like him' in communion with Christ and with one another.

Long Night's Journey into Eternal Day

BRENDAN PURCELL

Speaking to Australian aborigines in Alice Springs in 1986, Pope John Paul II said:

> Your culture, which shows the lasting genius and dignity of your race, must not be allowed to disappear … You lived your lives in spiritual closeness to the land, with its animals, birds, fishes, waterholes, rivers, hills and mountains. Through your closeness to the land you touched the sacredness of man's relationship with God, for the land was the proof of a power in life greater than yourselves.

Maybe we can learn something from those who built the mound at Newgrange over 5,000 years ago, where their symbols are a kind of preparation for the Gospel and the Eucharist in terms of how it lifts place, time and the passage from death to life into the profoundly sacred.

Sacred space

The great stone circle, once made up of thirty-five but now reduced to twelve massive standing stones, impressively marked the boundary between the sacred and the profane. Not only did the circle signify a divine presence within the sacred place, it also protected people from the danger they would incur by entering that place unsanctified, without having performed the right gestures of approach. The same ritual separation of sacred from profane was repeated even more emphatically by the huge kerbstones guarding the entrance to the passage.

Then the upward slope of the twenty-four-metre-long passage expressed a gradual initiation, undergone to approach the centre more worthily. The passage opens out to become a cross-shaped chamber.

Neolithic peoples represented the earth in terms of the four directions, with the point of intersection indicating its centre, located at the 'fifth' point at the intersection, which in archaic societies often indicated kingship. The corbelled roof above that point indicates that this is where the heavens intersect with the earth: this is the axis of the world, where passage between this world, the underworld and the heavens can occur.

Sacred time

The most striking enaction at that centre of the world occurs on that most important Sun-day, which is the first day of the solar new year. In this place, at the centre of the world, where heaven, earth and underworld intersect, the Boyne people expressed their experience of the mysterious answer to their search for participation in everlasting order. Here they deployed all their artistic, technological, astronomic and measuring skills to elevate mid-winter sunrise into a cosmic 'yes' between sun and earth at the zero point of their mutual forsakenness.

After the longest night of the year, at sunrise on the shortest day, the direct rays of the sun burst through the arrow roof box over the entrance, up the slightly winding passage, to the inner chamber, which explodes into light for nearly twenty minutes. Cutting through the heart of all reality, when darkness seems to have finally enveloped the world, light shines. At the time when sun and earth seem closest to the condition of death, the promise of a new year of life dawns. If death had overtaken the people's king, then, in this place at this time, a renewal of kingship is promised through attunement to the silent rebirth of the whole cosmos.

The passage from death to life

The fire dance at the centre of the world, at the dawn of each new year, culminates in the embrace of heaven and earth at the triple spiral, symbolically unique in human history – dualities (life/death, darkness/light, male/female) are common, but the triple could indicate a divine oneness underlying the duality. The five bands of the triple spiral may have indicated the golden thread of their representative kingship, penetrated by the divine-cosmic ground of being.

In and through their loving-suffering agony of attunement to the central place of the cosmos, at its own anxiously awaited time of rebirth, the Boyne people touched ecstatically for a few boundless, timeless moments the everlasting cosmic oneness at the heart of being. Radiating outwards from that oneness – renewing their kingship, sanctifying every corner of the earth's four quarters, eternalising every moment of cosmic time, bestowing hope and dignity to the people's otherwise mere mortality – was the happiness of belonging to the ultimately kind cosmic ground, the source of peace beyond the struggle between life and death.

Eucharistic significance

If we're humble enough to bend down and ascend Newgrange's ritual passageway, maybe the Boyne people can help us appreciate more deeply the divine presence of the incarnate Word present in the sanctuary of every tabernacle in our land. Each eucharistic Sacrifice is a re-enactment of the utter zero-moment of Jesus in his forsakenness on the cross, followed by his resurrection and ascension into heaven. And that paschal mystery is meant to be relived by his followers and brought to the four corners of Ireland and the world.

The 50th International Eucharistic Congress Dublin 2012: Communion with Christ and with One Another

LOUISE FULLER

THIS SHORT article offers some reflections on the Irish Church as the 50th International Eucharistic Congress, taking place in Dublin in June 2012, gets underway. The 1932 Eucharistic Congress was very much a spectacle and a triumphalistic celebration, perhaps understandably so, taking place ten years after the foundation of the Irish State – a time when consolidation rather than renewal typified the Irish Church. With this on his mind perhaps, Diarmuid Martin, Archbishop of Dublin, the host diocese of the 2012 Congress, has pointed out that if Christians work together, the Congress 'will not be simply an outward week-long spectacle or the triumphalistic celebration of an inward-looking Church.'[1] Instead, he points out, 'it can become a moment of real renewal in the life of the Church … and a true celebration of what the Church authentically is and should be.'[2]

When the Vatican Council took place from 1962–65, its vision was to renew the Church to make it more relevant in the changing times. Yet at that time the Irish Church authorities saw little need for renewal; it appeared to be in a very healthy condition and a certain complacency typified the mood.[3] Much has changed in the intervening fifty years. Archbishop Martin is now in no doubt that renewal is necessary and that it 'must spring from a new evangelisation, a vibrant re-presentation of the essentials of

---

1. Archbishop Diarmuid Martin's Chrism Mass Homily, Holy Thursday, Pro-Cathedral (21 April 2011), http://www.dublindiocese.ie.
2. Ibid.
3. Louise Fuller, *Irish Catholicism Since 1950: The Undoing of a Culture* (Dublin: Gill and Macmillan, 2002).

the Christian message to men and women who, though baptised and who were perhaps at one time active participants in the life of the Church, have in various ways drifted away from full sharing in that life'.[4]

In Ireland, weekly Mass attendance has fallen to somewhere in the 40 per cent range – still high by western European standards, but a very big drop from the heights of less than forty years ago.[5] The Archbishop's words provide clues as to why this has happened and the enormous challenge facing the Irish Church at this time. It is important to recall that while the Mass was always central in the Irish tradition, in the 1970s the idea of the reception of Eucharist as an integral part of the Mass was not fully appreciated by many of the congregation. As recently as the mid-1970s, a survey revealed that while 91 per cent of Catholics attended Mass weekly, only 28 per cent received Holy Communion.[6]

Before the reforms of Vatican II, because the Mass was in Latin, which most people did not understand, many said the Rosary or their own private prayers during Mass and the communal dimension of the Mass and Eucharist was often lost. Many liturgists were critical of the fact that people were 'passive' attenders at Mass. Expressions heard at the time told their own story: the priest 'read' Mass and the people 'heard' Mass.[7] The idea of Mass in the vernacular was that people would understand the celebration, thereby making it a more meaningful experience for them. Yet many felt that post-Vatican II, while changes designed to improve people's participation were implemented, they were not accompanied by a renewal of spirit, and an opportunity was lost.[8]

So the Eucharistic Congress will be seen as a welcome opportunity for spiritual renewal at a time when the Irish Catholic Church is experiencing a tremendous loss of morale, a consequence of the many scandals that

---

4. See notes from Archbishop Diarmuid Martin's speech at the press conference for the launch of the programme of the 50th International Eucharistic Congress, RDS, Ballsbridge (7 March 2011), http://www.dublindiocese.ie.

5. Recent polls have recorded weekly Mass attendance at somewhere between 45 per cent and 48 per cent, and in his recent book Fr Micheál Mac Gréil SJ has recorded a weekly Mass attendance figure of 42.8 per cent. See Micheál Mac Gréil, *Pluralism and Diversity in Ireland* (Dublin: Columba Press, 2011), p. 445.

6. See *A Survey of Religious Practice, Attitudes and Beliefs in the Republic of Ireland 1973–74*, report no. 1 (Research and Development Unit, Catholic Communications Institute of Ireland, 1975), p. 71.

7. Fuller, *Irish Catholicism Since 1950*, pp. 88–96.

8. Ibid., pp. 122–3.

have beset it since the early 1990s. The debate is ongoing as to the extent of secularisation in Ireland, but there is no doubting the extent to which the religious culture has changed and community is fractured. The theme of the Congress – 'The Eucharist: Communion with Christ and with one another' – reminds people that the Eucharist provides the spiritual sustenance which should overflow into people's daily lives in the family, the workplace and the political and economic arena.

While the Church might preach the importance of witness, solidarity and community, what the recent economic collapse and fall-out at different levels of Irish society has brought into sharp focus is that these very laudable aspirations are in short supply, and it is no exaggeration to say that a crisis of morale and of faith (in the broadest sense) and a sense of betrayal is palpable. Solidarity and community are not words which readily come to mind to describe the spirit of the times, and the fact that the institutional Church itself is seen to have fallen short has not inspired. Perhaps there never was a time when the Church in Ireland needed renewal so much, and the same goes for the Irish community at large.

In his address at the opening of the Second Vatican Council, Pope John XXIII stressed the importance of the Church engaging with the modern secular world – the challenge for the Council was the evangelisation of the culture of modernity. This challenge was only beginning in Ireland at that time; fifty years later it is well advanced. It remains to be seen whether the experience of the Eucharistic Congress can renew and re-energise the Irish Church at this difficult time in its history.

The Absent Presence[1]

DONAGH O'SHEA

T HE CROSS, called 'Absent Presence', that you see on the next page, stands in the meditation garden of Integritas, a centre for domestic spirituality in Ennisnag, Stoneyford, Co. Kilkenny, run by Patrick Treacy and his wife, Linda Rainsberry.[2]

In its simplicity, it makes clear the emphasis on ecumenism in this centre. In the Catholic tradition, the figure of Christ is shown on the cross but the Protestant tradition shows a plain cross. One says 'Christ has died'; the other says 'Christ is risen'. All Christians *say* both, of course, but it is difficult to *show* both together. In this cross the figure is cut out from its background and is then all the more visible; it is *present* by its *absence*.

The figure is quite stylised: a circle for the head, a crescent for the outstretched arms and a long rectangle to represent the body. When you look again you notice that it also represents the chalice and the host. This resolves with wonderful clarity a false contrast that people sometimes make between the Eucharist as shared meal and the Eucharist as sacrifice. Sacrifice may well *entail* suffering and death, as it did with Jesus, but the essence of Christ's sacrifice is not suffering and death but his total self-giving. If we come with a notion of sacrifice derived from animal sacrifice in pagan cults we will see blood as its essence, since the animal is not capable of offering itself in any conscious way. But Christ 'offered himself' consciously and completely. The expression 'body and blood' meant the entire self. This is what he offered at the Last Supper (and at every celebration of the Eucharist) and Calvary was the *measure* of how fully he

---

1. This piece and the accompanying image first appeared in *Spirituality* (November/ December 2011). We wish to express our gratitude to Rev. Tom Jordan OP, editor of *Spirituality*, for permission to reproduce it here. The photo of the cross is courtesy of Patrick Treacy SC, and we are likewise most grateful for the permission to use it.
2. www.integritas.ie.

Absent Presence. Integritas Centre for Domestic Spirituality, Ennisnag, Stoneyford, Co. Kilkenny. Photo by Patrick Treacy SC

meant it. This simple cross makes it clear that the self-giving of Jesus in the Eucharist *is the same* as his self-giving on Calvary: 'Christ Jesus ... emptied himself taking the form of a slave ... and became obedient to the point of death – even death on a cross' (Phil 2:7-8).

St Thomas Aquinas was once asked where he got his wisdom from. 'At the foot of the cross of Christ,' he replied. This simple cross expresses the wisdom of our ancient faith. 'Christ crucified,' St Paul wrote, 'is the power of God and the wisdom of God' (1 Cor 1:24).

List of Contributors

MOIRA BERGIN RSM has been a staff member of the National Centre for Liturgy since 1993, and is a member of the Advisory Committee on Church Music, Irish Episcopal Conference.

RACHEL BEWLEY-BATEMAN MA (Biblical Studies), is clerk of the Europe and Middle East section of the Friends World Committee for Consultation (Quakers) and secretary of the Dublin Council of Churches.

ELIZABETH BOYLE is a Leverhulme Early Career Fellow at the University of Cambridge, and a Research Fellow of St Edmund's College, Cambridge.

JOHN CAREY is a statutory lecturer in Early and Medieval Irish at University College Cork.

FINBARR G. CLANCY SJ is professor of Theology at the Milltown Institute of Theology and Philosophy, where he is also currently rector of the Ecclesiastical Faculty and acting president.

RICHARD CLARKE has been the Church of Ireland Bishop of Meath and Kildare for the past fifteen years, and is currently president of the Irish Council of Churches and co-chairman (with Cardinal Seán Brady) of the Irish Inter-Church Meeting.

HUGH CONNOLLY is a priest of the diocese of Dromore and is currently president of St Patrick's College, Maynooth.

EAMONN CONWAY is a priest of the archdiocese of Tuam and professor of theology at Mary Immaculate College, University of Limerick.

GEORGE CUNNINGHAM FSA is a former primary school principal with a lifelong interest in and commitment to Irish heritage.

THOMAS G. DALZELL SM is head of Theology at All Hallows College, Dublin.

ELIZABETH DAWSON is currently completing a doctoral thesis on Early Irish History in the School of History and Archives, University College Dublin.

MICHEÁL DE LIOSTÚN is a priest of the diocese of Limerick.

KEVIN DORAN is secretary general of the 50th International Eucharistic Congress and former parish priest of Glendalough.

MICHAEL DUNNE is head of the department of Philosophy at NUI Maynooth and dean of the Pontifical Faculty of Philosophy at St Patrick's College, Maynooth.

GEARÓID DULLEA is a priest of Cork and Ross diocese and is currently Executive Secretary of the Irish Episcopal Conference.

FRANK FAHEY is a priest of the archdiocese of Tuam and has served for many years as administrator of the historic Ballintubber Abbey, Co. Mayo.

GABRIEL FLYNN lectures in Theology at Mater Dei Institute of Education, where he is also currently Academic Leader for Research.

ALISON FORRESTAL is lecturer (above the bar) in Early Modern History at National University of Ireland, Galway, and a specialist in early modern Catholic and French History.

LOUISE FULLER is a historian working on the history of Modern Irish Catholicism. She is author of *Irish Catholicism Since 1950: The Undoing of a Culture*, which was published by Gill and Macmillan in 2002.

RAYMOND GILLESPIE teaches in the department of History, National University of Ireland, Maynooth.

≈

JOHN GILLIS is Senior Manuscript Conservator, Trinity College Dublin.

ANTHONY HARPUR has recently been awarded an MA from the University of Limerick for his dissertation 'Image, Symbol and Context: Reading the O'Dea Mitre and Crozier'.

MARTIN HENRY lectures in Systematic Theology at St Patrick's College, Maynooth.

HENRY A. JEFFERIES is head of History at Thornhill College, Derry.

PATRICK JONES is director of the National Centre for Liturgy.

EILEEN KANE is formerly senior lecturer in the History of Art in University College Dublin and continues to publish on the art of Avignon, Rome and Dublin.

DAVID KELLY OSA is visiting lecturer in Spirituality and Theology at Milltown Institute and at All Hallows College, Dublin.

FINOLA KENNEDY has been a lecturer at University College Dublin and at the Institute of Public Administration. She is the author of *Frank Duff: A Life Story*, published by Continuum International.

DÁIRE KEOGH lectures in History at St Patrick's College, Drumcondra (DCU). In March 2012 he was named as President-designate of St Patrick's College Drumcondra.

GILLIAN KINGSTON is lay leader of the Conference of the Methodist Church in Ireland and a part-time chaplain at University College Dublin.

BRENDAN LEAHY is professor of Systematic Theology at St Patrick's College, Maynooth.

FRANK LAWRENCE is a lecturer in Early Music History (medieval and renaissance) at the School of Music, University College Dublin.

COLM LENNON is a retired professor of History at the National University of Ireland, Maynooth.

BRÍD LISTON is an FCJ Sister from Banogue, Co. Limerick, and is currently director of Pastoral Theology at St Patrick's College, Maynooth.

MÍCHEÁL MACCRAITH is a Franciscan priest and recently retired professor of modern Irish at the National University of Ireland, Galway. He is currently guardian of Collegio S. Isidoro in Rome.

JOSEPH MCCARROLL, father and grandfather, is chairperson of the Pro-Life Campaign Ireland and a retired Educational Welfare Officer.

BRENDAN MCCONVERY CSSR is a native of Belfast and a member of the Redemptorist Congregation. He teaches scripture at St Patrick's College, Maynooth.

DOMINIC MCNAMARA is assistant to the president at St Patrick's College, Maynooth.

MARTIN MCNAMARA MSC is emeritus professor of Sacred scripture at the Milltown Institute of Theology.

EVIE MONAGHAN is an Irish Research Council for the Humanities and Social Sciences postgraduate scholar, currently undertaking a doctorate in eucharistic practice and belief in the Department of History, National University of Ireland, Maynooth.

MICHAEL MULLANEY is a priest of the archdiocese of Cashel and Emly, vice president and professor of Canon Law at St Patrick's College, Maynooth.

PATRICK MULLINS OCARM is professor in Systematic Theology at the Milltown Institute of Theology and Philosophy.

ROBYN NEVILLE is a PhD candidate researching Early Medieval Irish Christianity in the Graduate Division of Religion at Emory University and a visiting instructor in Historical Theology at Candler School of Theology, Atlanta, Georgia.

KEN NEWELL is an Irish Presbyterian minister who served as Moderator of the General Assembly of the Presbyterian Church in Ireland from 2004–05.

NÓIRÍN NÍ RIAIN is an internationally acclaimed spiritual singer. In 2003, she received a doctorate in Theology from Mary Immaculate College, Limerick, for which she coined the term 'theosony', meaning the 'sound of God'.

THOMAS NORRIS is a priest of the diocese of Ossory and was formerly professor of Systematic Theology at St Patrick's College, Maynooth. He is also a member of the International Theological Committee.

CIARÁN O'CARROLL is an ecclesiastical historian and is currently rector of the Irish College in Rome.

COLMÁN Ó CLABAIGH OSB is a monk of Glenstal Abbey, Co. Limerick, and a medieval historian.

CAITRÍONA Ó DOCHARTAIGH is lecturer in Early and Medieval Irish at University College Cork.

NEIL XAVIER O'DONOGHUE is originally from Ballincollig, Co. Cork, and is a priest of the Archdiocese of Newark, currently serving as Prefect of Studies at Redemptoris Mater Seminary in Kearny, New Jersey.

TADHG Ó DÚSHLÁINE. *Corcaíoch, file agus scoláire Gaeilge. Mórán foilsithe aige ar ghnéithe éagsúla de litríocht na Gaeilge. Ina léachtóir le Gaeilge i Má Nuad ó 1977 i leith.* Originally from Cork, Tadhg Ó Dúshláine is a poet and Irish scholar who has published much on various aspects of Irish literature. He has been lecturer in Irish at Maynooth since 1977.

RORY O'DWYER lectures in History at University College Cork.

FEARGHUS Ó FEARGHAIL lectures in scripture at the Mater Dei Institute of Education, Dublin.

KEVIN O'GORMAN lectures in Moral Theology at St Patrick's College, Maynooth.

JOHN O'KEEFFE is director of Sacred Music at St Patrick's College, Maynooth.

THOMAS O'LOUGHLIN is professor of Historical Theology at the University of Nottingham.

PÁDRAIG Ó MACHÁIN is a professor of the School of Celtic Studies, at the Dublin Institute for Advanced Studies.

PÁDRAIG Ó RIAIN is professor emeritus of Early and Medieval Irish at University College Cork.

DAGMAR Ó RIAIN-RAEDEL is a medieval historian specialising in the connections between Ireland and Europe during the Middle Ages.

JENNIFER O'REILLY is a member of the Royal Irish Academy and, until 2008, was a senior lecturer in Medieval History at University College Cork, where she continues to contribute to the teaching of Art History.

DONAGH O'SHEA OP is director of the Dominican Retreat Centre, Tallaght, and has lectured internationally on spirituality.

TOMÁS O'SULLIVAN, originally from Bantry, Co. Cork, is assistant professor of Early Medieval Christianity in the Department of Theological Studies, Saint Louis University.

BRENDAN PURCELL is a priest of the archdiocese of Dublin and former lecturer in Philosophy at University College Dublin. He is at present working at St Mary's Cathedral, Sydney, and teaching Philosophy at Notre Dame University, Australia.

JOSEPH QUINN was parish priest of Knock, rector of the shrine and episcopal vicar for Knock until his death on 1 December 2011.

ETHNA REGAN CHF is head of the School of Theology in Mater Dei Institute of Education.

KATJA RITARI is working as a postdoctoral researcher at the Department of World Cultures/Study of Religions, University of Helsinki.

SALVADOR RYAN is professor of Ecclesiastical History at St Patrick's College, Maynooth.

JANET E. RUTHERFORD is an Anglican theologian, living in the diocese of Meath, who works in the fields of liturgy and early Church history.

DIARMUID SCULLY lectures in Medieval History at University College Cork.

MICHAEL SHORTALL lectures in Moral Theology at St Patrick's College, Maynooth.

ISABELLE SMYTH, a Medical Missionary of Mary, has specialised in the field of communications.

GESA ELSBETH THIESSEN is originally from Germany. She lectures in Systematic Theology at Milltown Institute, Mater Dei Institute, and other theological colleges.

Acknowledgements

A publication with as many contributions as this volume necessarily accumulates a great debt of gratitude. We wish to express our sincere thanks, firstly, to each of our seventy-two contributors who responded so willingly to our invitation to offer a short article to this collection and for the timely fashion in which these were submitted. It has been a pleasure to work with each of you.

The inclusion of a large number of high-quality images would not have been possible without the co-operation and advice of various individuals and the permission of a number of institutions which have agreed to allow these to be reproduced here. For this we wish to thank especially Rev. Paddy Carberry SJ, Director, Manresa House; Mr George Cunningham; Rev. Paul Finnerty; Mr Anthony Harpur; Rev. John Hughes OSA; Mr John Gillis; Rev. Tom Jordan OP, editor *Spirituality*; Mr John McElroy; Mr Dominic McNamara; Dr Rachel Moss; Mr Tomás Ó Canainn; Rev. Dr Neil Xavier O'Donoghue; Rev. Dr Kevin O'Gorman; Dr John O'Keeffe; Prof. Thomas O'Loughlin; Dr Jennifer O'Reilly; Rev. Donagh O'Shea OP; Dr Niamh O'Sullivan; Dr Janet Rutherford; Rev. Dr Michael Shortall; Mr Patrick Treacy SC; Seán Ó Leochain; the Archdiocese of St Andrews and Edinburgh; the Board of Trinity College, Dublin; the Cathedral Treasury of Chur, Switzerland; Designbank, Leeson Street, Dublin; the Diocese of Limerick; the Hunt Museum, Limerick; Integritas Centre for Domestic Spirituality, Stoneyford, County Kilkenny; Manresa Jesuit Centre for Spirituality; the National Gallery of Ireland; the National Museum of Ireland; the National Science Museum at Maynooth.

The support of Mgr Hugh Connolly and the staff of St Patrick's College, Maynooth, as always, has made the editing of this volume all the more enjoyable. Finally, we would like to express our sincere gratitude to the staff at Veritas Publications for bringing this volume to completion with their customary professionalism, in particular Director, Maura Hyland, Commissioning Editor, Donna Doherty and Marketing Manager, Derek Byrne. Most especially, we extend our warm appreciation to Manager of Publications, Caitriona Clarke, and Editor, Julie Steenson, with whom we worked most closely on this volume and who helped to make this project such a pleasant experience.

Brendan Leahy & Salvador Ryan